T0399370

Humane and Sustainable Smart Cities

Humane and Sustainable Smart Cities

A Personal Roadmap to Transform Your City After the Pandemic

Eduardo M. Costa
Professor of Knowledge Management at the Federal University of Santa Catarina, Brazil

ACADEMIC PRESS
An imprint of Elsevier

ELSEVIER

Academic Press is an imprint of Elsevier
125 London Wall, London EC2Y 5AS, United Kingdom
525 B Street, Suite 1650, San Diego, CA 92101, United States
50 Hampshire Street, 5th Floor, Cambridge, MA 02139, United States
The Boulevard, Langford Lane, Kidlington, Oxford OX5 1GB, United Kingdom

British Library Cataloguing-in-Publication Data
A catalogue record for this book is available from the British Library

Library of Congress Cataloging-in-Publication Data
A catalog record for this book is available from the Library of Congress

ISBN: 978-0-12-819186-6

For Information on all Academic Press publications
visit our website at https://www.elsevier.com/books-and-journals

Publisher: Brian Romer
Acquisitions Editor: Graham Nisbet
Editorial Project Manager: Alice Grant
Production Project Manager: Swapna Srinivasan
Cover Designer: Victoria Pearson

Typeset by MPS Limited, Chennai, India

Working together
to grow libraries in
developing countries
www.elsevier.com • www.bookaid.org

Dedication

To Patricia, my wife, and to Nando, our son, "the Team."

Contents

Foreword

When I was invited to write the Foreword of this book, by my dear colleague and friend Eduardo M. Costa, the first thought that came to my mind was to concentrate on the various city brands that have been around us in recent decades. Then we were hit by the pandemic of 2020. In a way, looking at the past and present may inspire us to do the right and better things for the future of our cities, societies, and the planet post-COVID-19.

Our impact on the planet has escalated to a degree that the term Anthropocene has become an environmental buzzword since scientists—led by the Nobel laureate Paul Crutzen—proposed it as the new geological epoch in early 2000s. Rapid population growth and a net total growth of consumption of natural resources, combined with vigorous industrialization, urbanization, mobilization, globalization, agricultural intensification, and excessive consumption-driven lifestyles are to be blamed for the appearance of this epoch. In order to address the socioeconomic needs within the planetary limits without causing harm to the nature, various urban planning and development approaches are generated and put into practice. These approaches could be grouped under two schools of thought.

The first school of thought adopts an envirocentric viewpoint to conceptualize "sustainable urbanism." The origin of sustainable urbanism dates back to the "sustainable urban development" notion of the 1970s and the "smart growth" notion of the 1990s. This movement advocates planning strategies, including sustainable urban development, land use and transport integration, and use of appropriate tools and technologies, to address sprawl development and associated environmental externalities.

The second school of thought adopts a technocentric viewpoint to conceptualize "smart urbanism." The origin of smart urbanism dates back to the digital revolution notion of the 1990s and it is practiced through the intelligent city, smart city, and responsive city approaches. It advocates planning strategies, including enhanced liveability and prosperity in cities, unified experience for citizens to benefit from efficient and effective city services, and environmental sustainability through the implementation of relevant digital technologies, to address various problems of our cities.

Recently conducted research, however, indicates that both schools of thought have not managed the cities' problems adequately. For instance, a study we conducted on 15 UK smart cities found no evidence that urban smartness contributes to sustainable outcomes. Another research on Australian cities revealed the smartness of cities does not lead to sustainable commuting patterns. Furthermore, studies have shown that smart city wannabees are fascinated by the exogenous assets—such as imported goods and technology solutions—that have high carbon footprint. Unfortunately, the popularity of the smart agenda has already made policymakers and urban administrators turn their heads mostly away from the sustainable urbanism practices. Perhaps the main issue behind the failure of both sustainable and smart urbanism attempts is that they are still being performed within the boundaries of the unhealthy Anthropocene practice.

An out-of-the-box thinking is needed for us to be able to adequately address the problems we face. Following the adoption of such thinking, a healthy marriage of both schools of thought could be another good step forward—perhaps in the form of "smart and sustainable urbanism." In this perspective, smart and sustainable city can be defined as an urban locality functioning as a healthy system of systems with sustainable and balanced practices of economic, societal, environmental, and governance activities generating desired outcomes for all humans and nonhumans.

This new form of urbanism might sound just like a utopia for the time being. Nevertheless, it might be our last chance to avoid an urban ecocide and secure existence of humankind and other species on our planet for the millenniums to come. We need to urgently develop sound actions before it is too late; after all, future generations' lives are seriously at stake.

The unpredictable, sudden, and rapid emergence and transmission of COVID-19, during the last few months, have triggered significant public health emergencies and concern across both national as well as the global nature. Considering limited availability of clinically proven interventions and the infectious nature of the SARS-CoV-2's transmission, a global emergency developed in the form of a pandemic, resulting in implementations of lockdowns and restrictions in movement for citizens throughout the world. The resultant limitations have, thus, sparked a surge in the usage of online resources by the public, such as the usage of social media as well as the public's reliance on e-commerce services for the purpose of obtaining essential commodities.

During the pandemic, we have experienced less motor vehicle use, increased cycling and walking, traveling within the local catchment (travel self-containment within the 5 km range), discussions on finding a mid-way for the density of our settlements (neither urban core high, nor outer suburban low densities), a renewed sense of urban life that is connected with nature and pedestrian-friendly, and work-life balance (4-day work week discussions as introduced in New Zealand). While these are all well and good, unless these ideas are materialized rapidly, we will most likely find ourselves in a business-as-usual prepandemic situation again. Hence, as Eduardo's book advocates, it is the day of action.

Disruptive effects of the pandemic are way beyond the sole health implications. In fact, socioeconomic stability of almost every city and country is under threat. Following the pandemic, what awaits us are waives of recession, intensified climate crises, and biodiversity collapse. Cities are living organisms and cannot be taken into consideration without economic, societal, environmental, technological, and institutional mechanisms that give them life—or, in some cases, death. While we are thinking of the post-COVID-19 cities, we need to think radically to turn this catastrophe into an awakening moment to start solving the fundamental issues of our civilization ranging from socioeconomic inequality to climate emergency, and from ruthless capitalism and consumerism to malpractice governance. At this very point, Eduardo M. Costa's book provides a moral compass and a practical guide for us to rethink our places as more Humane, Sustainable, and, yes, Smart Cities.

Tan Yigitcanlar
School of Built Environment,
Queensland University of Technology,
Brisbane, QLD, Australia

Preface

I had been wondering for years why our cities were meant for cars, not for people. I even dreamt once of a village where cars would drive unnoticed to the back of the houses and people would go about their businesses walking out of the front door into a garden alley. When living in England during my PhD studies at Southampton University, I read of a place where they were trying something like that. Then I registered a reminder to go there some day but unfortunately have not yet got to it.

Years later, in 2012, I came across the "Smart City" concept and found it interesting. Not knowing a lot about it, I did what many professors do when they want to learn something, I decided to teach it! In the Spring term of that year, in the Graduate Program of Knowledge Management at the Federal University of Santa Catarina—UFSC, I conducted the first course on "Knowledge Cities, Smart Cities," which later became "Humane and Sustainable Smart Cities". It still runs once a year, and is my favorite course.

In that same year of 2012, through common friends, I met Dr. Alvaro Oliveira, a Portuguese specialist in the theme of *Human Smart Cities*, who already had, at that time, several projects under development for the European Union in his company, in Lisbon. It was "friendship at first sight" and that relationship lasts until today. He was launching a movement in Europe to change the concept of smart cities, which had been captured by the giant American tech companies, with the new concept of human smart cities, with focus on the citizen. I immediately joined the movement, which later became a real "movement" with a "manifesto" and slogans and all the rest of it. During the following years I attended and spoke at several of their conferences in European cities.

In the first edition of my graduate course in 2012, one of the students was Angela Amin, the former mayor of Florianópolis, who was finishing her PhD in our Program. What a privilege! As we were developing our first ideas on the subject, we had a real mayor, fresh out of office, to expand our ideas and talk about the constraints of government. In November, we both attended the Smart City Expo and Conference in Barcelona and could learn from other experiences in different parts of the world. This first course and the Barcelona fair convinced me to change my main research interest (up to then it was Innovation and Small Companies) to Human Smart Cities.

By 2014 I was one of the people in the Human Smart City bandwagon in Europe. Another member, Jarmo Suominem, from Aalto University in Helsinki, told me of a workshop methodology which they practiced, where they developed structural projects for cities in Finland. We decided to take the experience to Brazil and held the first Brazilian workshop in Rio, studying the Gavea Borough (the location of the Catholic University of Rio - PUC). Jarmo brought with him two professors and 12 graduate students from Aalto and I gathered 15 students from PUC in Rio and from UFSC in Florianópolis to participate in the workshop. We were sponsored locally by the Head of PUC's Incubator and my dear friend, José Alberto Aranha. The results of the workshop for the borough were so interesting that I went on to formalize the workshop methodology and apply it yearly in several other places in Brazil.

After the first workshop, I invited some senior members of the movement to conduct a "raise-awareness" tour in Brazil. Alvaro Oliveira, Jarmo Suominem, Ken Larson (MIT Media Lab), and I went to Rio, Campinas, Florianópolis, and Brasília, where we all spoke about the importance and the opportunity of bringing the new concept of Human Smart City to Brazil. In Brasília, the country's capital, we spoke at the Federal Congress and were later received by the Country's Minister of Cities.

One of the people who attended our presentation at the Brazilian Congress was my old friend Tadao Takahashi, the man who brought the Internet to Brazil when nobody even imagined what it was all about. Tadao was involved with a project to think about the planning of Brasilia (then 50 years old only) for the next following 50 years. He was immediately bitten and contaminated by the Human Smart City bug and became a loyal soldier afterward.

In 2016 Roberto Pacheco, my colleague at UFSC, invited Alvaro and I to write a chapter on Human Smart Cities for the "Oxford book on Interdisciplinarity, Volume II" which he was coediting. We accepted with enthusiasm and wrote the book chapter that was initially entitled Human Smart City. When it was returned for revision, the Oxford reviewer suggested we changed the word "Human" in the title for "Humane." I was furious and discussed it with Alvaro, "how dare he change our title?". But before answering the editor's questioning, I reached for the books to study it. And... the editor was right! "Human" and "Humane" translate to the same word "humano" in Portuguese. But in English, "Human" means "the human race," as opposed to, for instance, the animal race. Humane refers to the positive characteristics of the human race. Not all characteristics, but the positive only. Hate, for instance, is a human characteristic not found in animals. But we do not refer to hate as "humane." So, we humbly agreed with the editor and changed the chapter's title to "Humane Smart City."

Still in 2017 Tadao funded, through one of his projects, a study about the opportunities for Humane Smart Cities in Brazil. As part of the work we should produce a text explaining the concept. As we proceeded with the study, we realized that we should produce not just a text for Brazil but an international book on the subject. We would coauthor the book. Unfortunately, Tadao had some health issues in that year and had to leave the project.

The year of 2018 was very important for my work since we convinced another expert on the subject, in his case on "Knowledge-based Cities," Australian professor Tan Yigitcanlar, from Queensland University of Technology, to spend a year with us in Brazil. Tan's contributions to me in our discussions, to my research group, and to Florianópolis were invaluable. Amongst other things, Tan invited me to submit a book proposal to a series on Smart Cities he was editing for Elsevier. This is when this book project really took its final shape. I hoped to finish it by the second semester of 2019. Then it slipped a little. Then a bit more into 2020. The necessary confinement brought about by the pandemic crisis locked us all up at home. In my case, the elimination of travel time (I was traveling twice weekly on average) added an enormous number of working hours to my week, and helped me concentrate and focus on the book project. These extra hours came, at this time, as a blessing.

The book project took a long time to complete, but I can assure you, it has been a great pleasure to organize and systematize all the research and practical work we have done so far on this fascinating subject of more Humane and Sustainable Smart Cities. And it certainly helped me, during this confinement, to appease my worries about the world's terrible situation due to the pandemic.

If you fall in love with the subject as we all have, join the band and follow my suggestion in Chapter 8.

Thank you very much for your interest on Humane and Sustainable Smart Cities. Hope you use the roadmap presented here to transform your city after the pandemic.

Eduardo
Rio, August of 2020

Acknowledgments

To all my family, friends, colleagues, acquaintances, and everybody who helped me both in the research work that led to the book, and also with the book's content. In particular, I would like to express my sincere gratitude to:

Álvaro Oliveira (Alfamicro), Jarmo Suominem (Aalto University), and Kent Larson (MIT Media Lab), for bringing my attention to the subject.

Tan Yigitcanlar (Queensland University of Technology), for the foreword to this book, and for his contribution to my research and that of my graduate students during the year he spent in Brazil with us.

Javier Carrillo, Cathy Garner, Blanca Garcia, Ana Cristina Fachinelli, and Guenter Koch, from the World Capital Institute, who shared their knowledge with us in the Knowledge Cities World Summits in Tenerife and in Florianópolis.

My Ph.D. student and friend Eduardo Trauer, a gifted photographer, for his gracious authorization to use his photographs on the book cover and in Chapters 5 and 6.

My old friend Tadao Takahashi, for the early work on the book's project and fruitful discussions about its contents.

My dear friends and colleagues at the Graduate Program on Knowledge Engineering at UFSC, Neri dos Santos (my Guru on digital transformation) and Roberto Pacheco (my Guru on the commons theory), for our helpful discussions about the book's content and for the specific contributions in their respective areas of expertise in the sections of Chapter 7.

To the following list of family, friends, colleagues and students who searched for the examples listed in Chapter 5, Alexandre Biz, Andreici Vedovatto, Anne Aune, Arthur Sanders Jr., Carlos Olsen, Clarissa Teixeira, Eduardo Trauer, Emídio Costa, Estela Boiani, Fernanda Palandi, Fernando Costa, Hans van Bellen, José Aranha, Luiz Spinosa, Marcelo Guimarães, Marcelo Nierling, Marciele Berger, Mônica and Roberto Pinheiro, Mônica Carneiro, Neri dos Santos, Patricia Costa, Roberto Pacheco, Suelen Lazaretti, Tatiana Schreiner, and Thalita Souza.

To my colleagues at LabCHIS-UFSC, Jamile Marques, Tatiana Schreiner, Arthur Sanders Jr., Fernanda Palandi, Luciana Hervoso, Vanessa Eleutheriou, Estela Boiani, Adriana Kolenski, Laryssa Tarachucky, Daniela Jacobina, Thiago Furlani, Alexander Lara, Luiz Spinosa, Mônica Carneiro, Lucas Abdala, and Tatiana Whittmann.

To my colleagues at the Knowledge Management Department at UFSC, Gregorio Varvakis, Clarissa Teixeira, Patrícia Freire, Gertrudes Dandolini, and Francisco Fialho, for their support, whenever possible, to LabCHIS.

To all the participants and stakeholders that became involved in the nine workshops we organized so far in Florianópolis, Rio de Janeiro, and Salvador, amounting to more than 300 people—professionals, students, residents' associations, trade associations, NGOs, teachers, and many other helpful people.

To the institutions that contributed with their people's time and resources or financed some of our workshops, the Florianópolis City Hall (Cibele Lorenzi and Michel Mittmann), Fecomércio SC (Bruno Breithaupt), SEBRAE-SC (Carlos Henrique Ramos), Floripa Amanhã (Anita Pires), Instituto Lixo Zero (Rodrigo Sabatini), and Fundação Certi (José Fiates), in Florianópolis; State University of São Paulo - USP (Arlindo Filippi Jr.) and ArqFuturo (Tomas Alvim), in São Paulo; and ANPROTEC (José Aranha) and CGI-MCTIC (Demi Getschko), on a national level.

To the editors and other support people at Elsevier, who had the patience to stir my work all the way to its conclusion, Graham Nisbet, Alice Grant, Swapna Srinivasan, Indhumati Mani, and Ali Afzal-Khan.

To my dear wife, Patricia, and my son, Nando (who lives in New York City), to whom I not only dedicate the book but also want to express my gratitude for making these months of confinement all the more pleasurable.

To our family dog, Gloria, who inspired me in several parts of the work and gave particular contributions to Chapter 8.

To you, the reader.

Chapter 1

The concept of more Humane and Sustainable Smart Cities

"To the extent that we hyperseparate ourselves from nature and reduce it conceptually in order to justify domination, we not only lose the ability to empathise and to see the nonhuman sphere in ethical terms, but also get a false sense of our own character and location that includes an illusory sense of autonomy. The failure to see the nonhuman domain in the richer terms appropriate to ethics licences supposedly 'purely instrumental' relationships that distort our perceptions and enframings, impoverish our relations and make us insensitive to dependencies and interconnections."

Val Plumwood.

Content

You have probably heard the term "smart city." It refers to a place which has plenty of cameras, sensors, monitoring devices, lots of software, and one or two control centers. Most of the examples show how to improve the traffic conditions of the private car, how to control or ameliorate traffic congestion, how to find a place to park, how to pay electronically for the parking, how to find the best fuel prices or the best routes, etc. It is all about cars, not people. The assumption is that our lives will be better if our cars "lived" in a smarter environment.

May I beg to disagree.

There is, in our view, a fundamental mistake in the overall concept of the city today; it is designed for the car, not for the citizens. How did we develop this misconception? It all started in the 18th and 19th centuries with the industrial revolution and the invention of the automobile (see Chapter 2: Historical Overview: Cities From Medieval to Modern Times—What Went Wrong). Factories were at first built within the town's boundaries. But with the realization that they polluted the air and the rivers, and later on with the possibility of local transport by car, urban planners concentrated their efforts into building towns with segregation of the daily functions of living, working, and playing in different boroughs of the town. In the 20th century all

Humane and Sustainable Smart Cities. DOI: https://doi.org/10.1016/B978-0-12-819186-6.00004-X

major towns had one or more industrial districts, next to big roads where people could move around on a daily basis. Transport between the different boroughs was done by public transport initially, but eventually by private cars. It all went well when the number of cars was small (well, for the people who owned cars, of course) but it led to huge investments by local and provincial governments everywhere to construct the necessary infrastructure for the cars and trucks transporting goods: large avenues and roads, viaducts, even suspended roads. This transport infrastructure became a measure of the level of development of a town or a region.

Eventually, it did not work.

The level of air pollution in the cities became unbearable. A new movement started to take shape and emerged with force: the eco or green movement. The beginning of the movement is arguably set on December 24, 1968, with the photograph of our planet sent from his lunar orbit to earth by the American astronaut William Anders: it was sort of a rude awakening to the fact of how small and insignificant we were in the galaxy. Nature photographer Galen Rowell described it as "the most influential environmental photograph ever taken." The environmentalists and their ideas gained momentum over the following years, and, at the Rio-92 UN Conference on Environment and Development (also The Earth Summit), the 195 UN national states agreed on a set of principles, of which principle #1 stated:

"Human beings are at the center of concerns for sustainable development."

Right! And how did that translate into cities? In several ways: people started to question urban development based on the old ideas of cities for the car. Minorities started to voice their concerns. Diversity became a value. And planners and researchers began to rethink the city.

This new look at the city became an important field of study and gained different names over the years. Some of the ideas under these different denominations are similar, and some are particular to that term. We will show them here and try to group them later under the new denomination of Humane and Sustainable Smart Cities (HSSCs): the best findings of what we have studied this far—but with an anthropocentric focus.

Sustainable city

Richard Register was the first to coin the term eco-city (sustainable city) in 1987 (Register, 2006). Sustainable city was then defined as the one which cared for all aspects of sustainability (social, economic, and environmental) for today's residents without compromising this same sustainability for future generations. Or, in today's jargon, a city that offers the best possible quality of life to its citizens and visitors without compromising the environment (the lowest environmental footprint). The concept has been applied in several places as, for instance, in the redevelopment of Hammarby Sjostad, a former industrial precinct close to Stockholm's city center. It was such an acclaimed success that a study conducted by the Chinese Bank based on the "12 green guidelines for urban development" (Huang et al., 2015) awarded the project its highest marks in the world. The guidelines summarize the worries with environmental sustainability on the one side but also stress the necessary human connection on the other side.

1. **Urban growth boundary (UGB)**

   Every city should establish an enforced urban growth boundary (UGB). The UGB should be set based upon a rigorous analysis of ecological sensitivities, environmental capacity, and the efficiency and productivities of various land uses. The boundary can expand beyond the existing urban footprint only if there are no suitable infill locations as indicated by an intensity of urban land use of at least 10,000 residents per square kilometer.

2. **Transit-oriented development (TOD)**

   Cities should be built around their public transit systems. The area within 500−800 m of major transit stations, such as the metro or bus rapid transit (BRT), or within 500 m of nearest bus or transit stops (in case BRT or metro is not available) should have the building ratio (m2 built/m2 of land) at least 50% higher than the average of the district. For big cities, at least 70% of residents should live in TOD areas characterized by convenient mass transit service. Great accessibility (pleasant walking amenities to transit system within a 500-m radius) must also be offered.

3. **Mixed use**

   All residential units should be close to at least six kinds of amenities within 500-m radius of building entrance (amenities include schools, post offices, banks, retails, clinics, activity centers, restaurants, etc.). The job-resident ratio (the number of people employed divided by the number of residents) should be between 0.5 and 0.7 over every commuting district, which should have a spatial area that is no more than 15 km^2. Normally, these commuting districts are bounded by physical barriers for pedestrians.

4. **Small blocks**

   Blocks should be less than or equal to 2 hectares and 70% of the blocks should comply with this standard. Exceptions made for industrial areas.

5. **Public green space**

   Publicly accessible and usable green space should comprise 20%−40% of the construction areas (residential area should be at the higher end of this range). All residences should have accessible public space within 500 m.

6. **Nonmotorized transit**

   There should be dedicated and connected walking paths of at least 10 km in length per square kilometer, and dedicated and connected biking paths of least 10 km in length per square kilometer in urban areas.

7. **Public transit**

   All new developments must be within a 500-m radius of a bus or rapid transit station. For the city as a whole, at least 90% of developments should be within 800-m radius of a public transit station.

8. **Car control**

   Every city should have a strategy to cap car use. Where high-quality transit exists, there should be limits on parking.

9. **Green buildings**

   At least 70% of buildings should be MOHURD (Chinese equivalent to the western green bilding standard LEED) One-Star, 20%−40% of buildings should be MOHURD Two-Star, and 5%−15% of buildings should be MOHURD Three-Star within any development.

10. **Renewable and district energy**

    Every project should analyze the potential for district energy, such as combined heat and power (CHP), waste to energy, and waste heat reuse. There should be 5%−15% local renewable energy generation for residential areas and 2%−5% for commercial areas.

11. **Waste management**

    All buildings should have waste classification facilities. All household waste must be sorted and collection of hazardous waste must be prioritized. At least 30%−50% of waste should be composted and 35%−50% recycled or reused.

12. **Water efficiency**

All buildings must have 100% adoption of cost-effective water-saving appliances, and green spaces surrounding buildings must adopt low water-use plants. All water consumption should be metered and at least 20%−30% of water supply must be recycled from either wastewater or rainwater.

These 12 green guidelines cover a lot of ground and clearly point in the right direction. They are an important first step. People may challenge the actual metrics suggested but it is crucial, in any development, to have quantified goals to be met. Declarations of intent do not suffice. In China, since the bank is one of the main sources of finance for new developments, it is easier to enforce these rules and regulations. We will look back at these guidelines later in the book.

The ecological movement is a positive and fresh initiative, but its excesses may generate countereffects that go in the exact opposite effect of the original target. Take the feeling against high-rise buildings, for instance. Once the town prohibits the construction of tall buildings in its local code, the city sprawls as the population moves outside into the "green" belts around it. But as a result of daily transport to work and the heating and cooling needs of larger houses, the total consumption of energy increases substantially for the city as a whole. Glaeser (2011) suggests this is the biggest mistake that city planners have embarked on in the past decades. As the city uses a larger surface, the CO_2 emissions increase, not the opposite, as suggested by some people in the green movement. In the US, the move toward the outskirts is aggravated by federal subsidies in terms of income tax for people contracting loans to buy large houses in the suburbs.

Resilient city

The term "resilience" is often associated with the capacity to resist extreme conditions, mostly due to the weather, such as water flooding, snow storms, droughts, wild forest fires, rising tides, hurricanes, and tornados. In the context of cities, though the term takes also a broader meaning beyond the weather, encompassing threats and challenges of a different kind such as, for instance, terrorist attacks, corruption, social unrest, or power outages. In a sense, emergencies are scaled-up versions of everyday tasks in a city facing problems of floods, fires, traffic congestions, demonstrations, etc.

The number of recent disasters or threats in different parts of the world is growing and demand action from societies and their governments. How do we tackle recent major events such as the flooding in New Orleans, landslide in Rio, fires in California, terrorist, or hate attacks in several important cities of the world? Or, more importantly, how do we *prevent* or *avoid* them? The English Philosopher Thomas Hobbes stated that the purpose of the city is the preservation of life ("and a more contented life thereby") and it is now clear that a lot has to be done everywhere in order to fulfill that mission.

The Rockfeller Foundation (2013) launched and financed an important movement coined The 100 Resilient Cities program with the aim to "help cities around the world become more resilient to physical, social, and economic shocks and stresses." They first chose 33 cities and then grew to 100, out of a thousand applicants, and financed them to establish a basic infrastructure (including hiring a Chief Resilient Officer, responding directly to the mayor) capable of setting the agenda of resilience in the planning of the city's activities and of sharing good practices with all the other cities in the program and cities worldwide. Cities range from megalopolises, such as Mexico City and New York City, to old settlements, such as Athens and Rome, to newer cities, such as Porto Alegre and Sidney.

Local governments also started to take action and one of the results is the organization of 1500 of them in the International Council of Local Environmental Initiatives—ICLEI which organizes the annual Resilient Cities Congress with the first results already published (ICLEI, 2019). These results and shared experiences can be an inspiration for other cities worldwide.

In 2015 the 193 countries of the UN General Assembly adopted the 2030 Development Agenda titled "Transforming our world: the 2030 Agenda for Sustainable Development," with 17 Sustainable Development Goals (SDGs). SDG number 11 reads "Make cities and human settlements inclusive, safe, resilient, and sustainable." According to the United Nations Development Program (UNDP), an additional mass of 3 billion people will move to the cities up to 2050 (!), and 95% of that figure will happen in the developing world. Considering that most mega cities in the developing world face daunting challenges already, it is imperative that these cities be replanned in a different way, taking into account how to provide affordable housing, how to maintain sustainability, and how to make the city more resilient in face of a rapidly growing population.

Technology is here to help, but with a caveat: it is easy to lure mayors and city planners into buying technology as an end product or service. Let me stress this point here: they are not! Technology is a tool and, in general, a very expensive one at that. Its deployment should be preceded by careful evaluation of the benefits to the citizens and to the city, careful evaluation of alternatives, and very clear metrics on how to assess its impact. For instance, a sophisticated warning system for landslide has to be weighed against alternative systems for mitigation of the problem, or, even better, with alternative systems that may prevent the landslide altogether.

Sustainable cities and resilient cities point the right way forward: focus on the citizen and future generations of citizens.

All of these definitions and studies are important and we will take all of them into account as proposed by Chang et al. (2018) as we move toward the concept of more HSSCs.

Creative city

"Creative city" is a term coined by the Australian author David Yencken (2013) to describe places where the arts in general (painting, sculpture, literature, music, dance, etc.) play an important role in the economic fabric of a city and where local development is directly or indirectly connected to these economic activities. Later on, the concept was enlarged to also encompass nonrepetitive activities that are important in economic terms such as software, architecture, financial services, and any knowledge-based activities. In fact, "creative" activity may refer to everything that is not a traditional industry. Funnily enough, all of these nonrepetitive activities became known as the "creative industry." There are several explanations for this apparent oxymoron, but we prefer the view that the industrial activity is still ingrained in our thoughts as the "only" respectable economic sector. Thus even for instance the software sector likes to call itself the "software industry."

As we move away from the industrial economy into the creative economy (Howkins, 2001, 2013) or knowledge economy, it is only natural that we want to have creative cities where the creative economy may flourish. Howkins (2001) put together creativity and economics to stress the point that creativity is relevant once it is transformed into products and services, generating economic value. In 2013 he published a new revised version of his bestseller as a practical guide to success and the title read: "Creative Economies: how people make money from ideas" (Howkins, 2013). Cities soon jumped in to have their creative industry and substitute their industrial activity that moved to other parts of the country or overseas.

So how do you foster the transformation of a city into a creative city (Yigitcanlar et al., 2018a,b)? The answer is complex but one necessary condition is *people*—creative people at that. Richard Florida studied several cities in the United States and tried to figure out which are the common characteristics among these cities (Florida, 2014). His findings came as a surprise to many people when he included *tolerance* as one of these characteristics, suggesting that creative cities are places where heavy metal bands are abundant and where the gay community is large and active. Tolerance allows for the expression and circulation of new ideas that eventually may lead to innovations in the market.

It is understandable that the level of amenities is important to attract people to a city. But the Chilean architect Alejandro Aravena (2018) emphasizes the point that young workers are more mobile than their parents and they settle not only where amenities and resources are plentiful (called magnets that attract people) but they are also repelled by a city that enjoys a lesser quality of life (called bombs).

One factor missing from the creative city concept is the inclusion of less fortunate workers. The creative sector as a whole may draw better salaries than their counterparts in the industrial or the services sectors. But how to increase diversity if the focus is on the city for the creative class alone? Florida himself has been confronted with this problem and has developed some fresh ideas on how to cope with diversity in the city (Florida, 2017). San Francisco, for instance, is certainly listed as a creative city on any city rankings. But it is also sad to notice that people you meet on the streets are either entrepreneurs or beggars.

Knowledge-based or knowledge cities

"Knowledge Cities are cities that possess an economy driven by high value-added exports created through research, technology, and brainpower" (Carrillo, 2006). As our society moved from the industrial economy to the knowledge economy in the last few decades, and we installed the roots of a knowledge society it is only natural that cities that embraced the new paradigm faster be distinguished as the knowledge cities. Bilbao, in Spain, for instance, is a city that had a sharp decline in its industrial economy (as many other cities in the world) and faced a period of basque terrorism that left scars all over Spain. But in a short period of circa 25 years it transformed itself into a reference knowledge city (as few cities in the world did) based upon an architectural icon, the Guggenheim Museum. The Museum completely transformed the internal and external image of the city and shows a steady influx of 1 million visitors a year. Bilbao undertook several other parallel projects along with the Museum (Azua, 2006) and was awarded the prestigious inaugural Lee Kuan Yew World City Prize in 2010. In the following years, laureates of the biannual prize were New York City (in 2012), Suzhou (in 2014), Medellin (in 2016), and Seoul (in 2018). All of these city cases boast a transformational borough that become showcases and managed to impact the whole city. They are good examples of efforts to transform a city into a knowledge city.

A knowledge city depends upon the development of knowledge-intensive sectors in the town. These knowledge-intensive sectors strive where two conditions are satisfied simultaneously: policies of knowledge-based development (KBD), as proposed by Carrillo (2015), and knowledge workers (Florida, 2005). Yigitcanlar and Lee (2011) suggest that the main factor to attract knowledge workers is to adapt the city's urban planning with a focus on this very special and demanding population, hence the new study area knowledge-based urban development (KBUD).

The main characteristics of a knowledge city, besides the availability of knowledge workers, are creativity and cultural infrastructure, technology and communication, human capital, and urban development clusters (Yigitcanlar et al., 2008). Creativity and cultural infrastructure are key. Creativity has to be fostered and incentivized as a local value. The cultural infrastructure will help to attract knowledge workers. All of the characteristics impact each other of course. Technology and communication are key to the dissemination and accessibility of information. In a knowledge city, information has to be available everywhere and to everyone. Furthermore, education at all levels and different ages needs this infrastructure to offer services widely. Lastly urban development clusters provide examples, showcases that demonstrate the willingness of a city to transform itself (Costa, 2001). As we have seen here and will repeat again throughout the book, cities change step by step, borough by borough, and that is the way every city should start and proceed.

The concept of knowledge can be taken narrowly as scientific and technological knowledge (based, for instance, on the average number of school years of the population) but it can also assume a broader definition to include creative knowledge as well. In the latter case, the knowledge city gets closer to the concept of creative city that we visited just before.

Smart (or digital) city

Smart cities use information and communication technologies (ICTs) extensively. They have gone through a process that, in many sectors, is called digital transformation. But notice that if one googles the term "digital transformation," the first results point to equipment manufacturers, service offers, consulting services, and training. The fact is that suppliers captured the emerging trend of cities becoming smarter and grabbed the term to promote their wares. There is nothing wrong with private companies doing their marketing and sales activities in order to promote their stuff. The trouble is that this focus on technology sells the marvels of its deployment with little (or very little) reference to the benefits to the citizen (Yigitcanlar et al., 2018a,b). The fact that buying cameras, sensors, Internet of Things (IoT), software, and control centers is a good move to the city, and that it will eventually improve life of the citizen, is a given. It is the same attitude that cities have toward the car:

Q: Duplicating the number of lanes in an avenue is good for the city, right?

A: Well... It is not right. Not necessarily so.

But the appeal is strong. Consider the large software and hardware services company IBM and its strategy. The company has, for many decades, been successful in manufacturing state-of-the-art mainframes, the central processing unit that processed data for large corporations, governments, and institutions. Once installed, these huge machines gave the manufacturer an enormous advantage over any competitor: as everything at the time was proprietary, the user had to buy every new piece of software, peripherals, and add-ons from IBM. Over time, IBM changed its strategy to become a complete-services company, selling a full package of proprietary and nonproprietary items to their users. Then came the smart city concept. IBM embraced it fully and set its international strategy as being the company not only for smart city but for the "smarter planet." The new equivalent to the old mainframe is the control center, a centralized set of computer, software, and services that gives the company again a tremendous advantage. Once installed, the user tends to buy everything else from the company and the number of applications for the city is alluring. Such as:

Q: Want to know where your municipal police guards are?

A: Buy this piece of software here and hook it to the control center.

Q: Traffic control?

A: Another piece of software.

Q: A new demand that is not listed?

A: IBM will develop it for you.

Again, as in the old mainframe times, these purchase decisions demand no competitive bids, since everything has to be hooked to the control center and "better have one supplier only."

There is nothing wrong with IBM's strategy (a very successful one, by the way) but the point is cities and companies buy this solution to become "smarter." The image might be valuable for companies but for the city, where money is always scarce, every expense needs to be weighed not only against other options but also against other alternatives and priorities. And remember that the charm of new technology may be overwhelming and may lead to unnecessary purchases by the city hall.

One of the main technologies that are now available for city applications is sensors. Sensors for everything, really: rainfall, noise, air pressure and temperature, detection of presence, reading the various forms of barcode and QR code, lighting levels, pollution, and even smell. And they are very inexpensive since China is producing them on a very large scale.

Another interesting technology is the IoT. Technically, IoT is a system where a "thing" makes a decision based upon the information it receives from another "thing," without human intervention. But the term has been used in many less complex applications where sensors, software, and human intervention operate together. In any case, the number of possible applications in a city is huge. A special opportunity for the introduction of IoT in many countries has emerged with the substitution of lamps and poles of street lighting for LED sets that consume much less energy. The poles necessary to hold the LEDs are much smaller and lighter and, with proper planning, several sensors can be hooked to the poles during their installation in substitution of the old poles, making the deployment of new systems considerably cheaper.

Artificial intelligence and all of its variations (machine learning, deep learning) are another technology that has finally come of age. Information collected from the sensors, transmitted over the Internet and processed somewhere can be associated with Artificial Intelligence (AI) algorithms to produce amazing results for the city such as the capacity to predict natural disasters, anticipate and disseminate information to the correct receiver, process claims and forms in the city hall, etc.

Cities produce an enormous amount of data. Modern algorithms of big data can not only find patterns and behavior from large amounts of data but can also identify new intelligence in data that has not even been asked for. Although the technology is in its infancy, it promises very interesting results as it matures.

As all of these technologies and examples demonstrate, technology may be very good for the city. The trouble we face at the moment is the deployment of technology for its own sake with an almost religious faith and hope that something good will come out of it. For instance, several international rankings of smart cities register a parameter of the number of cameras in the city divided by the population. But frankly, who cares? We should not be concerned with how many cameras does the city center have but with how safe it is to walk in the city center at night time (Lara et al., 2016). Other ranking parameters relate to the ominous car: how can you find a spot to park in your own cell phone (making driving very dangerous...), how smart is the parking meter, how to handle fees, etc. Wouldn't it be better to measure how good and safe are sidewalks, how walkable is the city? How good and available is the public transport system? We will come back to this idea several times in the book.

Humane and Sustainable Smart City

We have seen that cities can be studied and defined in several ways, from sustainable to resilient, from creative to smart. The focus of this book is on an anthropocentric view of the city. How can we plan and implement a better city for its daily users without compromising the overall sustainability of the region? A word of caution here about the object: citizens are normally associated with people who are *residents* of the city. We refer here to "city users," for the lack of a better name, since it involves everyone who uses the city not only its residents. Take Manhattan, for instance. How can we plan the island city for its 1.6 million residents (including circa 100,000 who daily commute *out* of the city) without taking into account the floating population of 1.6 million working commuters, 400,000 out-of-town visitors, 374,000 local day-trip visitors, 70,000 commuting students, and even the 17,000 hospital patients (Morse and Qing, 2012)? The term city users might be a good reminder that the city is there to *serve* its users without compromising sustainability in the region.

A final word on the definition. It is important to refer to *more* HSSCs since the characteristic is a dynamic process, not a static condition. Cities should strive constantly to become more HSSCs.

So what is a more HSSC? Let us take the three adjectives in turn.

In an earlier version of this work (Costa and Oliveira, 2017) we had a discussion with the editor about the chapter title being "Human" or "Humane." Human refers to "a bipedal primate mammal (homo sapiens)," according to Merriam-Webster, as opposed, for instance, to animals. Humane, on the other hand, refers to the good characteristics of humans "marked by compassion, sympathy or consideration for humans and animals," according to Merriam-Webster. We all agreed that the term should be "humane" as we also use in the title of this book "Compassion, sympathy and consideration for humans and animals." Is there anything better to describe what we would like to be and to observe in our cities?

Sustainable here is directly related to the United Nations 17 SDGs for 2030 (United Nations, 2015). It is an objective agenda and following it should be in every city's priorities too. As we have seen already, SDG number 11 reads "Sustainable cities and communities" with the following goals:

11.1 By 2030, ensure access for all to adequate, safe, and affordable housing and basic services and upgrade slums.

11.2 By 2030, provide access to safe, affordable, accessible, and sustainable transport systems for all, improving road safety, notably by expanding public transport, with special attention to the needs of those in vulnerable situations, women, children, persons with disabilities, and older persons.

11.3 By 2030, enhance inclusive and sustainable urbanization and capacity for participatory, integrated and sustainable human settlement planning and management in all countries.

11.4 Strengthen efforts to protect and safeguard the world's cultural and natural heritage.

11.5 By 2030, significantly reduce the number of deaths and the number of people affected and substantially decrease the direct economic losses relative to global gross domestic product caused by disasters, including water-related disasters, with a focus on protecting the poor and people in vulnerable situations.

11.6 By 2030, reduce the adverse per capita environmental impact of cities, including by paying special attention to air quality and municipal and other waste management.

11.7 By 2030, provide universal access to safe, inclusive and accessible, green and public spaces, in particular for women and children, older persons, and persons with disabilities

11.A Support positive economic, social, and environmental links between urban, peri-urban, and rural areas by strengthening national and regional development planning.

11.B By 2020, substantially increase the number of cities and human settlements adopting and implementing integrated policies and plans toward inclusion, resource efficiency, mitigation and adaptation to climate change, resilience to disasters, and develop and implement, in line with the Sendai Framework for Disaster Risk Reduction 2015—2030, holistic disaster risk management at all levels.

11.C Support least developed countries, including through financial and technical assistance, in building sustainable and resilient buildings utilizing local materials.

Indeed! Everything we plan and implement in our cities has to be in line with these goals. Not only because we have to (for the signing countries, which means almost all countries in the world) but because most of us believe it is right to do so.

The third adjective in the title is smart. As has been said above, technology opens new roads for development in our cities. Once the city has set its priorities, always focusing on the user, technology should be deployed sparingly, weighing, at every step of the process, cost, and benefit to the user. It seems obvious but remembers that technology is "modern" and "cool," and planners may be lured by promises and political returns of huge screens, cameras, and such.

The book will tackle the characteristics of more HSSCs in the following chapters in detail. But let us introduce the concept here with three attributes of an HSSC: live-work-play in the same place; Citizen's (or users') wishes, interests, and needs; and mental deindustrialization.

1. Work-live-play within one-mile radius

In medieval times, villages existed along the sea (for transport) and rivers (for water). As villages started to move inland in Europe, away from the water, a common feature was a water well right in the middle of the village. In fact, the logic is reverse: the village grew around the water well. But it didn't grow much: to carry water home in heavy buckets of iron and wood, people could not go far. In fact, villages tended to be around one-mile radius each. Then they had an outside area for herds and crops. Life in the village was played within this one-mile radius. The concept of one-mile distance from the central source (the well) to the most remote user (consumer) was kept through the ages and is used still today (Deutschmann, 2017). In telecommunications, the distance from the switchboard to the wired user was limited to one mile and many people referred to this part of the network as "the last mile." In marketing, when they have to reach the individual customer, they refer to "walking the extra mile."

We will study the act of living, working, and playing within a one-mile radius in more detail in Chapter 2, Historical Overview: Cities from Medieval to Modern Times—What Went Wrong. But think of it as a characteristic of the HSSC: people being able to work, live, and play in the same borough. In that case, there is no need for local transport since one can go anywhere in town on foot. And, if you need to go from one borough to the other, you can use public transport. Sounds great! And we are all doing it in our cities . . . Right?

Of course not. For historical reasons and the overwhelming devotion to the car, our urban planners decided to segregate the daily functions of living, working, and playing into different parts of the city. One goes (or tries to go, pending traffic) from one place to another by car. By design! This separation is in general regulated by local laws and part of the city code: strictly residential, strictly commercial, and such. In most places, this segregation does not make any sense at all but it is still there. It is about time we review city codes to allow for living, working, and playing in the same borough.

A more HSSC plans its development with the old village concept of living, working, and playing in the same borough around circa one-mile radius (walkable) and with public transport to move people from one borough to the other.

2. Citizen's (or city users) wishes, interests, and needs

Most city officials claim that they are there to serve citizen's wishes, interests, and needs. But are they really? They tend to cloister at city hall and plan changes to the city without talking to anyone. They know better. Even when they hold public hearings about a city's project, they have designed the project already and want to hear minor modifications to it, if at all.

The staff of former Rio de Janeiro's mayor Eduardo Paes was surprised in a public hearing at Rocinha (a huge slum of 100,000 people)

when they showed the project of a local cable car up the mountain to local representatives of the community: the officials wanted to discuss number and location of stations and other minor detail of the project and the representatives argued that they did not *want* a cable car there. Before that, they wanted a proper sewage system, a good school, sports fields, and access to the Internet and many other services.

Hearing to people's wishes, interests, and needs is different. Priorities and the project itself should be developed along with the affected community. The city officials in Rio learned their lesson and the next big project in town, the "marvelous port," a reurbanization of the old harbor, was developed from the ground up, with much better results.

Sometimes even the city users can be fooled by appearances. In the island of Florianópolis (a state capital, south of Brazil) the city and all of its representatives have been discussing for years now where should the city build the third bridge between the island and the continent. The reason is that the two existing car bridges are completely jammed at peak hours. If one looks at the traffic congestion, it seems only natural that the island needs a third bridge. The answer to the question "how to alleviate car traffic congestion between the island and the continent?" is obviously the third bridge. But is this question correct? What if the question were "how to improve the transport of commuters from the continent to the island at peak time?" The answer would be completely different. The distance between the island and the continent is only 1 km. A passenger ferry service between the island and the continent, complemented with a good (and low cost) parking lot in the continent and a good (and low cost) public transport system in the island would be a much better solution. By far, Much less expensive, it would bring no additional cars to the island and would improve the public transport system for the local users as well.

Focus on the city user many times involves changing the question. For a start, we recommend the object of the question should *always* be the city user, not the car, or anything else.

3. "Mental de-industrialization"

Robert Palmer composed and sang "Addicted to love", one of the most famous rock hits of the 1980s (later sang even more powerfully by Tina Turner). One of the song's verses says "you might as well face it, you're addicted to love." This message comes to mind when we think of our relation with the word "industry." We all know we are not living in an industrial economy anymore. We are not an industrial society anymore. We know it. But we behave as if we didn't. We might as well face it "we are addicted to industry."

Take our working hours, for instance. Why do we work from 9 to 5 or 6 pm? All together? During the industrial era all the workers had to be there at the same time since the assembly or production lines depended on every worker doing his bit at the right order and in sequence. But today? Many companies have adopted the flextime system in which workers can shift their working hours up and down but be there at a certain "core hour." It is a beginning, but we still carry with us the mental model of being at the company at a certain time. In many places, companies register the time you go in and out in order to pay your salary accordingly. But what about all the work you do outside the premises talking over the cell phone, answering WhatsApp messages, making decisions based on information you received online on your tablet?

The schooling system is an even better example of our industrial mentality. Sir Ken Livingston, a British educator and a popular hit with TED viewers, explains humorously his ideas of the changes we have to promote in education, exactly on this mental hook to industry. If we compare a school with a prison, we will see very similar patterns: the use of a uniform, food, and play at prescribed times, gate bars, strict discipline and so on. How sad! No wonder, creativity, one of the bare necessities of the 21st-century worker, goes down with each year of schooling. The worst fact is that most universities in the world prepare their students to work at big companies (in many cases, industries) and do not even consider the alternative forms of work that exist today.

This addiction to industry reveals itself in other subtle ways as we mentioned before. How come, we call the creative sector of the economy the creative "industry"?

In order to promote our more HSSCs, we need to deindustrialize our thinking. For instance, in planning the transport system, we have to think of workers that do not follow the 9−5 paradigm and move around town at odd hours, including at night. In planning the opening hours to the public of the city hall services, we should think of odd hours (traffic jams would ease) and of one-stop shop for every service not making the user go to an office for a transport query, to another for a license, to a third one to pay overdue taxes, etc.

And finally, in our process of mental deindustrialization, we have to tackle industry's poster child—the car. We might as well face it "we are addicted to the car." Almost everything in town is planned for the car:

Q: Need a larger road?

A: Shorten the sidewalk.

Q: Want to please your voters?

A: Build a free parking lot downtown.

Q: Traffic jams in a spot in town?

A: Build expensive viaducts, underpasses, and new bridges.

Q: The cost?

A: Nobody cares.

Amazingly enough, in most cities nobody questions project costs related to improving the life of the car in the city. A new Music Hall in the City? The press labels it the "expensive white elephant of mayor so and so." The "Big Dig" in Boston? The fact that the US$24 billion project was the "largest civil construction project in the US" was heralded as a plus. Did anyone question it? Were there other alternatives to invest that sum? Apart from a few naysayers that were quickly identified as "working against progress," nothing is questioned, since the life of the car through Boston will be better.

What about the cost of the car to society as a whole? If one adds up the cost to build new roads, and new viaducts; the opportunity costs of parking places and parking lots in public spaces; the costs of air pollution and disposal of old tires and cars; and the medical and infrastructure costs of car accidents; the sum would be astronomic. Who should bear these costs? The car owner obviously. Is that happening? On the contrary. In many countries, governments give incentives of all sorts to car manufacturers and subsidize car buyers. Is it not insane?

The car is an expensive machine to the owner (as the old saying goes "the difference between men and boys is the price of their toys") and a very expensive machine to society. The owner should pay the full cost. Nothing less.

We will come back to these three attributes in the following chapter.

The book

The book draws its conclusion from the previous studies of sustainable, resilient, creative, knowledge, and smart cities and from field studies in several cities in the world, including a few practical projects in a developing country (Brazil).

This chapter recognizes that the term Smart Cities is probably well known. But that the humane and sustainable characteristics of a smart city are not. It introduces the concept of more HSSCs, detailing the evolution of the studies about our more modern cities and the meanings associated with the terms sustainable, resilient, creative, knowledge-based, and smart cities in the past 30 years. The difference between humane and human is also explained. It then emphasizes the need for an anthropocentric view of the development of a city rather than a technocentric view, stressing the point that a city exists for the well-being of its users in general, citizens and visitors, and technology is a tool toward that goal and not an end in itself. Three main drivers of the more HSSC are described: planning the city with live-work-play boroughs and focus on public (not private) transportation; focus on citizens' (and all other stakeholders in town) wishes, interests, and needs; and deindustrialization in the way of thinking—by far the most difficult driver to implement.

Chapter 2, Historical Overview: Cities from Medieval to Modern Times—What Went Wrong, recaps the history of the city from medieval times to the remodeling of Paris (the period when it was done right), and then from the industrial revolution through today (when it all went wrong). The first period, called here *the right*, describes the territorial expansion inland in Europe in Medieval times, when villages were set up away from rivers and seas. In that time, the human daily functions of "live, work and play" were basically conducted in the same location. Then the chapter focuses on Paris and its reurbanization in 1860 the last city to be planned in this *right* period. From there follows the *The wrong* period, from the industrial revolution through our times. Industrialization brought development, the private car for city transport and with its urban segregation of the daily functions of living, working, and playing. The chapter then lists facts and figures of the ensuing chaos and suggest what can be done.

In Chapter 3, From Smart Cities to More Humane and Sustainable Smart Cities: The World in Transformation, we dig deeper into the smart city context and all of its technologies such as cameras, sensors, IoT, AI, blockchain and big data, and their deployment in our cities. In whose interest is it launched? Privacy (or lack of) does impact on our daily lives? Are the giant tech companies good or evil? Then we discuss newer developments related to social changes in society as the millennials take over, such as the move from owning (the value of property) versus sharing (the value of usage) stuff. We then get back to the car and describe the perfect storm in the car industry (electric, shared, and autonomous) and its diminishing importance now and in the near future. Then we pinpoint the exhaustion of the smart city concept; discuss the emerging concept of the "3 Ds": Digitalization, decentralization, and decarbonization; and changes in public opinion. In order to clarify the HSSC concept further, this chapter suggests changes that can be proposed in any own in order to set the process of change in motion.

Cities evolve in very idiosyncratic ways in history, and no universal recipe applies to the development of their multiple features in time and space. For practical purposes, however, it is useful to conceive of a general framework to characterize cities in which a certain number of dimensions, each dimension referring to a set of desired functions or services, and each function/service with its readiness/performance indicators. Chapter 4, The Eight Dimensions of a More Humane and Sustainable Smart City, will suggest, for any given city, the set of indicators that will provide objective means to evaluate its situation and plan future actions. From the existing sets of characteristics of the existing definitions of new cities, this chapter details a framework to characterize humane, sustainable, and smart cities along "seven + one" dimensions, including economic development; people; public safety in general; use of the local historic, artistic, and cultural heritage; care of the environment; social inclusion; and citizen mobility, and plus one horizontal dimension, governance. Each dimension is described by the functions and/or services it is supposed to offer, and by the specific infrastructure demanded. Data from several sources are collected from well-known cities/places/projects in the world, in order to illustrate the proposed framework for practical use.

Usual listings of top "x" smart cities in the world invariably include "usual champions" such as London, Paris, Barcelona, New York, and Vancouver. Major cities in developed countries with plenty of resources and a long tradition of planning and management. But what about other cities, particularly in emerging countries where the largest megacities of the future are located today? What about medium/small-size cities which, for one reason or another, have gained prominence as more humane, sustainable, and/or smart than other cities? Chapter 5, Looking for Striking Humane and Sustainable Smart City Characteristics in Existing Cities, describes 30 examples of concrete project cases in the world, both from the champions and also places in that, albeit lesser known as exemplary textbook smart cities, exhibit at least one feature of an idealized HSSC or borough of an HSSC. Each case study example comprises of brief history of the place, the immediate challenge that stirred action, implementation aspects, the current situation, pending problems/difficulties, results for the citizens, future prospects, and lessons learned. Places selected include Palhoça, Curitiba and Caxias (Brazil), Singapore, Jyviskala (Finland), Nairobi (Nigeria), Barcelona (Spain), and many others. The main characteristics derived from these practical cases include starting small and continuously improving; enduring effort over (a long) time; and (pro-active) leadership.

Chapter 6, Where and How to Start in Your City, describes a methodology to transform an existing city. We suggest a guerrilla approach and course of action starting in a small borough, showing results, capturing hearts and minds, and moving forward. The one-week intensive workshop methodology developed by the author has been applied in a few boroughs already, and it includes the definition of participants and stakeholders for the workshop, materials to be distributed and format of the workshop, the use of the design thinking tool, the deliverables and expectations of participants, the actual results, and the governance of the project on the day after.

Then came the big blow of the pandemic 2020/21, depicted in Chapter 7, The Future: The Need for More Humane and Sustainable Smart Cities Postpandemic 2020/21. Although it is still occurring as we write this book, its effects and transformational power is already with us. It is not clear how we will develop from this crisis. We knew, before the crisis, that the knowledge society would evolve, with or without social inclusion, and that the social results did not look good that far. But the perception today by many analysts, including this one, is that KBD with social inclusion is now more viable than before. The crisis shortened the implantation of the "3 Ds" described in Chapter 3, From Smart Cities to More Humane and Sustainable Smart Cities: The World in Transformation, and the world's level of inequalities was thrown in our faces in the past few months. None of us liked what we saw. But the HSSC concept may be a helpful alternative to help create new forms of urban development *with* social inclusion. Other important concepts in Chapter 7, The Future: The Need for More Humane and Sustainable

Smart Cities Postpandemic 2020/21, as we look into the future, are that of The Commons, and the city as a Commons. This explains the importance of a new city and the buildup of citizenship of the "commons," followed by an improvement of relations between citizens and the local government as opposed to the provincial or the federal levels.

Chapter 8, Conclusions and a Call to Action, summarizes and draws conclusions on the work developed so far. If you are in haste, jump straight to this chapter, where you will find a summary of the book's findings. The chapter poses challenges for you, for me, and for us all. And it tries to frame the government in their proper capacity. The responsibility for change rests upon us, the citizens, not with the government. The chapter emphasizes the power of a single person. The book is then concluded with a call to action.

Read on.

References

Aravena, A., 2018. Interview to Arch Daily. <https://www.archdaily.com/906076/alejandro-aravena-shares-the-foundational-philosophies-at-the-core-of-his-socially-conscious-practice> (accessed 01.04.19.).

Azua, J., 2006. Bilbao: from the Guggenheim to the knowledge city. In: Carrillo, J. (Ed.), Knowledge Society: Approaches, Experiences and Perspectives. Elsevier, Oxford, pp. 97−112. , 2006.

Carrillo, J. (Ed.), 2006. Knowledge Society: Approaches, Experiences and Perspectives. Elsevier, Oxford.

Carrillo, J., 2015. Knowledge based development as a new economic culture. J. Open. Innov. Technol. Market Complex. 1, 15.

Chang, D.L., Marques, J.S., Costa, E.M., Selig, P.M., Yigitcanlar, T., 2018. Knowledge-based, smart and sustainable cities: a provocation for a conceptual framework. J. Open. Innov. Technol. Market Complex. 4 (1), 5.

Costa, E.M., 2001. Global E-commerce Strategies for Small Businesses. The MIT Press, Cambridge, MA.

Costa, E.M., Oliveira, Á.D., 2017. Humane smart cities. In: Frodeman, R., Klein, J.T., Pacheco, R.C. (Eds.), The Oxford Handbook of Interdisciplinarity, second ed. Oxford University Press, Oxford.

Deutschmann, M., 2017. The One Mile Radius. Advantage, Charleston, NC.

Florida, R., 2005. The Flight of the Creative Class: The New Global Competition for Talent. Harper Collins, New York, NY.

Florida, R., 2014. The Rise of the Creative Class. Basic Books, New York, NY.

Florida, R., 2017. The New Urban Crisis. Basic Books, New York, NY.

Glaeser, E.L., 2011. Triumph of the City. Penguim Press, New York, NY.

Howkins, J., 2001. Creative Economy. Penguin Books, USA.

Howkins, J., 2013. Creative Economy: How to Make Money from Ideas. Penguin Books.

Huang, C.C., Busch, C., Dongquan, H., Harvey, H., 2015. The 12 green guidelines. China development Bank Capital. <https://energyinnovation.org/wp-content/uploads/2015/12/12-Green-Guidelines.pdf> (accessed 15.03.19.).

ICLEI, 2019. Resilient Cities Report 2018. <https://resilientcities2018.iclei.org/wp-content/uploads/RC2018_Report.pdf> (accessed 19.03.19.).

Lara, A.P., Costa, E.M., Furlani, T.Z., Yigitcanlar, T., 2016. Smartness that matters: towards a comprehensive and human-centered characterization of smart cities. J. Open. Innov. Technol. Market Complex. 2 (1), 1−13.

Morse, M.L., Qing, C., 2012. The dynamic population of Manhattan. <https://wagner.nyu.edu/files/rudincenter/dynamic_pop_manhattan.pdf> (accessed 29.03.19.).

Register, R., 2006. Eco-cities: Rebuilding Cities in Balance with Nature. New Society Publishers.

The Rockfeller Foundation, 2013. 100 resilient cities. <https://www.rockefellerfoundation.org/our-work/initiatives/100-resilient-cities/> (accessed 19.03.19).

United Nations, 2015. The sustainable development summit. <https://sustainabledevelopment.un.org/post2015/summit>.

Yencken, D., 2013. Creative cities. Space Place Cult. 2013.

Yigitcanlar, T., Lee, S., 2011. Moving towards a knowledge city? Brisbane's experience in knowledge-based urban development. Int. J. Knowl. Organ. 1, 22−38. Available from: https://doi.org/10.4018/ijkbo.2011070102.

Yigitcanlar, T., Marques, J.S., Lorenzi, C., Bernardinetti, N., Schreiner, T., Fachinelli, A., et al., 2018a. Towards smart Florianópolis: what does it take to transform a tourist island into an innovation capital? Energies. 2018 11 (12), 3265.

Yigitcanlar, T., Kamruzzaman, M., Buys, L., Ioppolo, G., Marques, J.S., Costa, E.M., et al., 2018b. Understanding 'smart cities': intertwining development drivers with desired outcomes in a multidimensional framework. Cities. April.

Yigitcanlar, T., O'Connor, K., Westerman, C., 2008. The making of knowledge cities: Melbourne's knowledge-based urban development experience. Cities 25 (2), 63−72.

Chapter 2

Historical overview: cities from medieval to modern times—what went wrong

I think that cars today are almost the exact equivalent of the great Gothic cathedrals; I mean the supreme creation of an era, conceived with passion by unknown artists, and consumed in image if not in usage by a whole population which appropriates them as a purely magical object.

Roland Barthes.

The good...

Medieval villages

It would make no sense to further a romantic idea or depict life in medieval times as glamorous or interesting—even less when compared to today's standards, of course. But there are some characteristics of city living at this time that are important to this study and they will be described in detail here. We can learn from them.

The reference is to villages in Europe, between the 12th and 15th centuries. There are different definitions for the medieval era and even more of the subsequent era of the renaissance (Gies and Gies, 1969). But around medieval times, the world had four main different civilizations being developed in parallel: the European, the Chinese, the Hindu, and the Islamic worlds. They had very few interactions amongst them but albeit growing apart, daily life in these civilizations had several features in common mostly because the main activity was based upon agriculture for subsistence. Villages (up to 10,000 people) and a few cities (more than 10,000 but rarely above 100,000 people) were formed and grew, hosting families around some kind of rulers, such as princes, bishops, and lords, and some had a town council composed of merchants and craftsmen's guilds.

In order to defend themselves from enemies, many villages were fortified: They were enclosed inside a round wall at least 3 m thick and sometimes more than 10 m high. The local inhabitants lived and conducted most

Humane and Sustainable Smart Cities. DOI: https://doi.org/10.1016/B978-0-12-819186-6.00003-8

of their daily activities within these walls. Peasants went outside during daytime to harvest and hunt. The rulers, the clergy, and the merchants stayed in, apart from special times when they conducted specific campaigns such as battles, missions, or trade travels.

Life in the village consisted of the daily chores of preparing food, building shelter, sewing clothes, etc. The village churches announced the passing of time at regular intervals, some of them related to the time for prayers. Studying was reserved for boys and classes were taught by the local church where the bishop or some of his aides, taught Latin, mathematics, and philosophy. Entertainment was also within the walls and there were many festive days when everyone was in the village. Even for a peasant, life in a medieval village could be enjoyable, provided they had a benign lord and the year had a good harvest.

But the point that is interesting to this study is that everyone lived, worked, and played in a very restricted area, limited either by the fortified wall, or by the fact that they could not carry water very far from the main well in the village. Ken Larson, who researches smart cities at the MIT Media Lab (Larson, 2012), suggested this is the main reason medieval villages did not grow much more than a round area of 1-mile radius around the center square where the main water well was located. In fact this is the origin of the expression "the last mile" largely used in telecommunications and many other fields such as in marketing when they refer to "the extra mile": It means the distance between a source of some goods or services and the end consumer. In telecommunications, it refers to the distance between the old phone exchange and the subscriber. In a marketing campaign, it points to a means of reaching each individual customer.

The point here is that through the ages, from medieval times to the industrial revolution, people tended to live, work, and play in the same area. Traveling, when it existed at all, was mostly limited to the exchange of goods, mainly spices and cloths, or to military actions and conquests.

One tragic event of this era was the Bubonic Plague or the Black Death of 1348−50. It is estimated that the plague killed c.50% of the estimated peak European population of 73 million people within a very short period, due to several diseases but mostly caused by a bacteria hosted on black rats: Once the rat population was decimated by the disease, rat fleas carried the disease on to humans. It could only have happened in the cities since propagation would be much slower in the fields.

After the plague, both servants and serfs were paid more due to the shortage of labor and that had an impact on the development of Europe from there on, since serfdom was gradually eradicated and there was more money to buy goods and services. International trade boomed after that and led the way to the big transformation of Europe into the center of the world with the navigational adventures into foreign land and the riches they brought back in terms of tradable goods and precious minerals.

Cities continued to grow with the rapid expansion of the population after the plague and the beginning of the great navigations from Europe. But the medieval concept of living, working, and playing in the same area was carried through the ages and influenced the urban organization of cities up to the 19th century. The re-urbanization of Paris was emblematic of this period.

Napoleon III, Haussmann, and Paris around 1860

Let us now fast forward to the 1800s. Paris was a city with dreams of grandeur at the outset of the 19th century. But although it was the largest city in continental Europe, and some of the palaces such as The Louvre, Les Tuileries, and others were already there, the city was not a model for anything. It was dirty; streets in the city center and around town were narrow and unpaved. The central market at Les Halles was very unhealthy, with livestock and food displayed on the ground. Buyers mingled with stray dogs and cats and went by along with pushcarts that replenished the stalls.

Napoleon I, who ruled France at the time, wanted to transform Paris from the then 500,000 inhabitants to a vibrant 2,000,000 capital and a symbol of his reign. After becoming emperor, in 1804, he accelerated the work and developed new bridges, the new Madeleine Church, and a giant arch at the western entrance to the city (Arc de Triomphe). He also set up plans to provide access to safe drinking water, a major problem at the time. His power in Europe grew up to 1808 when he had a close grip on the country and its neighbors.

This period did not last long and he could not accomplish everything he planned. After the troubled period known as the Napoleonic wars, he had to abdicate in 1814, after a disastrous invasion of Russia in 1812 when the Russians managed to annihilate 5/6 of his 600,000 troops, in the beginning of a particularly severe Russian winter.

Napoleon's focus on the international scene did not leave much room for the planning and execution of his vision for the capital. After his definitive downfall in 1815, and for the next two decades, not much happened in the city until the arrival of the new mayor Rambuteau, in 1834. He was responsible for major changes in the old city center, including a new boulevard by the Les Halles market that had large sidewalks and that introduced a novelty at the time: gas street lamps. The new arterial road, that today carries his name, allowed for walks at night, which completely changed the commercial use of the area. Another of his great achievements was the new Place de la Concorde with the tall obelisk donated by the King of Egypt and that tried to eclipse the dramatic executions at the same place of King Louis XVI and Queen Marie Antoinette some 50 years before. Rambuteau also introduced greenery into the city with trees on all major boulevards and public parks. Before him, all the major parks in town were private. By the closing of his term, the new Paris had started to emerge: a startling city. A visitor, coming from the west, would enter the town through the Arc de Triomphe, descend Les Champs Eliseés to the new Place de la Concorde, through the Jardin de Tuileries and further down to the Palace de Tuileries, the king's residence. By far, it was the most impressive setup one could observe anywhere in the world.

London and other industrial towns in England dominated the economic and political world with the British Empire at its summit. France, after the defeat in the Napoleonic wars and all sorts of political trouble, concentrated its development as the cultural center of the world with Paris as a reference point for every manifestation of art. The city gathered musicians, writers, painters, and other artists from everywhere in Europe. Paris simply thrived with an artistic explosion of everything. People spent hours in the cafés in the large sidewalks talking about their ideas and dreams, day and night.

Prince Luis Napoleon Bonaparte arrived back in Paris in 1848 after 33 years in exile. He was a nephew of Napoleon I on both sides and carried a prestigious lineage. With the deaths of several of his relatives, he became the first in line in the Napoleon Dynasty. He had lived in London until then, but traveled extensively through Europe and even New York (a feat at the time), and had dreams of not only becoming the next ruler in France but of transforming Paris further into the most beautiful city in the world. He learned a great deal from short experiences he had living in other towns in Europe. The development of the city would build up from the recent improvements that had already established Paris as the cultural center of the world.

But the Prince needed power to transform his plans into concrete actions. France had become a republic on that same year of 1848 and, even before returning to France, Luis Napoleon managed to be elected for the new National Assembly, where he had a very modest term. But a few months later, came the first election for president in the country's history. Through a series of connections all over France and political maneuvering that testified to his political cunning; his understanding of the new world where the working classes would be, for the first time, allowed to vote; and to his last-minute allies that were certain that they would control him in power, Louis Napoleon managed to be elected with 74% of the votes in December 1848. An amazing accomplishment for a man that had been exiled, imprisoned twice, and deported before returning to France only months before.

At the beginning of his term, Louis Napoleon's presidency seemed to be destined to a transition period with him as a puppet of the Parisian establishment. But he quickly established links with the common people in the interior, the working classes and, most importantly for his plans, with the military. Three years into his term, a period that could not be extended unless of a constitutional change, he staged a coup d'état supported by the military and extended his presidency to 10 years instead of the original four. That bold move was followed, 1 year later, by a plebiscite where he was voted emperor under the name Napoleon III. The speech that led to his empire (historically known as the second empire) was read in a grand meeting in Bordeaux under the auspices of mayor George-Eugène Haussmann.

After a few months as emperor and with his reign firmly in place, Napoleon III felt strong enough to sack the existing Paris mayor Jean-Jacques Berger, and substituted him by his friend Haussmann. Berger had been adamant of running the city into debt in order to rebuild it—just to please the emperor. This replacement had a profound impact on the French capital and on the redevelopment of other cities in Europe and elsewhere. In the words of historian Stephane Kirkland (2013) "if there was ever an instance in history when the appointment of a civil servant brought together the appropriate aptitudes and capabilities for a specific mission, this was it! The combination of Napoleon III and George-Eugène Haussmann would change Paris forever." And the world too, one might add, considering the impact the Paris had over other cities in Europe.

After his inauguration as the new mayor, Haussmann was taken by Napoleon III to his private office, adjacent to the main office at the Palais de Tuileries, where he had a model plan of Paris and several drawings in color of new boulevards, squares, and new buildings. The emperor had a vision for the grand new capital of his empire. Haussmann was put in charge of executing it. They immediately set afoot to start *les grands travaux* (the big works) in the city. The goal was to have the new Paris glittering for the second World Exhibition (the first was held in London in 1851) to be held in town in 1855. It all started with the already planned extension of Rue de Rivoli, followed by several other boulevards and streets.

The trouble was financing. The city had difficulty approving an extended budget through the City Council for its first steps. But once the new avenues were done, there was not enough capital to build the new facilities. The private sector was weary of the new regime in its first years, not knowing for sure how long it would last.

So besides fighting the city's bureaucracy, Haussmann had also to convince wealthy individuals to invest in new buildings, hotels, and commercial buildings. That is when some of his friends devised a new financial instrument. Up to that time, existing banks lent their own money to customers. The new instrument would have to be based on a much wider pool of capital coming from the private sector. So, they launched the idea of private funds to invest in real estate that would be repaid with the results of the ventures. A new mortgage bank was formed, the Crédit Foncier de France, that exists still today.

The move spurred other novelties and another Societé Générale de Crédit Mobilier was formed to invest in the private sector where loans would be guaranteed by the actual ventures financed, the same way real estate guaranteed the mortgages. When the new bank launched its shares in the French stock market, it was a huge success. It then went on to finance most of the infrastructure projects in Paris and in France as a whole, later expanding to finance foreign governments as far North Africa. The first venture was the real estate project along the extension of Rue de Rivoli, just opposite from the Louvre. The centerpiece of the project was the Grand Hotel du Louvre, a massive structure with 700 rooms and an aristocratic shopping mall on the ground floor. The owners of the bank included a bastard half-brother of the emperor that was a usual guest at the court. He brought privileged information from the government to the bank and that helped the bank thrive for years.

Government's concessions of state assets combined with the new financial mechanisms helped develop new buildings, canals, railways, and buildings in the new streets of Paris, and were fundamental to the ensuing development of the new capital.

Haussmann planned his transformation of Paris initially for the old town, where he completely redesigned arrondissements 1, 2, 3, and 4. With the success of his intervention, he was then authorized by the emperor to rebuild the whole 20 arrondissements of the City into what is pretty much the urban design that we can appreciate today.

Paris influenced other major cities In Europe. Everyone who visited Haussmann's Paris returned home with the idea of doing something similar in their own city and country. The new Paris architecture was carried to cities such as Barcelona, Budapest, Vienna, Milan, and many others, including some cities in the new world of the colonies. Rio and Buenos Aires, for instance, in Latin America, show clear influences of the Paris plan still today such as the Avenida Central (now Rio Branco Avenue) in Rio and Buenos Aires's large avenues plazas and sidewalks, developments that were built in these countries in the beginning of the 20th century.

One example of Paris influence over cities in Europe was the work of engineer Ildefons Cerdà in Barcelona, who won a commission to plan the expansion of the Catalonian Capital (the Eixample, expansion in Catalan) in 1859. Cerdà believed that the expansion of the new industrial cities such as Barcelona should combine the best aspects of both the rural and the urban life and planned the new blocks with two rows of buildings and space in between them for growing vegetables. Buildings were low rise and the new blocks ended at a 45-degree angle with small plazas, much as he had seen in Paris. Some of his original plan was diverted though, in order to please eager builders with occupation of the open spaces and with licenses to build higher buildings. But most of it remained, such as the avenues and streets that were 20 m large with 5 m of sidewalks, a feature that has been admired by visitors ever since, and that impresses people who visit the city still today.

Cerdà compiled his work into a book published in 1867 called the *General Theory of Urbanization*. The very term urbanism is accredited to him and his ideas influenced back the French in the new research area called *urbanisme* and the American and English areas of Town Planning. From then on, towns and cities started to plan their expansion before actually building them, designing streets, plazas, housing, commercial and other facilities according to the social needs of the population at the time.

In the early 20th century, urban planning was a trend in most of the then developed world and cities began to work according to zoning codes, which established the allowed uses for the land in different parts of town. In these codes, building heights were limited (say 4 stories, up to 20 m, downtown, and down to one or two stories, up to 11 m, further out from town). Land coverage was also established ranging from say 40% in the outer boroughs to 75% downtown.

But the medieval principle, the one that was kept in the redevelopment of Paris, of working, living, and playing in the same area was later challenged by the consolidation of the industrial revolution and the need to segregate functions within the city. That was when things started to move in the other (wrong) direction.

The bad. . .

The industrial revolution

The industrial revolution started somewhere along the 18th century in different countries in Europe, with the substitution of the artisan work for rudimentary machines in the production of basic goods such as shoes and clothes. Some historians even dislike the term *revolution* since it would be the result of an *evolution* from rudimentary machines to the invention and use of the steam engine. The steam technology was based on the simple fact that heated steam exerted pressure and provoked movement, and this principle generated all the different machines that followed.

But it was only in the second half of the 19th century that the impact of the industrial revolution was spread from England to other countries in Europe and other places with the use of the steam engine for trolleys in mines and to propel boats and rail locomotives (Roberts, 1980). It also had profound social and economic impacts with the emergence of a new class of rich people with no traces of nobility: capitalists and industrialists, later followed by merchants and all sorts of intermediaries that moved the industrial goods from the factories to the end consumer.

On the urban side, the new industries, initially set up in the city, had to be removed further out of town because of pollution and dirt produced by the industrial process. That was the unfortunate beginning of the segregation of the daily functions of living, working, and playing

The industrial revolution's poster child: the car

Of all the marvels of the industrial revolution, none has attracted more attention, and commanded more loyalty, akin to the creation of a "motordom" (Schwartz, 2015) or a "car kingdom" than the automobile, or popularly, the car. Not surprising: It was really a machine that changed the world (the computer might be a runner-up in this contest). Suddenly people could move from one place to another, provided there were passable roads and streets, swiftly and at their own time and will. It is a very useful tool, no doubt. But the fact that it commanded that much reverence and loyalty, and carried them up to our times, is just amazing.

It was the ingenuity and engineering skills of Henry Ford and other entrepreneurs at the beginning of the century that produced the miracle. They invented and launched the serial production industrial line and managed to cut the final cost of the new machine to the customer to a reasonable level. At the turn of the 20th century, there were only a few cars in the United States, belonging to the upper classes, and their driving on a city street was followed by pedestrians as a true novelty. With the standardization of Ford's model T in 1908 though, and its commercial success, the number of cars grew steeply: By 1924, Ford alone was turning out 500,000 model Ts a year and grabbed 50% of the US market.

From there on, production went further up. And it is curious that 100 years after that, the car is still running the show and with very few innovations. The changes in the original idea of the car are dismal compared to, for instance, what happened in, say, the communications sector or the house appliances sector.

Until now.

Maybe the car industry is not as healthy as before, but this will be detailed later on in this chapter.

With the introduction of millions of cars to the city streets in the United States, a battle started to unravel for the "right-of-way." Streets used to be for everyone and for diverse use. But with cars running around, they became dangerous: in the 1920s, between 20,000 and 30,000 people were being killed a year in the United States due to traffic accidents. This tragic number peaked to 50,000 per year in the 1980s and is now down to 36,000 a year, including drivers, occupants, pedestrians, and bikers.

Motordom became so powerful in the United States that it won a definitive battle for the right-of-way over everything else in a panel convened by President Hoover in 1926 composed of 31 people: 25 representatives from the car and rubber industries, the automobile clubs, and the yellow cab companies against 5 representatives from the rail industry and 1 from the pedestrians. The car lobby won, of course, as we can notice almost everywhere, and took not only the pedestrian out of the way, but also the electric bus, by then a very viable and cheap means of mass transport in many cities.

But perhaps the major victory of motordom is the absurd concept that everything needed for the car infrastructure (streets, roads, viaducts, bridges, and even downtown parking) is the responsibility and cost of the City Hall and indirectly the local taxpayer's (driver or no driver). The amount of this subsidy is difficult to measure, but it is huge, and unfair. We will return to this point in the book.

Modernism and urban planning

With the advent of urban planning as a discipline and a practice, many people started to have ideas about how to regulate the use of different parts of the city for different uses. Of all these people, three were particularly harmful not only to the practical implementation of their ideas in existing or newly planned towns, but also for the 20th century thinking of urban planners and city officials, a malady that is widespread still today: Englishman Ebenezer Howard, the famous Swiss-French architect Le Corbusier, and the then Chicago mayor Daniel Burnham.

Ebenezer Howard was a court reporter in London and took city planning as a hobby. Accustomed to the lives of the royals, he disliked the exterior signs of poverty in London (with every reason) and devised a new town plan—he baptized it the Garden City—instances of which would be built outside the capital, thus thinning out London and moving most people to the country. The Garden City would have 30,000 people living in well-developed residential areas, around a "downtown" where commerce of all basic necessities (defined by city hall) would happen. Everything else was also planned: schools, parks, amenities, etc. The Garden City would be surrounded by agricultural land and the local government would keep strict control of everything. Howard's plan did not go far, and only two villages were built (one in England and one in Sweden), but his utopia did influence city planning all over the world. One of the nasty side effects of the Garden City concept is the segregation of functions within a city: in particular, the segregation of living, working, and playing in different parts of the town, a common mistake that can be widely observed still today.

The French architect Le Corbusier expanded the Garden City idea in another direction, in order to make it more practical for larger populations: tall buildings for living and working, well separated from each other, and grass everywhere. In fact, in his plan, land coverage should be reduced to 15% in residential areas and 25% in commercial areas. And cars should be used for everything. He called his model city the Radiant City.

The Garden City advocates did not like the novelty: They wanted to spread people around, not concentrate them. But the same "bad trip" of central planning was there. The trouble with Le Corbusier's ideas is that it directly influenced the design of several new towns in the world such as the Brazilian capital Brasília, built from 1958 to 1960. The solid concept that a resident would behave, the way he was planned to, in everyday life cracks dramatically when faced with reality. In Brasília today, many people wonder how is it possible to live in a city that has no or very few sidewalks and where every kind of service is grouped in clusters (to the extreme of an absurd "pharmacies block")?

Le Corbusier had a large impact on architectural thinking and an enormous contribution to modern architecture for buildings (Mumford, 2018), mainly official monuments. As for his urbanistic ideas, there is much less to praise him for.

Apart from the Garden City and The Radiant City, another instance of the same "bad trip" of total central planning is the City Beautiful concept, popularized by Chicago mayor Donald Burnham. It started during the Chicago Columbian Exposition of 1893 and gained momentum in several places in the early 20th century with the construction of monuments for public use in beautiful places such as parks and new boulevards but completely detached from the existing city. It did not work, of course, and since the monument did not offer the city services around it, it had to allow for parlors and tents selling low-quality stuff to be set up in the lawn, completely beating the purpose of the city beautiful. Check in your city: There may be some monuments that follow this pattern.

Jane Jacobs was the first to bash these concepts and defend the need for diversity in cities and the maintenance of old buildings and the reorganization of existing poor dwellings (or slums) instead of just wiping them out. The very first phrase of her delightful and insightful book *The Death and Life of Great American Cities* (Jacobs, 1961) sets the tone: "This book is an attack on current city planning and rebuilding."

Her influence in the second half of the 20th century was significant. Her denial of modernism and the "system" was soon to be identified with the hippie movement of the late 1960s, a few years after the publication of the book. She was not a great critic of the car though and did not see it as a major problem in the city as many other people do (including this author). Maybe because her work was centralized in New York, a place where the car was already losing ground at her time while in the rest of the world (and indeed still in the developing world today) urban planning is still based on motordom.

Modernism and urban planning in the 20th century solidified the concept of segregation of living, working, and playing in separate areas of the city and, along with it, crowned the car as the winning species that had to be taken care of in the city. This misconception was not was not apparent at first, but it was predominant in city planners' thoughts anyway.

As for the existing cities, "unstudied, unrespected, cities have served as sacrificial victims" (Jacobs, 1961) to the new theories of urbanism that modeled cities in the first half of the 20th century. The effects of these theories left us with ugly problems in our cities that we now have to tackle.

And the ugly...

Urban chaos

The results of planning cities for the car, only worked reasonably, while the number of cars was small. When everyone and their dog have a car, cities do not work well. In fact, they are not working at all in many parts of the world, in particular in the developing countries. São Paulo, a megalopolis in Brazil, is a city of 12 million people and many problems, where traffic jams, for instance, are a nightmare. So many people have predicted that São Paulo is going to come to a complete halt, that a group of academics actually bothered to meet and define what is and when the city will actually come to a halt. The result points to the day when one particular deadlock in traffic will be so bad that it will take 24 hours for the last car to disentangle from the mess! And when is that going to happen? It will be a heavy rainy Friday, before a long weekend (with a holiday on Monday). How far in the future is that particular day? No consensus here. Some predicted it in months, and others in weeks. But soon enough... And, to make matters worse, the city alone is licensing 800 new cars *per day*.

But traffic jams are not the only problem. Disposal of parts and pieces of old cars, and in particular of used tires, is a difficult problem to solve worldwide. There are some new technologies that propose to use them for something useful like road pavements or buildings, but nothing materialized in any large scale up to now. Valuable space in the cities is taken as parking lots, as has been shown before. Air pollution from CO_2 emissions from fossil fuels burning is again one of the main causes of the degradation of the environment and of the dangerous climate changes the world is suffering in modern times.

There is still another social problem derived from traffic jams that enervate drivers outside their limits of good behavior. Argentinian film *Relatos Salvajes* (2014) shows how two apparently normal people can get so angry in a road dispute that they try and manage to kill each other as a result. What is the social cost of the overall aggravation from traffic jams in our towns? Further down in this chapter there is a side effect on commuters complaining to their children against traffic in the streets. But the fact is, the situation is not good. And, in many places it is certainly getting worse, before anything is done in the right direction. Some possible "right directions" are suggested in the way forward section of this chapter.

The car as a problem

The number of traffic-related deaths (mostly cars and motorbikes) in the world is up to 1,350,000 in 2016, according to the World Health Organization. That number is just unacceptable. It is much more than any contemporary conflicts between countries. And worse, it is not even known by the population. TV news that report accidents and war conflicts on a global scale every night everywhere does not refer to this gruesome statistics. It is by far the largest cause of nonnatural deaths in the world. And it is worse than the total number of deaths by the major coronavirus pandemic of 2020. Think of it again: Traffic in the cities kills more people than the pandemic 2020, and it happens *every year*! What is the world doing about it?

Very little. A few campaigns against drinking and driving (alcohol is one of the main causes of accidents) and speeding, and life goes on, unabated. Even for the families of those involved in the accidents. It is as if this carnage were a fact of life!

Most of the accidents happen in town. Besides the social cost and misery brought upon the families of the deceased, there is the economic costs of treating the crippled, disabled, and injured in these accidents, an even larger number, between 20 and 50 million of them a year in the world.

The city has a problem that must be tackled, now.

Social disintegration

The number of suicides worldwide is almost just as bad, over 1 million a year. Statistics are not published widely in this case and some countries just do not classify or count it. But it is big. The social causes of suicides are a different subject altogether and will not be dealt with here. But since more than half of the world's population is in the city (and the numbers are growing) it seems reasonable to believe that an improvement in the livability of our cities will help in solving this tragedy too.

Hopelessness and anxiety are other problems related to the modern life in our cities (Harari, 2015). Once the sense of neighborhood is lost, the feeling of loneliness and all other social dysfunctions increase. A lone killer in Boston in 2001 entered the office where he worked and killed several people there at random and then killed himself. The police went, soon after the crime, to the place where he lived for several years, in search of motivations for the shooting and other connections. They found nothing. Nobody knew him in the building or in the borough where he lived. Only one of his neighbors reported remembering seeing him once in the elevator, "because of his long beard." A young man lives in a building in a city for years and nobody remembers him? There is something wrong in the city and that certainly needs change.

Slums are another cause of the growth of our cities, mostly (but not only) in the developing world. But as pointed out by Glaeser (2011) slums are, to a large degree, a solution, not a problem, since the living conditions of the people who moved there from the hinterland, from wars, from racial persecution, and other causes, although terrible, are actually better than what they had before, where they escaped from hunger, assassination, or abuse. They left in search of jobs, opportunities, and education for their children, and that could only be found in the city.

From this section of current life in the city today, it looks as if people would be running for the gates to get out in search of a better living. But no, they are flocking in. The city has the best job opportunities, the best schools, the best entertainment, and the feeling of being part of the real world. What is needed, and this book is about, is how to keep the good things the cities present us with, while trying to get rid of the bad things that cause so many of the problems reported above. And improvements are at reach, with small changes. Keep reading.

The way forward!

The millennials are the generation that was born after 1980 or 1984, according to different definitions. Predictions about their behavior have been actually wrong but the actual observation and measuring of their behavior signal at least one remarkable change: For the first time in our recent history, they are driving less and are less interested in cars than before, at least in the United States and in Europe. Until 2004 the total mileage driven in the United States had been going up every single year, apart from wartime, major crises, and fuel shortages. After these disruptions, the upward trend resumed and in some years at an even stronger pace than before, up to 2004, and that was *before* the major crisis of 2008. In this crisis it did go the furthest down, but the number did not grow afterward. In fact, it continued to go down. The millennials are just not that much interested in cars as their parents were.

The reasons for this are many. Their generation is more attuned to experiences of living and less on possessing stuff. Their parents bought many pieces of household appliances and equipment that their grandparents did not have. Millennials are used to these commodities and are not excited about them. In the case of the car, they evaluate the benefit of having it against the actual costs involved and the balance is not alluring. The end result is that a large percentage (varying from country to country) of this generation do not even bother to apply for a driving license. Curiously, one of the reasons for this attitude, according to transport specialist Sam Schwartz (2015) is that millennials that were driven everywhere by their parents, especially those commuters from the greenbelts (boroughs in the outskirts of large cities with lots of greenery and large houses) to the cities where they worked, spent their teen years listening to both their parents' complaints against the traffic, the price of fuel, the cost of maintenance of their cars, and such. The complaining happened in their car trips and at their dinner table, where one of the favorite subjects was how bad was their commute on that particular day. After hearing these whinges for years, it is small wonder the millennials are not interested in the source of so much aggravation.

Such a major change in behavior has not yet been fully accounted for but it will have a profound impact in our cities.

In the developed world the move from suburbia (the green belt) back to town in a generation or two will leave empty millions of unwanted large houses far from major cities. American planner Arthur Nelson estimates that in the United States alone there will be some 25 million unwanted green belt houses by 2025 (Nelson, 2006).

In the developing world, the process of urbanization is different. It means moving large populations from the countryside, where there are no more jobs, to the cities, where these people hope to find better opportunities.

The compound effect of people returning to the city from suburbia in the developed world with the needs of the new population in cities in the developing world points to a pressing need to plan and implement new facilities in our cities to accommodate this new demand. UN estimates that by 2050 2/3 of the world's population will be living in cities.

A few guidelines are suggested here.

Live-work-play in the same area

As we have seen, in the 1900s, the urban planning trend was to segregate the daily functions of living, working, and playing into separate boroughs of the city. As most of our cities grew enormously during this century, most of our cities are the result of this planning. In other words, most people in the world today have to commute from home to work and from either one to any kind of entertainment. And any people do this using their private car. The city code regulates this segregation so you cannot have, for instance, a bakery at the corner of a residential block in a gated community. People's attitudes and behavior are difficult to standardize but even taking into account the risk of slipping into generality, it is very difficult to think that the residents would not want a bakery there.

Once the city starts to think of integrating boroughs with the three basic functions of living, working, and playing, mobility of the locals takes a completely different direction. Suddenly, sidewalks, bike lanes, and public transport gain a new status of importance. Let us tackle them in turn.

Care of the sidewalks has been neglected in most of our cities as a nuisance. In many cities, all over the world, they have been even *reduced* to make way for the car, either as new lanes on the streets or as parking spaces. It is very common to provide free parking space downtown for cars that take that precious public space for the whole day (and the cars took only one person each to work) while thousands of pedestrians try to make their way through a tiny stretch of sidewalk next to the parked cars. It is difficult to think of anything more stupid and unfair in terms of public use of the land. Yet, nobody questions this arrangement because the car kingdom is just too powerful, and city officials don't dare to propose anything different. It is just insane!

The difficulty to change this situation is being tried in different cities with small measures to attract public support. For instance, the parklet is a small wooden deck that takes the street space of, say, two parking slots next to the curb, decorated with plants and benches, and that stretches the serving area of a restaurant or café. Once people get used to the idea and find it nice, other places start to implement the parklet and eventually it is there for the whole block and a precious area of public space is reclaimed back from the car to pedestrians. It is a guerrilla tactic but works well and can be tried anywhere. It requires some kind of change in the city code, but since it looks small initially, it does not spark the same revolt as a full reduction of public parking would.

Tourists that walk around the Champs Elyseés in Paris or Las Ramblas in Barcelona marvel at that large sidewalk and interesting places to shop, go about, and visit. It does not cost much to have large sidewalks in some of the avenues in your city. Why not?

Citizen's wishes, interests, and needs

Each and every elected politician says in her speech that she is there to represent and answer to the needs of her voters and the population as a whole. The same is true of City Hall politicians and administrators. But then again... no, that is not what actually happens. There is a haughtiness in most administrations that makes them behave like royals from previous times. In Portuguese speaking countries such as Portugal and Brazil, when a citizen puts a case against the state, he is legally referred to as the supplicant ("suplicante" in Portuguese). One can almost depict the picture: the citizen on his knees pleading for or begging for mercy. Jane Jacobs (1961) refers to city hall administrators as the "emperors." Funnily enough, Jacobs' "emperors" are in fact civil *servants*! Explanation for this paradox is beyond the scope of this book but suffice it to recognize that that is true and act upon it accordingly. Attitudes must change. Administrators are there to *serve* their constituents. To begin with listening to their wishes, interests, and needs.

It is important to define the word citizen in this context. Citizen, for the lack of a better word, is defined here as anyone that lives or uses the city on a regular basis. Besides people who actually live there, it includes merchants, daily or nightly workers who commute there, regular visitors, tourists, etc. It would be foolish to plan Manhattan, for instance, for its population of 1.5 million residents not taking into account the floating population of workers, visitors, etc. that double this number on a typical working day.

How to make citizens engaged in the solution of their city's problems? It is not easy, but one hint is to try and create the atmosphere of the old neighborhoods where everyone cared about everyone else (in the good and in the bad sense of course). People tend to unite around specific problems. For instance, many cities in the world have neighborhoods that practice the "crime watch" concept. If they spot, see, or suspect something, they report it immediately. In order to implement this, of course, one needs a system of surveillance/action in place and trust of the local police force. It is of no use just to post a placard in the borough's entrance.

In order to really listen to the population, it is much wiser to divide the city into several administrative districts as proposed by Jane Jacobs. Only local people, living, working, or regularly visiting the place, have full account of its needs.

Paris and Barcelona are two of the denser cities in Europe (respectively, first, with c.20,000 people per square kilometer, and fourth, 16,000). They are two of the most admired too. That is not to say that to have a better city it should be denser, of course. It points to the fact that quality of life in a city has to do with many other factors and that density alone is not an indication of anything. In fact, in many cities, it is much better to allow for an increase in density in order to avoid city sprawling that is very costly in terms of the provision of services by the City Hall and costly in terms of transport and energy consumption.

One of the mantras of city planning should be the provision of good data for decision-making. Janette Sadik-Khan, New York's former Secretary of Transport, under Michael Bloomberg's administration, reports in her public talks that the mayor liked to repeat this phrase: "In God, we trust. Everybody else, bring data." Not surprising, of course, coming from an entrepreneur who made it big producing financial data in the successful company that bears his name. But very appropriate as well.

Following this practice, Sadik-Khan wanted to study a better use for Broadway in Manhattan. New York has a well-known classical grid of parallel streets at mostly fixed intervals, crossed by parallel avenues a bit more spaced in between them. The only diagonal avenue is the large Broadway, all across the city. Janette was well aware that any changes in the number of lanes for cars in Broadway would face an uproar of protests. So, she first started with data. How many people use the street daily by car/buses versus pedestrians? The surprising number showed the proportion of four pedestrians for every motorized user. That being the case, the precious public space of that road should be used proportionally 4 to 1 in favor of pedestrians. But how to implement this? If you asked local merchants what they thought about closing a car lane in the avenue, most of them were radically against it. So, the Transport Secretariat produced a plan to close down a few blocks around Times Square during the weekend and measure the population response to it: Pedestrians and bikers loved it, of course. But merchants liked it too, since they reported an average increase in revenues for the weekend as 50% (Sadik-Khan and Sollomonow, 2017). This was due to the fact that people on foot or on a bike are much more likely to stop and buy something than people driving by. Obvious, isn't it?

But obviousness for city plans and decisions is not enough. It has to be backed by numbers. With these numbers in hand, the Secretary of Transport could plan a new use for the space at Broadway and implemented it all the way in stages. Most people in Manhattan were very pleased with the change and the results are there today to be admired by everybody: large sidewalks, plazas, places to sit outside restaurants and cafés, new urban equipment such as benches and tables, segregated bike lanes, etc. But it has to be remembered: It was not easy to implement. It took talking, listening, convincing, prototyping, measuring, changing, and trying again. It is the classical Deming's circle of Plan-Do-Check-Adjust with the notable addition of talking-listening or even better listening-talking to local people. The recipe is clear.

Edward Glaeser, a Harvard professor, wrote an impressive "contra" book *The Triumph of the City* questioning not only the planning of the cities but also the environmentalists and residents that suffered from the not-in-my-backyard syndrome and never thought of the city as a common good. He challenged the common notions that higher density is bad, green is good, and asphalt is bad, and the overprotection in the city code of some city's characteristics that may be positive. For instance, when density avoids a city's urban sprawl, it is good for the environment, for the city and for the residents. As with Janette Sadik-Khan's, his ideas are backed by numbers and he demonstrates their feasibility.

Mental deindustrialization

The concept has been referred to in Chapter 1, The concept of more Humane and Sustainable Smart Cities. Yes, we live in a postindustrial era. No, we do not acknowledge that in full, and behave as if we did not!

The way forward in our cities begins with the full realization that most of our workers, commuters, and people in general, move about town at different times and that trend is going to continue as we fix working times more flexibly and set opening hours of commerce and services accordingly. Take, for instance, a new company that develops software to identify ringtones worldwide that may appeal and seem more interesting for different segments of society (this company exists and employs 27 people in Boston!). Workers should meet sometime to exchange ideas, share projects, and exchange knowledge of their trade. But do they need to work from 9 to 5? In fact, do they need to work in the same place at all?

The success of the new office sharing facility known as coworking is a manifestation of this trend. People share office space at different working hours and different days of the week. WeWork, the largest company in the new business, founded in 2010, has now more than 500 offices in 36 countries and hosts almost 300,000 workers worldwide. And one might think this is only for startups and such but one in five of their members is an employee of a large corporation. WeWork has long passed the mark of a "unicorn" (startup that reaches a market valuation of US$1 billion) and is valued at around US$50 billion! Their offices have extended working hours (in some places 24 h × 7days), and the workers, entrepreneurs, and employees tend to live nearby and commute by foot or bike. Some of their facilities have living spaces in the same area or even in the same building. And where are these offices located? You guessed it: close to the cool areas in town, where restaurants, cafés, and shops are plenty. This trend will accelerate in the postpandemic 2020/21 era, as we indicate in Chapter 7, The future: the need for more Humane and Sustainable Smart Cities postpandemic 2020/21.

Part of the process of mental deindustrialization is to deal with legislation. In the industrial area, workers needed protection against greedy capitalists that wanted to overwork them to the limit. Not anymore. Companies have to try and look modern and trendy in order to attract the best possible talent. It should be left to them the endeavor to please their staff. Working at night or on weekends, for instance, may be a plus to the worker and should not be taxed differently as it is in many countries. Change in the existing labor laws is a must in most countries.

A change in the working hours will lead to better transport both individually and in the mass transit. A small change in that direction may make wonders. Smartness in transport is not only centralized control centers. For instance, a change of opening hours of the public services tendered by City Hall may just do the trick.

The next move in the deindustrialization process is to face the challenge of changing the school system. Our schools everywhere are modeled, you guessed it, for the industrial area. Children are taught discipline, conformity, and uniformity. In an assembly line, workers should do what they are told to do, in that order, at that time. Our schools prepare the students for this. But in an era when the most sought-after characteristics of a new recruit are flexibility, creativity, ability of group working, and similar such soft skills, schools do not fit anymore. Times changed. Schools did not. And this is true not only of primary education. Universities are just the same. They prepare students to work in big companies (in particular, industries). Only a small percentage of their student output will eventually work for big companies but that is the training students get. No wonder the numbers of dropouts are large and, in many countries, increasing.

And finally, yes, the car. The poster child of the industrial era has to be put into perspective and taken care of. We have seen that most cities were and are being planned for the car. For instance, every city has a Traffic Department. Danish architect and smart city specialist Frank Gehl asks: How many of them have a Pedestrian or a Cyclist Department (Gehl and Svarre, 2013), or, at least, a Mobility Department instead of a car Traffic Department? Aren't walking and biking just as important?

Public parking is another issue. Street area is one of the most valuable assets of the city. It should be put to better use according to the benefits it provides to the citizens. Janette Sadik-Khan has shown the way in Manhattan. On the one hand, there are cities such as London and Singapore that are controlling car access downtown with tolls and taxes, which is the right thing to do. On the other hand, there are cities segregating valuable real estate for car parking. Worst of all, public car parking is free in some towns, encouraging people to use their cars to go downtown. It just does not make any sense. People should get incentives to use public transport not to use their own car when traveling to the city.

Millennials are not eager to buy their first car and that is a welcome novelty. Let us not give incentives to change their minds.

Car manufacturers are feeling the blunt of the change. They are suffering a situation that can be referred to as a perfect storm: At least four major changes are happening at the same time.

- New generations are not so keen on their product.
- Power is coming from electricity, so long-term partners, the fossil fuel companies, are no longer allies.
- Cars are becoming autonomous, driven by software, so ownership does not make that much sense anymore.
- Car sharing is becoming more popular. If the trend continues, who will be the car buyer?

Car manufacturers and their supply chain are big companies and are seeing the changes and threats, as everybody else. So, they react. How? Adverts. In many countries, the proportion of car advertisements to the other products and services in the media is increasing enormously. In order to lure the new generations, the advertisement depicts cars that are capable of going anywhere, off-road, and face any challenge. In the advertisements, a nice looking young professional takes her car to the streets (clean, free of other cars, etc.) or beautiful advertisements, and then, suddenly, decides to turn to a side tarmac road, where the car can demonstrate how well it will perform in a rugged road, crossing a small stream of water and arriving at a mountain top with a wonderful view, where it swirls on an impressive dust wave! This ad is so prevalent in TV commercials that one can only guess that ad companies are too busy with work from all other car companies and are just repeating the script... Since the advertisements are so similar, the end result is that no one associates the ad with the car maker!

And that is not the worst. One particular ad company in Brazil tried to innovate and changed their advertisement for a car company from this standard and shows in their TV commercial... a good-looking young professional that takes his car to a beautiful road by the sea and, suddenly, spots a mermaid in the water. He immediately parks the car, jumps in the water, kisses the mermaid and ... poof!... the mermaid goes off, driving his car, and leaves him there in the water! It makes one wonder, what is the actual message of this advertisement? Buy this car, kiss a mermaid, and she will run off with your car and leave you in the water?!? And she drives with the long tail and all, a tribute to sophisticated engineering

A few decades back, most commercials were about cigarettes. With the conscientization campaigns against smoking, cigarette companies went into decline and in many countries, advertisements are forbidden or must display compulsory warning messages about the maladies of smoking. It seems as if car manufacturers may be following the same track: Deluge them with advertisements in order to try and avoid decline! Brazilian architect and city planner Jaime Lerner, known for his audacious transport plan for Curitiba during his tenure as mayor (12 years in alternate periods between 1971 and 1992), compares the two industries and decrees: "The car manufacturers are the cigarette companies of the future!"

References

Gehl, J., Svarre, B., 2013. How to Study Public Life. Island Press, Washington.

Gies, F., Gies, J., 1969. Life in a Medieval City. Harper-Collins, New York.

Glaeser, E., 2011. Triumph of the City. Penguin Books, New York.

Harari, Y.N., 2015. Sapiens — A Brief History of Humankind. Harper-Collins, New York.

Jacobs, J., 1961. The Death and Life of Great American Cities. Vintage Books, New York.

Kirkland, S., 2013. Paris Reborn: Napoleón III, Baron Haussmann and the Quest to Build a Modern City. St. Martin's Press, New York.

Larson, K., 2012. Brilliant Designs to Fit More People in Every City. TedX Talk, Boston. < https://www.ted.com/talks/kent_larson_brilliant_designs_to_fit_more_people_in_every_city > .

Mumford, E., 2018. Designing the Modern City: Urbanism Since 1850. BW&A Books.

Nelson, A.C., 2006. Leadership in a new era: comment on "Planning Leadership in a New Era. J. Am. Plan. Assoc. 72 (4), 393–409. Available from: https://doi.org/10.1080/01944360608976762.

Roberts, J.M., 1980. The Pelican History of the World. Penguin Books, London.

Sadik-Khan, J., Sollomonow, S., 2017. Street Fight: Introduction for an Urban Revolution. Penguin Books, New York.

Schwartz, S.I., 2015. Street Smart: The Rise of Cities and the Fall of Cars. PublicAffairs, New York.

Chapter 3

From smart cities to more Humane and Sustainable Smart Cities: the world in transformation

Smart cities do not mean creating jungles of concretes or sophisticated cities of glasses with HiFi technologies. But a smart city means a city, where humans, trees, birds and other animals can grow with all their glories, imperfections, freedom and creativity.

Amit Ray.

Smart cities

Smart cities are places that use information and communication technologies (ICTs) extensively. These modern technologies involve sensors, cameras, smart devices, software of all sorts, and interconnectivity to the Internet and amongst devices throughout the city. As every new technology has shown us in the past, they can be used for the good or for the bad. But in this particular case of modern ICTs, they look nice and can be shown off also as a sign of "modernity" (Lara et al., 2016). They might be very helpful, of course. But they can also be useless. We will go there later. For the moment, let us get a closer look at what they are and how they can be used constructively in our cities.

Cameras and sensors

Security and public safety have become major concerns in every city, even more so in the developing world. This was the perfect opportunity for vendors to push into administrations the idea that a set of cameras and sensors would do marvels to the security of their buildings, gated communities, commercial installations, and walking precincts. In fact, the system has undeniably helped improve security a little in buildings and shops: We have all

Humane and Sustainable Smart Cities. DOI: https://doi.org/10.1016/B978-0-12-819186-6.00005-1

seen, in news programs on TV and on social media, recordings of thefts and aggressions that might have helped the police in identifying and eventually capturing the actual perpetrators. So much so that, when we enter a shop with camera surveillance and spot ourselves on the screen, we feel as if we were part of a burglary scene.

The results of the installation of such systems in cities are much less noticeable and striking though. For instance, in Rio (Brazil), the Traffic Control Center has been installed in a new and special building downtown that looks like a NASA rocket launch control center: a big wall with 100 or so large TV screens, where one can watch the main arteries in the city and realize how bad the traffic jams are. When we visited the scene in 2014, we could see on the wall panel that the traffic on the main road leading to the international airport was flowing at an average speed of 12 km/hour. Someone mentioned then that that was the speed of the chariots that carried passengers in England in the 19th century.

Check the "development": Two centuries later, we witnessed that, using our wonderful cars that can zip from 0 to 100 km/hour in 7 seconds, we reached the same transport speed of the chariot! And that is not the worst finding about that figure. If one watched the average speed on that artery for the 5 working days of that week, the result would be the same or very similar, since traffic congestion there is a chronic condition. And the following weeks could be even worse. (Think again of the city of São Paulo which issues 800 new license plates... a day!)

Cameras and sensors do help in our security in many places. But their deployment in the city should (and oftentimes are not) be preceded by careful evaluation of what are the expected results of the project and, more importantly, how these results are going to be measured once the project is completed and in operation.

Besides this point of efficacy, privacy concerns need to be openly addressed from the start. There might even surface a compromise between privacy and public safety in the sense that we, citizens, might be willing to concede part of our privacy in favor of a better security. But the discussion about this issue must be open to the public and the people concerned need to understand what exactly is at stake and what are the practical consequences for them of any possible project implementation.

The main trouble with cameras and sensors is that they look nice and they look modern. Mayors love them. But they might, very well, also be useless.

Internet of things

The Internet of things (IoT) is a technology where a "thing" makes a decision based upon information collected from another "thing." But, as with any fancy new technology and acronym, IoT has been misused in all different sorts of applications where sensors send information to humans who make the decision. This is not IoT. When humans make the decision after receiving input from sensors, there is not much novelty, we have had that kind of application for many years. The new technology in IoT is that things make decisions on our behalf, a situation that introduces difficulties for practical implementations in the city, as we will show below.

In any case, the IoT technology has come of age and will have a considerable impact on our daily lives. IoT is a combination of sensors and computer software. Sensors collect data that are relevant in a particular situation, and send it (in general through the Internet accessed by cable, Wi-Fi, Bluetooth, or any other communication means) to a processing device where a software program will analyze this information and act accordingly, making the decision that was once a step only taken by humans.

Think of the autonomous car: The computer software program in the car control unit receives information from the car itself and from sensors on the road and speeds up or down and turns the wheels according to a program that interprets this set of "sensed" data.

As computer software upgrades itself from tools that help us make decisions, to tools that make decisions "instead of us," several questions emerge. For instance, let us go back to the autonomous car example for a hypothetical case: The car is driving itself on a road and, as it bends a curve, it finds a dangerous slippery situation on the road. Further up the road, the car camera spots a zebra crossing with a young girl crossing it and an old man standing on the sidewalk. Calculations in the car control unit indicate that if the car does not break, it might kill the girl. If it does, it might kill the man on the sidewalk. Which decision does it take?

If the original program were written by an Asian programmer, it would probably risk the girl's life, since their culture values more the accumulated knowledge of the old man than that of a child. If written by a Western programmer, it would probably risk the old man's life, since their culture values more the future possibilities of the youth! A question of life and death would then be decided depending on the nationality and the cultural beliefs and practices of the original programmer.

The reader might not like the example, but the concern is real. The full-scale adoption of IoT will raise many sorts of ethical questions as we hand over decisions to computer software written by programmers under the auspices of private companies (and their interests) and/or governments (and their interests too).

IoT technologies are being used in several other applications in our economic system, not only in cities. They are very useful in industry (connecting machines to machines), modern agriculture (deciding about the perfect mix of fertilizers, for instance, sensing the conditions of the soil, or the current amount of sun exposure or overall weather conditions), and health sector (both at hospitals and as sensors of patients' conditions).

Artificial intelligence and its derivatives machine learning and deep learning

Jeremy Achin, DataRobot CEO, speaking at the Japan AI Experience Conference in 2017 gave a short and simple definition of AI:

> *AI is a computer system able to perform tasks that ordinarily require human intelligence... Many of these artificial intelligence systems are powered by machine learning, some of them are powered by deep learning and some of them are powered by very boring things like rules.*

Artificial intelligence (AI) applications, with all of their different denominations, are very important in the cities. The obvious examples are in traffic control, synchronization of semaphores, and opening of green-light corridors for emergency vehicles, but they also extend to several other areas: monitoring and control of viruses and disease spreading, urban planning, smart street lighting, etc.

The other two terms, *machine learning* (ML) and *deep learning* are subsets of the general AI field.

ML is an expression that refers to the result of a set of algorithms extracting information from data without specific instructions from humans. It can be further subdivided into supervised ML, when algorithms apply, to a new set of data, what they learned from similar sets of data in the past. Think of a set of data about traffic patterns at a specific semaphore: an ML algorithm may plan how to signal the traffic lights in the future based upon what it learned from the past behavior of similar data in the past. The other subdivision of ML is unsupervised ML, when algorithms extract patterns and try to make sense of a set of raw data, without references from the past. Think of an investigation of a hospital's intensive care unit where an unusual number of casualties is being reported: An unsupervised ML algorithm may sieve through all the extensive and diverse data generated by sensors and medical equipment in the ICU and identify a pattern or something relevant but unusual as a possible cause of the problem. Human investigators might not even have guessed that particular possibility.

Deep learning, the other buzz expression, refers to the application of a specific technology called neural networks to tackle unsupervised ML applications.

AI is relevant to cities and will be even more in the near future, as we continue to extract and process data, information, patterns, and logical insights out of the huge amount of data that is registered daily in a city about its functioning and about the comings and goings of its citizens and visitors.

For instance, from the GPS in the citizens' cell phones it is possible to draw a mobility map of the entire city with links of where-from and where-to people actually go. Then, through simulation, and AI, one could design, for instance, what would happen in the town if the City Hall facility were moved from a building here to another building there, in another part of town. Or they could figure out what would happen if the working hours of the schools, shopping, or public buildings were changed. The new simulated mobility map would show a completely different picture and could suggest structural urban planning changes or just urban acupunctures (Lerner, 2011), small interventions in a limited part of the city.

Another example would be the actions to monitor and control the spread of a dangerous virus such as the deadly coronavirus in 2020/21. South Korea managed to limit the initial impact of the pandemic there with the use of AI tracking algorithms. They monitored the focus points of the virus, even on an individual level, and were able to identify, through analysis of the location of infected people and patients' records in hospitals and clinics (both people with and without symptoms of the disease), who might be infected. These people were treated separately from the others, in several cities. The algorithms also acted directly on warnings for suspects and also indicated to the responsible authorities what was the best course of action in terms of social distancing, segregation of groups of people, and/or lockdown of particular areas of the cities most affected by the virus.

Big data

The vast amount of consumer data, combined with new AI technologies, creates opportunities to generate value from data while respecting personal data protection regulations and laws. The trouble is that the amount and speed with which these data are generated and modified create an enormous difficulty in dealing with them. That is why we needed new technologies and algorithms to face the challenge.

Big data is a relatively new field of science to study, evaluate, and generate value out of increasingly vast repositories of data generated not only by sensors everywhere, but also by normal users on the Internet, and *things* communicating through IoT systems.

From the inset, as with any other new field of science, we needed an acronym to make big data popular: In this case, it was the three "V's". *Volume*: Big data refers to large structured and nonstructured databases collected everywhere; *Velocity*: data that is produced and stored in a high speed and its processing and use need powerful processors capable of analyzing and extracting information from them in almost real time; and *Variety*: Big data comes from a variety of sources, and processing them requires alternative methods and techniques beyond those already found in traditional database studies.

Impressed by the original three "V's" some sources rushed in to add three more "V's". *Veracity*: that deals with how trustworthy is the information available in this data being generated from different sources; *Value*: that evaluates to what extent is this data relevant to anything or anyone; and finally, *Variability*: that accounts for situations in which data vary significantly over time due to unprecedented conditions or to any other unforeseen situations.

In any case, in the city, the amount of data generated is huge and its potential for value is high, very high indeed. Since most of us are living in cities, data related to us are being generated and collected systematically. And with the new IoT systems, and the explosion in the number and variety of sensors, big data is being created full time and may be used to help in the generation of useful information and intelligence for several purposes, public and private.

And it is not only in the outbreak of the Coronavirus in 2020 that big data algorithms were used to track, predict, and help in the diagnosis and containment of the spread of diseases. The same is true for other areas of public health such as air pollution control, or water contamination, or even psychological illnesses such as isolation and depression.

Weather forecasting and natural disasters are other areas where big data systems are useful in the city. On the economic side, large corporations are using big data from cities to generate value, with or without users' consent. For this reason, some of their activities are being challenged because of invasion of personal data but we will deal with that later.

On the democratic election front, big data algorithms are being used to track and manipulate voters' sentiment and behavior, leading to unforeseen election results: the Brexit vote in the United Kingdom, for instance, showed results that were different from the opinion polls immediately before the actual voting (results came outside the *certainty* range). A movie by the same name explains in detail how big data algorithms were used to track, influence, and change voters' behavior and feeling about the subject. It is likely that there will be other "surprises" in the next open elections all over the world, until such time as the opinion polls will themselves use big data algorithms to deliver their forecasts.

In many countries, the law restricts how the information is mined from voters, exactly to *avoid* manipulation of the opinion poll returns. Because of that, it is difficult to predict what will follow in our democracies with the extensive use of big data and social media in the elections. As everything is changing so fast, the law, as is often the case, does not follow suit and is way behind new technological advances. Observe how dysfunctional for our society this is: Legal systems are at a stage where they are trying to regulate the old media against abuse, but the will of the voter is in fact being influenced and maybe manipulated by the new social media such as Instagram, Facebook, and WhatsApp, or by some kind of new cell phone app launched only last year that the legal systems do not even know of. It is difficult to respond swiftly to all the changes that are happening in the technology front at such a fast pace.

Blockchain

Blockchain is the technology behind bitcoin and other cryptocurrencies. Because of that, it is being confused with the digital currency bitcoin, its first real use. But the technology carries the possibility of a much greater impact altogether than all the cryptocurrencies that use it. Marc Andreesen, of Netscape fame, claimed that blockchain is "the distributed trust network that the Internet always needed and never had" (Fung, 2014).

The origins of blockchain and the bitcoin are sort of mythical. A person named Satoshi Nakamoto (real name or pseudonym, unknown up to today) published a white paper "Bitcoin: A Peer-to-Peer Electronic Cash System" where he proposes an electronic ledger system that would record transactions of any sort in a manner that was secure, and needed no central authority or intermediaries. Ironically, and probably on purpose, the first block (block 0) of the blockchain recorded the cover news on *The Times* on January 3, 2009: "The Times 03/Jan/2009 Chancellor on brink of second bailout for banks". Nakamoto, whoever he is, was probably making fun of the fact that banks were not to be regarded as trustful intermediaries, which of course he claimed his technology was.

But how does the blockchain work and, more importantly, why is this relevant to our cities?

The blockchain is a technology that records electronically and in a peer-to-peer distributed network, with no intermediaries, every transaction that needs and wants to be recorded. The peer-to-peer network of personal computers is widely distributed and does not belong to anyone. The system is decentralized and distributed. Each block knows the hash-code of the preceding block and uses heavy-duty encryption to produce its own hash-code that links itself with the following block. The information that is recorded in the block may be a financial transaction, a contract, a title deed, or anything worth recording for any reason. Once recorded, the transaction cannot be altered by anyone (this would change the hash-code) and the proof of its existence is publicly available in all the nodes of the network. In other words, once recorded, the transaction cannot be disputed because it is nonrefutable. Think of it for a minute: one can *trust* the information there. Compare the blockchain and the Internet. On the Internet you find all sorts of information from trusted and nontrusted parties. Fake news, for instance, are unfortunately abundant and very difficult to track all the way to the original posting. In a blockchain application, every transaction is recoverable and trustful. How many applications will it entice? There is a lot of movement in the venture capital industry to fund new technologies and applications based upon the blockchain technology, and new developments, products, and services will most likely spring up in the very near future.

And what about the application of blockchain to the city and to its citizens? Apart from the obvious applications for local governments that could then have a trustful ledger of everything that happens in town, there are many possible applications in the IoT realm, presented above. As things will decide on our behalf based upon information from other things, it will become paramount to keep records of the history of that information and of the algorithms that were used in each single occurrence and decision made by machines.

Identification of a person and privacy

In the smart city, in some cases, one should be able to identify precisely a person, provided that his/her privacy is protected and that the identification is used only with his/her knowledge and consent. Easy?

Nope. It is difficult to identify precisely a person, and it is even more difficult to protect privacy. And, to make things worse, there are (arguably) practical needs of public safety that preclude previous agreement by the subjects. In the 2020 pandemic, for instance, governments had to track people's movements in several countries in order to control the spread of the disease. In face of that kind of catastrophic emergency, simply there was no time to ask anybody anything in a practical way. But then again, many people feared that governments could and would use that valuable information for political purposes thereafter. And that is not the only problem: We must take into account that more than 1 billion people in the world have no registered identity whatsoever.

Let us check technologies for identification first. There are many and they are at different levels of maturity and cost for practical use (World Bank, 2018). But in order to understand the complexity of the subject, think of the identification process: One might be interested in verifying if this person here is the one he says he is (one to one, as in a bank), or if this person here is any of these people I am looking for (one to many, as in a police checkpoint), or who is this person here (one out of the world population, as in a border control). There are different levels of demand that require different technologies.

Biometrics encompasses most of the technologies of choice today. Fingerprint recognition, iris recognition, vascular (the vein patterns) recognition, face recognition, DNA recognition, and behavior recognition may be used since each one of us has a unique set of these biometrical characteristics. The trouble is how to measure, register, and store them, and, later on, how to identify them in different checkpoints in a rapid, easy, and cost-effective way. The situation today is that all of these technologies are being used to some extent in various countries in different situations: One might use one's fingerprint to enter the office building for daily work, iris or facial recognition to enter another country, vascular recognition to be treated after a car crash at the hospital, DNA recognition to prove or deny parenthood of a claiming unrecognized son, and behavior recognition to access the bank account.

Biometrical recognition has had another boost with the widespread use of smartphones with built-in biometrics. It also helps as a second proof that "you-are- you" since you are porting your cell phone and know your password. The combination of smartphones and biometrics is being used for several purposes and will be prevalent for identification in the next few years, given the wide availability of these devices.

But a big question remains, of course, and it is "what about privacy"? This essential human right is at stake here. We are already mesmerized by the amount of information about us and our behavior that many companies and governments (and who else?) have. When your cell phone asks you for the first time how did you like restaurant X where you have just dined, you find it strange. But then, after many occurrences, it becomes natural. But when they combine that information with the GPS tracking of your cell phone, your credit card purchases, and even the daily tracking of your electricity bill, someone might figure out that you bought this loaf of bread at this supermarket (through your credit card statement), and toasted two slices of bread at 7 a.m. at your house (through the surge in electricity consumption at your dynamic meter). Where is the limit here? Set by whom? Should we care?

Smart for whom?!?

We need a change in focus. "Citizens first" should be the norm (Eleutheriou et al., 2017). Which is certainly not the case today. But who are the offenders, welcoming and making way for the technology juggernaut?

Technology is charming

Technology is a display of modernity, as we have seen already. For that reason, it is easy to convince local administrators that their city needs this wonderful control center with cameras everywhere, or this display system for the free(!) parking lot downtown that directs an entering car to an available space. In the latter example, with the added "bonus" that once you make the driver's life more comfortable, you get more people going downtown by car, instead of using the public transport system.

Cities are complex systems, no doubt. So, every single project, measure, or regulation must be weighed against its cost and its benefits to the system as a whole. In the car park example, the display system is a nice feature but is it *worth* it? Do we want more cars downtown? Is the car park a good use for the public land downtown anyway?

Tech companies are TOO powerful

The five most valuable companies in the world (by market value in the US Stock Exchange), the so-called FAAMG (Facebook, Apple, Amazon, Microsoft, and Google), are worth something in the staggering region of US $1 trillion each! This is such a huge number that we are only used to seeing the word trillion associated with entire countries' gross domestic product (GDP)! And not many countries at that (15 countries only). To put this number in perspective, the world's GDP, that is, the sum of everything that is produced and sold in the world, is c.US$90 trillion.

Is the big size of these companies a real problem?

Yes. It is.

A company that is too big, with its army of good and well-paid lawyers, and its big-budget marketing campaigns, is capable of turning every decision, every regulation, every law, and ultimately every vote, in their favor. That is not good for the democratic system.

Bria and Morozov (2018) argue that the "folly of technological solutionism" propagated by the big tech companies has not solved *any* of the world's real problems and has achieved only the obscene enrichment of their owners. Again, there is nothing wrong with becoming rich through ingenuity. But that rich? And is it bringing along everybody else? More on that in Chapter 7, The future: the need for more Humane and Sustainable Smart Cities postpandemic 2020/21.

The next battlefield is data. A resource that is more and more valuable. And owned and manipulated by a small number of big companies. In the words of Takahashi (2018) when you use any nice free app that you cannot figure out what is the app's provider business model, the product they sell is you (your data)[1]!

"Enclosure" of public spaces and public data is happening already

The term "enclosure," in this context, refers to some public resource that used to be shared by people and has been appropriated privately by big corporations, in some cases legally, in others, without being noticed. In the former case, corporations take hold of land, water, or services through government-approved regulations, public tenders, or licenses (not always fairly disputed), and go on to explore it in the most profitable way. An example of the latter case is data (Ekkehard, 2019).

We are all users of the Internet and social media applications in one way or another. Over time, some of us started to feel uncomfortable with

---

1. As the old saying goes: "in a poker table, there is always a bozo. If you are playing at poker table and you cannot figure out who he is, it is you!".

information about us that some companies hold. Some people even report that companies, through unauthorized access to their home computers, "hear" what they talk about in the privacy of their homes! That assumption, if and when confirmed, in our view, clearly crossed the line of reasonability.

Ekkehard and other progressive thinkers suggest we treat data as a "commons" resource to be shared by everyone agreed to by each data provider. Maybe the provider may even accrued some of the value generated by that data.

Social and generational changes

Yes, the world is different today. But is it that different from what our ancestors would have noticed or written about say 50 or even 100 years ago? My hunch is, well, no! They would also say the world was different in their time. Even the terrible pandemic of 2020/21 has been, to some extent, experienced before, in the "Spanish" fever of 1918−19, on the sanitary side, or in the Great Depression of 1929, on the economic side.

But what is singular of our times (and may be worse in the future) is the *pace* of change. So, the world is indeed different today as well, but the changes now are happening at such a lightning speed that we face difficulty in grasping them. Figure the astonishment of an elderly person, which has finally agreed with her grandchildren that she should have a Facebook account only to learn from other people that maybe that is not the right tool any more, and that using Facebook is kind of "old school."

Consider the social changes we have experienced. There are still incidents of intolerance all over the world, about all kinds of different issues of race, religion, ethnical background, etc., but the fact is that we are in the process of evolution from a patriarchical, chaste-based, male-dominant society to a new order based upon diversity in ethnic descent, sexual orientation, age and income levels, and so on. And one of the reasons for this evolution is the fact that most of us (coming to 2/3 of us, according to the UN) now live in cities where education is more available and where the daily chores of city living put all of us in close contact, which tends to break or at least tame prejudices. For many people, including this author, changes have not actually gone far enough but that is another discussion. Suffice it to point out here that the city must allow for these changes in its urban planning and development of new projects.

A combination of societal and technological movements has hit our society in recent decades at an unprecedented pace and the ensuing changes are still unfolding and will do so for the next decades.

Digitalization

Firstly, the most obvious, *digitalization*. The impact of the Internet and ICTs in general on all sectors of the economy is striking, with new products and services being launched at a mind-boggling pace. It took airlines 64 years to reach 50 million users; Netflix, 7 years; the new Disney + channel achieved this figure in just 5 months with school kids under lockdown in 2020. But figure this: generation Z propelled the HouseParty app to 50 million users in just 1 month!

In some countries this digitalization impact may be even greater, since several basic demands of society have not yet been met. Take education, for instance. The setup and the human and physical infrastructure to build and maintain good schools used to be very large. It still is, but technology has helped shorten the distance between poor students and the best education, as online platforms such as Udemy, Coursera, and Khan Academy have shown us.

The digitization of society has changed customers' views on companies and the interactions they expect from key service providers such as transportation, security, health, energy, and administration. In many segments of the economy, such as finance, entertainment, e-commerce, and online services, customers are already used to high-quality services. Their requirements to local governments will follow suit. Consumers are citizens somewhere and they will be increasingly looking for high-quality, personalized products and services from their federal and local governments that are accessible 24/7 through mobile and social media. And we all know how far governments are from addressing this need.

In most countries, services provided by governments are infamous for working in the old paradigm of a different location for each service offered by the same government, which does not make any sense; bored and, in general, badly paid clerks; long queues for any simple service. Nothing short of a shock is needed here in order for governments to attend to this demand of society.

It is common and understandable that people see electronic devices as the key enablers of the digitization of society, but the real revolution is actually happening in software, not devices: four out of the five most valuable companies in the world are software companies and only one a hardware company. Interestingly enough though, this one, Apple, chose to outsource manufacturing of almost all of its products and parts: the company designs, develops, and tests new products and services in the market—but full-scale manufacturing is outsourced. We are living in the age of software. A new business model is that of "softwaring" products and services by replacing the value of fixed assets (hotel rooms and cars, for example) with systems for accessing, selling, and distributing those assets (Airbnb and Uber, for example).

In the city, the *softwarization* movement (i.e., software in all processes, equipment, and devices) has not yet occurred, but it will come: it is up to the most dynamic companies to drive this change. Established companies that supply services to the city (such as power and water utilities) are the ones mostly at risk. They are in danger of being overtaken by new, more aggressive entrants, more familiar with the new "digital" world of today's society.

Same for government functions, which are in a process of becoming totally irrelevant. Think of a government service by the zealous Ministry of Tourism, using an army of evaluators, that rates hotels in terms of number of stars, for instance. Is anyone interested? Or do they all go to TripAdvisor and other online services to evaluate where to stay? Local governments are under the same kind of pressure. They regulate and evaluate the cab services in town but users trust much more the users' evaluations shown by Uber and Cabify instead. Isn't it time the government itself digitalizes its operation?

Decentralization

German-born British economist Schumacher, of "Small Is Beautiful" fame (Schumacher, 1973), in one of his talks recorded in tape and kept at the Schumacher Society in Amherst, MA, strongly states "Unity is God!, Uniformity is hell!", to the delirium of his followers.[2] His work suggested new forms of distributed sources of energy that might save the world from catastrophe. Notwithstanding the importance of Schumacher's work, acclaimed almost as a cult culture in his time, it was subsequently dismissed as one of the ideas of the "hippie" era of the late 1960s. Unfortunately, and in the name of efficiency, the world moved exactly the other way and followed the mantra "the bigger the better." In the energy sector and in many other fields of society. In the computer industry at the time, computers became so huge that they needed special buildings and refrigerators to cool down the beasts. It was only in 1981, that IBM launched the personal computer—the IBM PC, a revolution in the computer industry that changed it upside down.

IBM is a case study in adaptation to technological change. The large corporate mainframe computers produced by IBM in the 1960s and 1970s were being challenged by new entrants such as Digital that produced departmental mid-size computers. Then IBM went one step further and launched the PC. Along the following years, the computing power and some of the functions of the PC were being replaced by the cell phone. IBM then decided to get out of the small computer business altogether and sold its PC division to the Chinese manufacturer Lenovo in 2005, and went on the change path and became a services (mostly software) company where it is still successful today.

The computer power in people's desks today is just amazing for those of us who have struggled with limited computers for decades. In fact, the

---

2. The author visited the place for two weeks in the Fall of 2001, while working on one of his earlier books. The book's final chapter was written there and very much inspired by Schumacher's ideas (Costa, 2001).

computing power in people's hands (the cell phone) is even more amazing. Decentralization went a long way here, from the central processing unit of the big mainframes of the 1960s to the laptops, tablets, and cell phones of today.

In the energy sector, as it often happens in history, Schumacher's ideas are now back, 60 years later. Electricity used to be provided by increasingly bigger power plants, be them thermal, nuclear, or hydroelectric. The huge installations of the Itaipu power plant (in the triple border of Brazil, Argentina, and Paraguay), and the Three Gorges power plant, in China, were the last facilities built under the cult of "the bigger the better." The trend is now reversing and smaller plants are being built all over the world. In the solar energy sector, in particular, power plants have been reduced to such an extent that a small power plant can be installed on a single house rooftop, making it economically viable for an individual consumer and his family. In some sunny places, the roof of a house covered with solar panels may produce more energy than that required by the house itself, and the owner is entitled to *sell* (not buy) the surplus energy to the local distribution company. Consider the change that is needed in the culture of the incumbent power distribution companies: From unquestioned monopolies in distribution they saw their customers become their *suppliers* also!

In the commercial office space, as a result of the pandemic 2020/21, big offices are being questioned. It is not yet clear what will be the outcome of the huge involuntary home-office experiment that was taking place, but it is likely that the large coworking facilities provided by companies such as WeWork may be substituted by several mini coworking facilities in several different parts of town, where people and companies want to and eventually will implement their leave-work-play strategies.

This new trend will eventually come to government. Citizens may want to participate in their local government not only as taxpayers, but as active participants of decisions, regulations, maintenance, and care of their cities.

Governments, welcome to the future!

Decarbonization and the UN's sustainable development goals

Global pressures toward a low-carbon economy are already significant and tend to grow even more. In 2015 195 countries ratified the Paris Agreement whose objective is to reduce the world's greenhouse gas emissions and to enable a healthier future for the next generations. The Paris Agreement's central goal is to cap the earth's temperature rise this century at 2% above preindustrial era temperature, and to take active measures to limit it even further to 1.5% rise until 2030.

In order to achieve this ambitious target, each signatory will have to achieve quantitative reduction of carbon emission by 2030. A series of indicators will track each country's performance in 17 sustainable development goals (United Nations, 2015). One of the biggest impacts of this agreement is the substitution of energy from fossil fuels by other alternative sources of energy in several products. One striking example is the new electric vehicles. The electric car is a paradigm shift with several structural impacts on the economy (see the car industry below) and, of course, a unique opportunity for cities to reorganize their relation to the car as a major transport facility, and to reorganize their energy sources toward a less polluting energy matrix. It is also an opportunity for new companies, aggregators, service providers, and such, those with innovative business models.

Another major example in the decarbonization of our societies in the increase in demand for photovoltaic panels in the developed world, whose cost has dropped significantly, as we mentioned earlier. The change to cleaner energy, from today's use of fossil fuels such as oil and coal to produce electricity, will happen by the offer of new technologies, by the enactment of new laws and regulations from governments, or by strong demand from concerned citizens. Or by a combination of the three factors.

The perfect storm for the car industry

We have introduced the subject in Chapter 2, Historical overview: cities from medieval to modern times—what went wrong. But let us dig a little deeper into it and figure out what it means for the future of our cities.

Who needs a car?

A dream of older generations, the first car was for the adolescent a symbol of everything a young man (and then young women too) needed: freedom, status, even beauty. Either you had it or you would be part of a "lower" class. Fast forward to our days: when you take a car somewhere, you must worry about where to park it and at what cost. Down went your freedom. As for status, the car is losing importance as youngsters in the developed urban world value other affluence signs. As for beauty, many cars today are driven from a high-rise residential building garage to a, say, shopping mall garage, not seen by anyone on the way there. So, what is the point? Who needs a car today in the city? Isn't it better to use Uber?

The new generation focuses more on experience than on property. The private car must provide a better "experience" than that provided by a transport app. Does it really? Well, in the city, no! Or at least not always. More often the private car means a loss in terms of time (where to park it), drinking possibilities (due to personal safety and police road checks in many towns, with sometimes zero tolerance to alcohol), and worry (is the place where you parked safe?). Even youngsters who do have a car are reconsidering their options after they weigh the pros and cons of having a private car. In many cases people of different ages retain their cars just because they always had one—a situation similar to what happened to the landline telephones at home. The reduction in number and eventually the decay of the landlines has been slower than their effective use indicated because people faced the inertia of changing something that had been there for so long.

Youngsters that live in cities, and some of their parents too, are indeed changing their habits. The rate of change will vary from country to country, of course, but the change is in the direction of diminishing interest in owning a private car. Bad sign for the car industry and for all of its huge supply chain and related services.

Anthony et al. (2017) identified five early signs of disruption for any large company. The first one on his list is a "change in loyalty from your customers." As the younger generations mature, they look at the car not as a consumption dream but as an offender of quality of life in the city. If one goes through Anthony's list of other disruptive signs (venture capital investment in the competition, for instance), one would rush to sell his/her shares of not only car companies, but all related companies, one of the largest sectors of the world's industrial economy. But read on. There is more bad news for the industry.

Electric cars, autonomous cars, and shared cars

The overall auto and auto parts industry is huge, corresponding, in the United States, to c.20% of retail sales and 3% of the country's GDP, according to the U.S. Bureau of Economic Analysis (2019). Similar percentages can be found in other countries. Any structural changes here will have a profound economic impact.

And the car industry is being challenged by technological advances from all sides, in the United States and everywhere else. First, by the emergence of the electric car. Apparently, this should not be a problem since it is still the same car; you only change the power source. Yes and no. The auto industry has been forever an interested bedfellow with the oil industry that produced gasoline. Looking at the automotive sector as a whole, you also find the gas stations, the auto parts industry, and other related services. They will all be hit hard by the new technology. The auto parts industry, because of new and, in some cases powerful, entrants which are more akin to the new technologies; the gas stations, because electric power stations might be totally different from gas stations and might be localized in different lots in town. And the car-related services sector, because the new electric parts tend to be more integrated and, along with the push to automation, cars will require much less manual service and constant visits to the services shops.

Second, the autonomous car. We might be pushing the argument too far here, but we think that the car owner relation to his car will be different once it is autonomous. You do not need the driving skill of the owner anymore, you do not speed up at the driver's will, and the driver is not in control anymore. Will the car owner retain the same level of attachment to his/her car in this scenario? If the prospective buyers are not driving their future cars anymore, will they be as willing to buy new cars instead of using transport apps?

Third, and even worse for the industry, the trend toward shared cars will diminish the need for new cars. The market for cars is already stagnant in the United States and optimistic projections point to flat markets for the following years. And that does not take into account the Covid-19 crisis of 2020/21, whose impact in the car industry is yet to be evaluated. Besides this, shared cars will be owned by whom? The apps companies? The City? And in any case, is the industry prepared to sell their cars to this new kind of buyer? With much less emotion and subject to reasonable arguments to make a purchase decision? Our hunch is no; they are not prepared.

The three factors combined project a perfect storm for the auto industry as a whole.

The new cigarette industry?

From the evidence above and the facts we have seen in Chapter 2, Historical overview: cities from medieval to modern times—what went wrong, the auto industry is in deep trouble today. As the cigarette industry before them, they became a symbol of times past. Not seen as such by the population as a whole yet, but aging nonetheless.

Is this good for the city? During the coronavirus pandemic of 2020/21, the number of cars on the roads was reduced dramatically as we all noticed. What was the result? People who did not get the disease breathed better than before in all big towns, pollution was reduced, and people started to see sunsets in places such as Mexico City, Shanghai, and São Paulo. Also, badly needed hospital beds for the sick with the terrible disease were made available because of the drastic reduction in the previous numbers of car accidents and related casualties.

The point here is not to ban cars from our cities. It is to take them for what they are: very expensive, very dangerous, very costly to society, and very inefficient means of transport for people to commute (in general, one person per car) to work.

A radical change of perspective by our societies is needed here.

Toward more Humane and Sustainable Smart Cities

Some of the initial ideas to start changes in your city are very simple (Costa and Oliveira, 2017). Basic. Back to the beginning, when cars were not kings of the roads and streets. When streets were basic items of infrastructure, shared (almost always peacefully) by people who lived, stayed and played there, and by people who were passing through as pedestrians, bikers, horse and carriage riders, car drivers, and bus commuters.

Changes are not easy. We have lived with cities-for-cars for many years. Although the following suggestions are relatively simple, their implementation needs a lot of talking to and convincing people. But it is worth it. Be prepared. Have data on hand that may be used as an argument. And good luck! You will need it.

Enlarge sidewalks

Sidewalks are the most neglected item of a city infrastructure. It may have to do with the fact that they are used by poor people, the ones that are not "lucky enough" to own a car. And they have been reduced, several times over the past few decades, in order to make way for new car lanes. Or for curbside parking space (parallel to the curb, 45 degrees, or perpendicular).

Curbside parking is a particularly bad use of public space. In many places, people go to work by car and park at the curbside for a full day. If this is downtown, you can see hundreds, maybe thousands of people struggling to get by on foot on a narrow sidewalk just by these curbside parking spots. And, in many places, parking is free. It is just insane!

Some of these parking spaces are around underground stations and occupy part of the space of bus stops. In many cases, these car owners could take public transport if they so wished. If it is so stupid and illogical, why is the system kept there as it is? Again, and again, remember the "cities-for-cars" planning mistake.

Yet sidewalks are still the basic item for citizens moving about, including car drivers, for the final leg of their journey to where they are going. On foot. When Transport Secretary Janette Sadik-Khan convinced then New York City mayor Bloomberg to enlarge Broadway across town, she used recently surveyed data about how many people used the avenue on foot and in cars (data in the survey showed four times as many). "If four times as many pedestrians used the avenue as car drivers, the *public* (remember: public!) space should be allocated accordingly," stated Khan at the time in as many places as people would care to hear. After the initial acrimony from businessmen and citizens, it was implemented and, they ALL loved it.

We visit and marvel at the promenades at Las Ramblas in Barcelona or Le Champs Elysée in Paris and do not bother or care to do the same in our cities. In fact, in most large cities in the world sidewalks have been *reduced* over time, in order to make way for new car lanes. It was a sign of progress, remember? Not anymore.

So, what can you do in your town? Start with a visible place downtown. A place where many people already flock the street as pedestrians. Transform into pedestrian use a street lane that is currently used either for curbside car park and or a drive lane. You may hear that this is impossible!

That car traffic will become a nightmare! Well, most likely, car traffic is already a nightmare and the change may in fact *help* and not hinder people transport in town as a whole, as more people decide to use the new sidewalk space as pedestrians and avoid short trips by car downtown.

Another possibility is that of the parklet, which is tantamount to a guerrilla tactics. Parklets are sidewalk extensions that occupy the space of a couple of parking spots and are used as little plazas where people can meet or rest, and also as places for more tables and chairs for restaurants and cafés. In many places, they really look nice and, once adopted by the population, it is only natural to enlarge the sidewalk along the whole block. It may also need new legislation but it is much easier to get started since it is only taking a few parking spots.

And why are sidewalks so important to the livability and the well-being of its citizens? Because that is where the city pulses. That is where we build a sense of community. Jacobs (1961) stresses this point and finds value even in the local trivia (the new shop, new items in a shop, better prices here and there, the new neighbor) and in the local gossip (who is dating whom, who was seen in the bar, who had a problem with the police) that are exercised in casual encounters on the sidewalks and in local shops that need vibrant sidewalks to attract customers.

Speed limit in town up to 40–60 km/hour

Major thoroughfares in big cities face congestion in parts of weekdays. But people have commitments and appointments that are important to them and, once cleared of the major roads, they take the inner roads and streets that are less congested and speed up there. We are all excellent drivers and we know we can stop suddenly using the car brakes when necessary. Right?

Wrong! At least for the 1,350,000 (2016 figures) people killed in the world in traffic accidents per year. One-third of them (in low and middle-income countries) were pedestrians and bikers. Think of these numbers for a minute. One person in the world is killed every 25 seconds in a traffic accident. As you read this page, there will be 120 new fatal casualties in the world related to car accidents. Isn't it time we do something about this?

What about your town? First, get hold of these gruesome statistics locally. Find an academic group (in case you are not part of one already) that might be willing to work with you in a study of how you can dramatically reduce the number of accidents in your town by limiting the car speed in streets and avenues. Say, 40 km/hour in streets and 60 km/hour in avenues. The study should also appoint what is the cost to the drivers in terms of minutes lost per average trip in town with the new limits (this figure tends to be ridiculously low). Armed with these numbers, go to the local Legislative and find a member that is interested in the subject and that is willing to table this change.

Once we limit speed in town, there will be no need for the cars we use today. At least not for use *within* the city. This realization will then open space for a new car or a new urban transport vehicle that consumes much less power and is much more environmentally friendly.

Reclaim useless streets and corners

The results of Janette Sadik-khan and mayor Bloomberg in the Broadway project in New York City demonstrated the benefits of reclaiming street space for sidewalks, bike lanes, and recreational spaces. From that initial inspiration, several other parts of the town started to check useless stretches of streets that could be put into better use. And this is still going on all over town. One particular target is the streets that limit triangle blocks: In general, one or two sides of the triangle can be easily reclaimed as pedestrian precincts or square extensions.

Find those opportunities in your town. It is important that you have an iconic place to start the change. It will take time to get people convinced of the benefits of this change. Many doubt it, at first. Even some of the direct beneficiaries of the change such as merchants and cafés and bars' owners. But, again, is it one of those projects that, once implemented, people begin to ask themselves: Why haven't we done this before?

Establish a policy of no free parking anywhere

Most uses of a city public land are charged by the city. A lot pays land taxes, a house pays land taxes, a commercial joint pays land taxes, and everyone pays taxes to use public spaces. Not cars. Think of it. Why is that so? Is it one of those things that is there because it has been there forever?

One of the immediate measures to transform your city into a more Humane and Sustainable Smart City (HSSC) is to enact in law that there is no free parking anywhere. We can hear the outcry already! Maybe even from you who is reading this book. But before you close it and go do something else, we invite you to reflect a bit on the subject. The actual charges and taxes will have to be studied and planned well in advance. For instance, in residential areas, there might be parking rights for residents, but there will be licenses for that, and these licenses will have to be paid for annually. Paid curbside parking downtown will be allowed, but only in certain streets, for a limited time, according to the interests of the city functioning as a whole and not as a function of the car driver's best comfort. Remember that, at any given time, between 10% and 30% of cars on the streets are looking for a place to park, which is one of the worst possible uses of the public space that is allocated to car driving.

Secluded bike lanes and bike transport as a system

Once bike lanes became fashionable, several cities in the world decided to paint them in red in parts of existing streets, either the full lane or just the separation between the bike lane and the driving lanes. The bike lane looks nice on the street, the mayor gets praise for the change, and bikers start to adopt it.

It also does not work.

Car drivers, when stuck in a traffic jam, get particularly angry. And when they observe that a bike lane is empty by their side, they imagine that that piece of real state has been "stolen" from them. And they hate it! To a point they invade the bike lane to avoid traffic and sometimes kill a biker. The bike lane painted on the street is a potentially dangerous setup.

Bike lanes need to be secluded from the driving lanes. *Really* secluded, that is, in the sense that car drivers cannot drive through it without injuring their cars. The ideal situation is to have a hard, concrete, separation between lanes (blocks or a sidewalk, for instance) but there are other alternatives on existing roads using cement or hard rubber blocks to create the separation wall.

Besides the actual bike lanes, the use of bikes as a transport means must be incentivized as a system. City planners need to look at the full system of purchasing a bike, maintaining it at home, riding it to work, keeping the bike there safely and as close as possible to commercial office buildings where people actually work, and returning home—sometimes already in the dark. What is the price and financial conditions to buy bikes (in some places, government taxes on bikes are higher than on cars)? Do residential buildings have bike storage places that are safe? Does the public transport system allow for bikes? Does the city code for commercial buildings require biking space and showers in the building? The bike *system* needs someone at City Hall looking after its operation. A pedestrian and bikers Department. Don't we have people there (sometimes hundreds of them) in the existing Traffic Authority taking care of car rides in town?

Maintain existing parks and create a few new gardens and plazas

Most cities have squares and gardens and parks. Some of them are nice places to visit, stroll, and relax in. But many are deteriorated to a point that they are occupied only by homeless people, drug addicts, drug dealers, and prostitutes. The latter situation, mostly in degraded downtowns.

This is a good starting point for a change in the city (Costa, 2020). Treat the existing public spaces for recreation with care. And it should be done with direct participation of citizens particularly impacted by the change, such as residents, merchants, and companies.

One interesting contribution has been provided by Bollier (2019) with the idea of a public-commons initiative, as opposed to a public-private initiative. In a public-commons initiative for a square, the government shares responsibility and maintenance over a public space with a group of interested individuals and merchants. This arrangement can produce marvelous results. In the public system, in order to buy a spade, for instance, governments need to go through a lengthy tender process that may take months. By sharing responsibility for maintenance of a park with the civil society interested in its use, the government may deliver a much better service to the city (Dalmazzone and Boilier, 2010).

Besides the existing parks and plazas, there is room for new ones in several parts of the city: old public buildings that became useless over time, reclaimed streets that are not used, car parks (yes, car parks!) that can be put to better use, and other public land that, for any reason, has become underused over time.

Conclusion

Yes, it is possible. Cities can improve, and it is not only a matter for the local government. It depends on the direct involvement of citizens, in particular, *your* involvement.

One major change and almost self-explanatory is to return the city to its citizens and abandon the city-for-the-car model. There will always be opposition to this change at first, but once implemented, it is widely accepted and acclaimed.

Several ideas for change within the concept of more HSSCs have been shown here, and you will find concrete examples in Chapter 5, Looking for striking Humane and Sustainable Smart City characteristics in existing cities. But each city must pursue its own path to a better life. In this path it is important to follow the mantra: metrics from the perspective (and only from the perspective) of the citizen. Everything else is irrelevant.

After the pandemic of 2020, many changes are expected in our society. People will probably spend more time at home and require more services from the neighborhood where they live. Isn't this the time for the live-work-play model to be tested and launched in the city?

We will get back to the subject in Chapter 7, The future: the need for more Humane and Sustainable Smart Cities postpandemic 2020/21.

References

Anthony, S.D., Gilbert, C., Jonson, M.W., 2017. Dual Transformation. Harvard Business Review Press, Boston, p. 272.

Bollier, D. 2019. Free, fair and alive: the insurgent power of the commons [video]. <https://www.youtube.com/watch?v = 5Elxr73IT10> (consulted on 22.04.20.).

Bria, F., Morozov, E., 2018. Ripensare la Smart City (Italian) Paperback. Codice, Italy.

Costa, E.M., 2001. Global e-Commerce Strategies for Small Businesses. MIT Press, Cambridge, p. 202.

Costa, E.M., 2020. Framework: smart cities can be more humane and sustainable too. In: Augusto, J. (Ed.), Handbook of Smart Cities. Springer, Cham.

Costa, E.M., Oliveira, Á.D., 2017. Humane smart cities. In: Frodeman, R., Klein, J.T., Pacheco, R. C.S. (Eds.), The Oxford Handbook of Interdisciplinarity, second ed. Oxford University Press, pp. 228–241. Available from: http://doi.org/10.1093/oxfordhb/9780198733522.013.19.

Dalmazzone, S., Boilier, D., 2010. This land is our land: the fight to reclaim the commons (DVD), The Media Education Foundation. Int. J. Commons 5 (2), 557–558. <https://doi.org/10.18352/ijc.314>.

Ekkehard, E., 2019. Big data and its enclosure of the commons. Social Europe blog. <https://www.socialeurope.eu/big-data-and-the-commons> (consulted on 23.04.20.).

Eleutheriou, V., Depiné, Á., Azevedo, I., Teixeira, C., 2017. Smart cities and design thinking: sustainable development from the citizen's perspective. In: Anais da IV Conferência de Planeamento Regional e Urbano (Annals of the IV Conference on Urban and Regional Planning), Aveiro, Portugal.

Fung, B. May 21, 2014. Marc Andreesen: in 20 years, we'll talk about bitcoin as we talk about the internet today. The Washington Post.

Jacobs, J., 1961. The Death and Life of Great American Cities. Vintage Books, New York.

Lara, A.P., Costa, E.M., Furlani, T.Z., Yigitcanlar, T., 2016. Smartness that matters: towards a comprehensive and human-centred characterisation of smart cities. J. Open Innov. Technol. Market Complex. 2 (1), 1–13.

Lerner, J. 2011. Urban acupuncture. Harvard Business Review. <https://hbr.org/2011/04/urban-acupuncture> (accessed 12.05.20.).

Schumacher, E.F., 1973. Small is Beautiful: A Study of Economics As If People Mattered.

Takahashi, T., 2018. Private conversation.

U.S. Bureau of Economic Analysis, 2019. GDP by industry, value added by industry, value added by industry (A) (Q). Annual industry data, lines 21 and 22. <https://apps.bea.gov/iTable/iTable.cfm?ReqID = 51&step = 1> (accessed 20.04.20.).

United Nations, 2015. The 17 sustainable development goals. <https://www.un.org/sustainable-development/development-agenda/>.

World Bank, 2018. Technology landscape for digital identification. Washington, DC: World Bank License: Creative Commons Attribution 3.0 IGO (CC BY 3.0 IGO).

Chapter 4

The eight dimensions of a more Humane and Sustainable Smart City

We do not grow absolutely, chronologically. We grow sometimes in one dimension, and not in another, unevenly. We grow partially. We are relative. We are mature in one realm, childish in another. The past, present, and future mingle and pull us backward, forward, or fix us in the present. We are made of layers, cells, constellations.

Anais Nin

Vision Zero is not just my goal in this city and in this region. We are all a part of this movement. We all play a role in curing this threat to public health.

Muriel Bowser.

Introduction—the Humane and Sustainable Smart City characterization

There are many possible forms of characterization of the more Humane and Sustainable Smart Cities (HSSCs) we want to develop, depending upon the focus one wants to emphasize or wants to tackle first. We have seen in Chapter 1, The Concept of More Humane and Sustainable Smart Cities, that the transformation of cities has gone through several denominations such as sustainable cities, resilient cities, creative cities, knowledge cities, digital or smart cities, and, the one we propose in this book, more HSSCs, which is an evolution of the concept presented in Costa (2020). As with all other previous denominations, our HSSCs show a set of characteristics, which we call here "dimensions." They are Sustainable Economic Development; People; Quality of Life; Historic, Artistic, and Cultural Heritage, including Tourism; Environment; Social Inclusion; Mobility of People; and Governance. The latter is a "horizontal" dimension since it is an enabler of all the other seven dimensions.

Humane and Sustainable Smart Cities. DOI: https://doi.org/10.1016/B978-0-12-819186-6.00001-4

This set of eight dimensions evolved in steps from the six characteristics of smart cities defined by a study in the European Union (Giffinger et al., 2017). We started to change them over time as they were applied in nine instances of a practical planning workshop that we developed in several boroughs of different cities in Brazil from 2013 through 2020.

In each of these instances, we asked all the stakeholders involved (officials, residents, merchants, visitors, tourists) what were their main wishes, interests, and needs for the transformation of their cities. These demands were grouped into dimensions and as they evolved from one workshop to the next, we settled for this set of eight dimensions. It is, of course, an evolving concept and may change again in the future. But this set of dimensions presented has proven in practice to cover the most important aspects of any process of change in our cities today.

The dimensions are interconnected, as the reader will soon realize. Development depends upon the right People, who want or do not want to live in that particular city depending upon the dimensions of Quality of Life and the Environment. Social Inclusion relates to public safety, the Mobility of People depends upon the right Environment, and so on. It is therefore natural that HSSC projects more often than not tackle more than one dimension in their strategy for development.

The eight dimensions are:

- Sustainable Economic Development (DEV)
- People (PEO)
- Quality of Life (QOL)
- Historic, Artistic, and Cultural Heritage, and Tourism (HAC)
- Environment (ENV)
- Social Inclusion (SOC)
- Mobility of People (MOB)
- Governance (GOV)

The Sustainable Economic Development dimension

Economic development can be pursued using several strategies. An "old school" mayor, for instance, might want to attract a car manufacturer to install a plant in his city in order to foster its development. Fiscal incentives up to the possible legal limit are granted to the manufacturer in order to bid for the project. But the trouble is the project will probably create very few jobs in the city, will generate little fiscal income, and, in some cases, will pollute the local river and landscape. In the developing world, it is even possible that the city will offer a large manufacturer exemption from environmental restrictions! This is *not* the economic development path we want to follow in our HSSC city. So, what is this path?

We want a sustainable economic development that is clean, offers high-paying jobs and work opportunities, and that is in tune with the city's vocation, mission, or strategic planning.

The creative sector is a starting point. Software development is—and will be even more in the future—a promising sector. But it is not for everyone, for sure. You need a significant pool of talented young professionals coming out of the local schools and a city that can demonstrate it is attractive to these professionals. Several cities in the world are graduating young software engineers only to see them "migrate" to more interesting cities, where they will find people who work, look, and behave like themselves. A study by Depiné et al. (2017) showed that the two most important factors to attract and retain young professionals to the creative sector in Florianópolis, Brazil (one of the innovation hubs in the country) were the availability and quality of graduate courses in local universities and the group of likeminded professionals that already lived there.

It is important to foster the entrepreneurial spirit and attract entrepreneurs who will create the startups that propel the new economy. There are several ways to do this but it is better to think of it as an encompassing support system that includes private, public, and academic incubators; attractive coworking spaces; private and corporate accelerators; venture capital companies, funds, and angel investors; and, perhaps most important of all, well-publicized success cases: "Success breeds success," they say. Thus successful startups breed new startups.

Another important aspect is the intangible symbolic image of an interesting place. A name, such as Silicon Valley (in the United States), Porto Digital (in Brazil), or 22@ (in Spain), does wonders to foster development of a city. But many other cities tried to copycat these successful symbols and they did not work. So, better not try to create your own "Silicon Avenue" or "Digital Forest" and such. Coming to think of it, Silicon Valley is already a misnomer: Originally, it concentrated several microelectronics companies (microelectronic devices are manufactured in wafers of silicon) that spun off out of mother womb company Fairchild, thus Silicon Valley. Today though, successful companies in the "Silicon" Valley are most likely software companies, not microelectronics (or even hardware, for that matter) companies, and many are in downtown San Francisco, not in the valley.

Tales from our workshops

In the Ressacada workshop, in Florianópolis, South of Brazil, in 2019, participants of the DEV working group came up with the idea of an impressive symbolic building to be planted just facing the airport's exit. The building should transmit an idea somehow associated with the local culture, history, or culinary tradition. Someone immediately shouted: "Oyster!" the building could be an oyster... Oysters are popular in Florianópolis, which is the largest producer in the country. Well, not sure the reader is familiar with oysters. But the shell looks awful and the actual oyster meat looks even worse! (in fact, many people do not eat oysters exactly because of their looks). So, no, that idea did not go ahead. But one of the rules of the workshop (and of any other design thinking exercise) is to never scorn any suggestion...

Examples in the book

We selected diverse examples for the book, shown in Chapter 5, Looking for Striking Humane and Sustainable Smart City Characteristics in Existing Cities. But note in the examples that a DEV dimension project may be related to something very tangible such as the Marina Bay in Singapore, where a full new city downtown was planned and implemented based upon the HSSC concept, or to some intangible asset such as the Open Data project in Paris. The latter opened opportunities for entrepreneurs and helped transform Paris into an innovation hub for information and communication technologies.

Your interventions

Entrepreneurs and established businesses' executives are not particularly good at pushing their ideas forward. They are too busy developing their businesses and cannot waste time looking at the other side of things, no matter how interesting. So, it is your job to go after them and listen to what they have to say. A good DEV dimension project is a combination of the local vocation, which you should be aware of, the wishes of the business community, and the existing city planning from City Hall. Talk extensively to all of them before you start anything.

The People dimension

The popular Styne and Merrill song reads "people, people who need people?". Well, we do, in our HSSC city.

The average number of years of formal education per working adult is one important and relevant measure of smartness. But be careful here, it is not the only one. Along with software developers, architects, designers, and engineers, creative people, who will develop our creative city, also include artists, musicians, artisans, etc. They may not have that many years of formal instruction, in the traditional sense, but are relevant to the local development as well.

Other important aspects of the people dimension are tolerance, flexibility, diversification, multiplicity of ethnical background, cosmopolitan spirit, and participation in public life. And these can be fostered by a local administration through special programs. The soft skills of tolerance, cosmopolitan spirit, participation in public life, and flexibility, for instance, may be taught in informal programs—but it is important that the local system be organized to incentivize a culture of life-long learning.

We have seen that creative people attract creative people but how to enhance diversification and multiplicity of ethnical background? One possible solution is to target the missing cohorts in special programs: giving incentives for women in technology, importing talent from neighboring countries (Startup Chile attracts young talent from all over Latin America), and even being creative in the diversification itself. For instance, French multinational Total placed an ad in several airports in the world praising the company's policy of "valorizing young talent." Now, can you think of any company in the world that in their right mind would not valorize young talent? No novelty here! Frequent travelers have run past these ads several times. Those belonging to older age groups (a majority of travelers) would probably think: Wouldn't it be nice to read for once an ad stating, "valorizing mature talent"?

The push toward diversification though should not be expressed in ads only, there is a need for concrete steps. Inclusive design (Sander and Taylor Jr., 2012) must be a necessary component in any city project: Will the new development be available for the blind, for the hearing-impaired, for people in wheelchairs? And remember, the cost of inclusive design when done at the initial phase of a project is marginal. Corrections, after the project is operational, are much more costly.

The mantra here is how to form, attract, and retain as many creative people as possible, of all ages, ethnic background, gender, sexual inclinations, and country origins. The common characteristics amongst them are creativity, flexibility, and a talent for innovation.

Tales from our workshops

During the Gavea workshop, in Rio, in 2014, a cartoon, drawn by one of the students from Portugal, summed up the situation in the target region. Gavea is a sophisticated borough in town, home to one of the best universities in the country, the Catholic University of Rio. Next door to the borough, there is a large slum, one of the largest in town. The cartoon depicted how one side of the social divide imagined people on the other side. In the drawing, on the Gavea side, a middle-aged lady sat at the window of her apartment, with the curtains drawn. As she looked outside through a small opening in the curtains, she imagined what was happening in the slum, and "saw" heavy-armed marginals that looked threatening... On the slum side, a group of youngsters were happily playing a "roda-de-samba" (a small gathering of samba players) with their tambourines, imagining what was happening on the Gavea side and "saw" a group of aristocrats in a penthouse being served by servants in livery by the pool. So much for prejudices...

Examples in the book

Examples in the book range from tiny Guaporé, in Brazil, to New York City. Both these examples concentrate on formal education, one for students in one end of the spectrum (basic), the other for graduate students. But it is interesting to notice the problems that they wanted to solve by way of the People dimension. In Guaporé, they needed a good school for their children, way above what the public school had to offer. And residents took it to themselves to solve their need and did not wait for the local government to act.

In the Roosevelt Island project, they needed sophisticated entrepreneurs. The dream of the then mayor Bloomberg was to establish New York City as a rival to Silicon Valley for new startups. In the past (recent past, i.e., 30–40 years ago), innovation was based upon microelectronics and hardware and needed the well-trained engineers and IT professionals from Stanford, Berkeley, and the other quality universities in the California State educational system. But in recent years, innovation has been based more on design ideas and marketing talent. Also with the availability of venture capital. And which city had all three basics in abundance? New York City! Bloomberg then decided to invest in a region in the city that was not so expensive and had good connections to the major areas of Manhattan, and settled for Roosevelt Island. The project deserves a study by the interested reader both about the Cornell Tech project (www.tech.cornell.edu) and about its results to the small island (rooseveltislander.blogspot.com), but for the purpose of this People dimension, the main pillar of the project was to start a graduate course with the best possible teachers and the best possible students. An international US$100 million tender posted by the City of New York in 2011 chose a consortium formed by NY's Cornell and the prestigious Technion— Israel Institute of Technology to establish a graduate engineering and applied science course (DNAinfo, 2011). And, in order to attract the best students, they were offered a package of incentives to study and to transform their studies into new startup companies in the sequence.

Your interventions

The main *caveat* here is that you need the proper place to attract and retain talent. Do not try to fulfill a politician's desire to have a tech park in his constituency. It will not work. One of the characteristics of talented people is that they can choose where to work. You can always improve the chances of an existing region that is already partially attractive with new features. But be reasonable. Las Vegas was a city built from scratch in the desert. It worked! But it is a single and striking case. Do not rely on that particular case for the success of your endeavor. Do not try to erect an innovation hub nowadays in a place that is a desert of creative people.

The Quality of Life dimension

This is the dimension that has to do with "feel good" in a city. What makes you feel good? It is very personal but certain characteristics help, and cities must strive to show them to their existing or prospective citizens. The all-important creative class, as we have shown, besides being creative, is also volatile. They can choose to live wherever they please. Four of the characteristics to attract them, and keep them there, are: public safety, health security, well-being, and life-long learning.

Public safety

The reader might remember small interventions conducted in New York during the 1990s by the then mayor Rudolf "Rudy" Giuliani (mayor from 1994 to 2002) in order to reduce criminal activity in New York. By means of a policy that became known as "zero tolerance," he managed to reduce the violent death rate in the city by 57%, transforming New York into one of the safest large cities in the United States. The policy determined that the police should not overlook "small crimes and violations" such as not paying public transport, breaking windows, painting graffiti on walls and trains, practicing prostitution, and pickpocketing. The policy worked, as reported by Malcolm Gladwell—he called it the "no-broken-windows" policy (Gladwell, 2002) and many cities all over the world tried to copy it, with unfortunately many different levels of success. Apparently, what worked in New York did not travel well to other latitudes.

There may be other reasons for these different results. Best-selling book *Freakonomics* (Levitt and Dubner, 2005) advances the argument that the reduction of the crime rate in New York in the 1990s may well be due to a completely different reason altogether: The authors, following theories of behavioral economy backed by compelling statistics, argue that there is a significant reduction in crime rate in any city around 18 years after the passing of abortion legalization laws (!), implying that unwanted children tend to fall into misdemeanors once they reach adult age—in their absence, crime rates decline. Malcolm Gladwell counterarguments that if that theory were true, the adoption and widespread use of oral contraceptive pills in the 1960s should have produced the same effect, and it did not. In fact, crime rate in the United States in the 1980s (20 years hence) was at its peak.

Anyway, this book is not the place for this discussion, but the interested reader might refer to a delightful post by Gladwell in his blog where he elegantly discusses the two arguments on the subject at length (Gladwell, 2006).

Suffice it to point out here that what worked well in terms of public policy in one city may not work well, or even not work at all, in another one. Therefore it is important to learn and study good and bad experiences from as many places as possible in the world, but to plan *your* own strategy in *your* city. Public safety is a must to attract and maintain residents.

Health security

Health security is defined by the World Health Organization as "the activities required, both proactive and reactive, to minimize the danger and impact of acute public health events that endanger people's health across geographical regions." The health system (hospitals, clinics, policies) in a city that conducts these activities is a major concern of the citizen, even more so after the terrible pandemic caused by the new coronavirus in 2020/21. The crisis started to show its deadly impact in the most sophisticated boroughs of major cities, since residents of these places were the ones who brought the virus home after returning from international travels. But once it spread to poorer parts of these cities, the impact was considerably worse, since the virus spread wildly amongst residents that lived packed together and the local hospital conditions were not only poor but totally unprepared to tackle the disease at such short notice.

Health security became an issue and its importance will be even greater as the population ages everywhere over the next few decades. The immediate reaction to the social distancing measures taken by most major cities in the world to avoid the spread of the disease was for people to start working from home ("home-office"), as we shall see in Chapter 7, The Future: The Need for more Humane and Sustainable Smart Cities Postpandemic 2020/21. But at the time, many people started to dream of going to live in a country chalet—only to realize that no residents may want to move their home from downtown to a nicer borough farther away but not too far, to a point of not having a guaranteed health security system in place.

Life-long learning

Graduation ceremonies are grand events in students' lives. They are now ready to go to the world and apply their acquired knowledge to work for existing companies or maybe open their own. Their relationship with their alma mater ends there. They might return only for the annual reunion.

Then they start work in the real world. To their surprise, some of the things they learned at their course are already obsolete. The tools have been updated. The language is different. And, worst of all, companies now tell them they also need some "soft skills" such as being able to work in groups, being flexible, resilient, ready to adapt to new circumstances, innovative... Help!

Well, back to school, not necessarily to universities, but to all kinds of different courses and institutions. Some of the demanded courses will be online, others still in the classroom, and some will be hybrid. Welcome to life-long learning!

Cities that want to be competitive with their sisters have to offer all kinds of alternative courses to attract creative people. They have to get ready to offer courses that will be required by the working environment, and also courses that will be demanded by the creative people themselves—on new social skills or even self-help courses that these people need or which they want to attend just to make social contact with their peers.

Well-being

These are the city's characteristics that make the citizen feel good about living there. It has to do with natural beauties such as beaches, forests, and parks, but also with man-made equipment such as bike lanes, pedestrian precincts, nice squares with flower beds and clean benches, and sports complexes.

The bar scene, diverse restaurants, and cultural and entertainment life are also especially important. The city can also capitalize on intangible characteristics associated with it. For instance, New York City is "the center of the world," Paris is "romance," Rio is "fun," Florence is "culture," and Vancouver is "garden."

There are also negative intangible characteristics that may hinder the city's effort to become an HSSC. Cities associated with famous crimes or natural disasters of large proportions have difficulty in offering residents and visitors a "feel good" sensation. That being the case, there are two possibilities to revert the "feel bad" sensation. One is to try and use the incident as an attraction (Dallas, for instance, with the assassination of President Kennedy). The other is to demonstrate how the incident was solved and what were the lessons to be shared with other towns that may face similar disasters (flood, hurricanes, fires, etc.). In any case, the city's image must be treated seriously by the administration as one of its most valuable assets.

Tales from our workshops

In the Hercílio Luz Bridge workshop in 2017, one of the projects suggested by the participants of the QOL dimension working group called the attention and became dear to all the participants. Florianópolis locals have the bridge in high esteem, as a symbol of the city; it is commonly referred to as the "old dame." The bridge has a special lighting at night that defines the contours of the structure and this light is visible from several different angles in a major part of the island. So, the project idea was to develop an app where the locals would register their feelings for that day. Sad, angry, happy, hopeful... Then, using a color code, the lighting on the bridge would express, every night, what the citizens were, on average, feeling that day...

Examples in the book

Examples in the book concentrate on the use of parks as playing grounds for everything in New York, Mexico City, or Vancouver. But the case of the Cheonggyecheon park in Seoul is emblematic. There we have a river, across town, that became polluted and provoked floods in the city. Years ago, it was covered by concrete and asphalt to solve its problems and to make way for *motordom*. Now the situation has reversed completely. They tore apart and removed the concrete cover, worked on the transformation of the river banks into a park with walking and bike paths, and built small resting places where people can eat, talk, or simply relax away from the big town above.

Your interventions

The number of alternatives for interventions related to this QOL dimension is almost limitless. You must study the city or the target borough carefully and look for interesting opportunities. They exist, be sure of that. But one more, as we have stressed time and again, it is important to listen to the locals, people of all different backgrounds, income, and social position. Remember, the city is there for its users, be them residents, commuters, workers, or visitors.

The Historic, Artistic, and Cultural Heritage, and Tourism dimension

One of the richest sources of inspiration for change in a city is its historic, artistic, and cultural heritage, not only for residents to experience a sense of belonging, but also as a magnet for tourism and economic development.

Economic benefits

There are several positive impacts of heritage preservation in economic terms. The first is tourism. In the tourism segment of the economic activity, trips associated with visits to historic, artistic, and cultural heritage are the fastest growing sector worldwide. Tourists want to visit them, to learn the interesting narrative, to understand the case, and to apply what they experienced there to their own places. But the presence of tourists must be managed carefully, since preserved sites are delicate and may be harmed by the very people they attract. Tourists may flock the place in excessive numbers, and be badly educated or ill-informed about what they can and cannot do in the place. These sites must convey the idea that the heritage is there for this generation of visitors to enjoy and for future ones also.

Another benefit is the number of jobs created. Jobs related to the presence of tourists in the hospitality business, but also those created in the actual remodeling, transformation, and maintenance of preserved sites. There is also the benefit of transforming the borough into a nicer place capable of attracting nontourist-related businesses and people as we mentioned in the previous item.

Projects may be major endeavors such as the Guggenheim Museum in Bilbao, the Sidney Opera, or the Tomorrow's Museum in Rio, but they can also be small investments in interesting ideas of use of the local narrative of historic, artistic, or cultural heritage. Think of the "Camino de Santiago" in Santiago de Compostela in Spain, that invites visitors to follow the steps of Saint Thiago in his pilgrimage around the town which eventually adopted his name (see example in Chapter 5: Looking for Striking Humane and Sustainable Smart City Characteristics in Existing Cities). Or the "high-line" in New York, a bottom-up development of an ugly and abandoned train line that was transformed into a sequence of small linear parks devised by the local community, and that attracts 5 million visitors a year.

Projects can also use bad moments in the city's history to make interesting cases for tourism such as the "Salem Witch Trials," women who were tried and executed in that Massachusetts city in the 1800s—now a successful touristic attraction; the 9/11 Memorial and Museum in New York City; or the Apartheid Museum in Johannesburg and the Auschwitz concentration camp, in which the visitor has an emotional experience through the observation of registered facts and images of these terrible events—they leave with the intended message of "never again" printed in their memory!

Social benefits

Heritage preservation projects help build a sense of community in the area. Residents associate their culture and even identity with these places and may transform their own environments into better areas after a preservation project is implemented. Radical activist Leopold Kohr, in his polemic book *The Breakdown of Nations* (Kohr, 1957), suggests that a way out of poverty in the slums of Puerto Rico, a poor unincorporated U.S. territory in the Caribbean, would be to build a castle there, right in the middle of the largest slum. Every resident in the neighborhood would strive to make his house more presentable—and that would change the landscape altogether. The example might be a bit far-fetched, but the main idea holds true: The local administration can renew and maintain a local historic site, for instance, and residents will hopefully respond in earnest.

Environmental benefits

Preservation of the city's history and culture brings also environmental benefits. For instance, old buildings consume much less energy in a retrofit project compared to the amount necessary for a new building in the same place. Preservation of historical sites helps maintain the environmental conditions in selected areas in town. But one must be careful here: Preservation must be justified by real significance. Buildings should be kept where they are considered relevant for historic or cultural reasons. There is no point in limiting the development of the city by keeping old buildings just because they are old (Glaeser, 2011). The net effect is to make the remaining areas too expensive (for being scarce) and to favor sprawling of the city into outside areas that will be very costly environmentally. The "green belts," portrayed as a sequence of tree-lined wonderful streets in the American film "American Beauty," may be green in their neighborhoods, but the CO_2 emission by the resulting car trips to practically anywhere is very "brown" indeed.

Tales from our workshops

In our experience of the workshops (one of them is described in Chapter 6: Where and How to Start in Your City) the working groups that deal with this dimension are always highly active and come up with the most interesting findings. All major cities have a history to show and transform into something that is worth a visit.

Once we planned a workshop for the restoration of an old street in Brusque (Brazil)—Rua Azambuja, that went into decay after years of abandonment by the local government, and was now left to drug dealing, prostitution, and poor housing. Studying the area, we found out that the bungalow houses with a small shed at the back, typical construction along the street, were in fact business-residence arrangements: The front house used to be the sales shop at street level, and the family residence was upstairs. The shed was a small primitive textile joint that produced the garments to be sold in the shop. The whole family used to be involved in the business.

Adjacent to the local church there was an almost unnoticed museum of church antiques, one of the only ones in the country. And, at the end of the street, a small road led to a grotto and small oratory connected uphill to a pure water well. Water from this well had magical and healing powers that attracted the faithful to pray and ask for indulgences. According to a local tale, the grotto was even visited annually by an aristocrat lady from Europe who was convinced of its healing power.

From an old and abandoned derelict street, we now had an aggregation of small businesses with a church and an interesting "ars sacra" museum on the corner and a fantastic story about a secret well to convey to visitors. The structural projects defined in the workshop suggested the installation of a training facility for small business entrepreneurs by the local Small Business Agency, incentives for them to establish their new ventures in the old houses, restoration of the sacred and religious art museum, and a historical study of the origins of the water well tale, and of its practical use to attract visitors.

Examples in the book

The examples listed under this HAC dimension here are concentrated in Spain, one of the most sought-after countries for historical tourism (Italy is another example) for all its treasures. But the most interesting example is, in fact, "El Camino de San Tiago." Narrative of the pilgrimages of the catholic saint in the region had attracted pilgrims for centuries. But up to the 1980s, only a few pilgrims registered their journey at the local Santiago registry annually.

From then on, a partnership between the local government, private companies in the hospitality business, and interested individuals launched a project that organized the original main route from France to the city of Santiago, publicized it to a larger audience (not only Catholics), and transformed the region. It is today one of the best-known places to go and look for solace, reconnect with one's inner-self, change the direction of one's life, and also, pray, although that is not the reason for the success of the project. Every Sunday, at 10:00 a.m., thousands of pilgrims gather at the Santiago church to celebrate their journey and the ceremony includes the swinging of a giant 53 kg censer in the "botafumeiro" ceremony that is impressive and really moving, even when you do not share the same religious beliefs as the Catholics.

Your interventions

Search for something interesting about the local history of the region under study. An intervention and new planning for a borough are much easier to implement when it refers to or has a connection to a narrative that is dear to residents and occasional visitors.

The Environment dimension

A more HSSC takes care of the environment. For real, not only as a fuzzy, non-binding and innocuous declaration of principles, because smart environment is much more than just an ecological issue. It involves the preservation and expansion of green areas, clean sources of energy, better transportation systems, garbage collection, and even collective gardening.

Green areas

We have seen the importance of preservation of green areas such as public parks, commons, and green fields in the city. One of the first actions to start action in a city is to prepare an inventory of every green area the city possesses. And to identify clearly what is private and what is public land in the inventory with the respective attributes in the local zoning law for every piece of land. This basic information is a good starting point to a "greening" project in the city.

But two other elements must also be present: environmental education and investments in the green economy. Schools have invested quite a lot in the development and application of environmental content in the classroom. Children love the idea in fact. But an eco-friendly attitude must also be responsible: Kids observe their teachers and parents attentively and expect them to act in an eco-friendly manner too. For instance, in a recent environmental meeting in the United States, one of the presenters surveyed participants and found out that 50% of them drove an SUV to the meeting. Alone! The best one can do about the environment is to act responsibly oneself. Not only *talk* about the environment but do your part in order to preserve it.

Investments in the green economy relate to the role that companies from different sectors can play in the better management of the natural resources they use to produce their goods and to operate their businesses. Check the Vienna example in Chapter 5, Looking for Striking Humane and Sustainable Smart City Characteristics in Existing Cities. Considering the growing importance that consumers give to the environment, an investment in the green economy can be not only right but also good and sound business. Consumers want to have access to eco-conscious products and services; in fact, they might even be willing to pay a little more for a clearly identified and environmentally certified product.

Energy

The best-known sources of clean energy are the wind and the sun. Windmills tend to be huge facilities more appropriate for installations in the fields, outside cities. Solar panels, on the other hand, can be multiplied in several places in the city bringing to reality Schumacher's dream of "Small is Beautiful" (Schumacher, 1975). Solar panels for electricity are now available in such small sizes that they may be economically viable for installation on ordinary homes' rooftops. But there are municipal large buildings such as schools, garages, office buildings, and such, that can be converted to use solar energy.

The solar energy solution may need a few incentives for private companies to adopt it, but governments can do it especially for new buildings where the additional cost for the new structure on rooftops can be absorbed by the overall project. Many municipalities in several countries are adopting this strategy to transform their cities into a "cleaner energy" place. A good place to start is in public schools. The solar panels, besides providing clean energy for the school and reducing operational costs, have a didactic purpose for the school such that teachers can "show and tell" their pupils about the importance of preserving the environment (see, for instance, Stanford News, 2019).

Other sources of clean energy should also be tried in the city and they may also help in other areas. In Brazil there is an ambitious program to use ethanol and biodiesel as substitutes for fossil fuels such as gasoline. It helps diminish pollution since ethanol use sugarcane as a source, a plant that is already abundant in the country and that is also used for sugar production. Several countries are experimenting with biodigesters of several sizes that may help in waste disposal in the city. Other alternatives such as burning other forms of waste (paper, cardboards, grass clippings, etc.) in waste-to-energy plants are also being tested (in the United States, see, for instance, eia.gov, 2019).

Transport

No, we are not going through our usual diatribe against the car. Cars are bad for the city when used for private commute downtown, as we have seen repeatedly. But the questions here are pollution and waste. Electric cars, for instance, pollute much less, of course. But even with electric cars, a good public transport system shows so many advantages over the use of private cars that they are a must in any city. Transport vehicles such as buses, trams, and light-rail vehicles should be nonpolluting as well. Besides electricity, alternative energy solutions from other fuels such as fuel cells from liquid hydrogen (that can be filled up at recharging stations) are being tested (The Economist, July 4, 2020) and should be tried in other places.

Used tires and abandoned cars are other sources of problems in the city. It is really disgusting to observe ugly abandoned cars parked in several cities in the world. The question, in many places, is legislation. City hall cannot collect these cars and dispose of them, unless they go through a lengthy process and procedure in court. This situation is plain stupid and can be solved by your local legislator. As for tires, several technologies have been developed to transform them into something usual such as building material but unfortunately none has yet matured to a point of general acceptance. And another problem with them is that abandoned used tires combined with rainwater are ideal spots for the procreation of dangerous mosquitoes such as the infamous *Aedes aegypti*, which transmits tropical diseases such as dengue and chikungunya.

Collective gardening

Several projects of collective gardening are being developed in different countries. A group of residents in a borough gets together to plant herbs, greens, and vegetables for local consumption. It is a marvelous endeavor for the actual local food production, but it is also a means of social interaction that is so desperately needed in many cities around the world.

In one of the examples of Chapter 5, Looking for Striking Humane and Sustainable Smart City Characteristics in Existing Cities, in London, the organization of collective gardening also has a therapeutic motivation, gathering people with minor physical or mental deficiencies to work in the actual planting of shrubs and bulbs. It also fosters volunteering and receives incentives from companies that want their employees to practice volunteer work for a number of days per year (which is compulsory in some countries).

Garbage collection

Garbage collection is a major function in any city. It is also responsible for various types of pollution. Not only the sites for garbage disposal but also the transport system to collect and process the waste. But new technologies are being developed now to improve waste management and there is a clear possibility in the near future that companies may be willing to *pay* for garbage, rather than the other way round, since different waste materials in the garbage may be sources for production of other goods or even energy, as we described earlier.

A new consumer?

Difficult to tell. But the pandemic of 2020/21 raised some questions that consumers knew of but preferred to ignore in the past: Am I eating well? Eating well is obviously a must for a healthy living, but its effect on our immune system has been brought to our attention brutally by the Covid-19 disease. Health authorities used to call our attention daily about the need for a healthier diet in many countries. Many other people in government have tried to do this in the past (former First Lady Michele Obama, in the United States, is a good example). But the change in our daily bad habits (that have been hammered into our heads daily with ads from the food industry) could certainly be procrastinated before. Not now. It became a question of life and death. Eat well, build up your immune system, and resist the virus! Or else...

It is still early to figure out whether this change in consumption patterns will extrapolate to other consumer goods such as gadgets and clothes and all kinds of bric-a-brac. But we are hopeful we will emerge from this crisis in better shape in this respect. And the environmental education of our children may help foster consumption habits aligned with the concept of sustainability. It would lead to a search for consumption of local products and services of ecological appeal, and to a change in consumption patterns. As we know, in many cases, the acquisition of a good is only the result of preconditioning to consumerism, as we have seen in the car ad example in the previous chapter, or the TV ads that we watch daily where they show celebrities consuming food items or wearing brand clothes, not a real need and maybe not even a pleasure. Kids, for instance, get bored easily over their new toys. Some countries now provide a service whereby you sign up for a toy rental service that, based upon the age group of your child, send you two new toys (used toys, but they are sanitized and in perfect condition) every month!

Tales from our workshops

One of the workshops we conducted in Florianópolis, in the South of Brazil, commissioned by the Federal University of Florianópolis, was for the region known as Primavera (Spring) around an innovation hub that sprang out of a large garden and flower shop by the same name. During the 1-week workshop, in 2015, the group that worked with the Environment dimension surveyed the area in search of interesting spots for project ideas for the environment. One of the things they found was an almost abandoned institution called "City of the bees" where they cultivated beehives and that was struggling to increase funding for maintenance of their activities. The place belonged to ... the same University! Although the workshop was organized by the University, nobody was aware of the "City of the Bees" there. The group eventually proposed, as one of their resulting structural projects for that dimension, the organization of a touristic environmental circuit in the region including a stop at the spot. Entrance fees would help to revamp and maintain the place.

Examples in the book

Examples that we selected in Chapter 5, Looking for Striking Humane and Sustainable Smart City Characteristics in Existing Cities, will demonstrate different characteristics of possible interventions in the city. The Smart Campus in Vienna is all about clean energy. The Green Legacy in Addis-Ababa concerns both a response to deforestation and an interesting educational tool for children and ultimately for everybody in the country. But pay special attention to the Green Alleyway in Montreal. The idea of renewing, transforming, and taking care of back streets may apply to many different situations everywhere and maybe an idea for your city.

Your interventions

The environment is a "no-brainer" intervention spot in any city. It is something most people agree that we should do something about. It has great appeal for children, it moves parents, and eventually it clearly demonstrates to be a benefit for everyone. If you are in doubt where to start, try this ENV dimension.

The Social Inclusion dimension

In most descriptions of smart cities in the developed world, Social Inclusion is a lateral subject approached as a horizontal dimension to be taken care of, if and when applicable, in the other dimensions. As we started to study the subject of more HSSCs in the developing world though, we realized very quickly that the subject of social inclusion is not only very important in itself, it can also help in the solution of other relevant problems of other dimensions in the city. It became central to our studies. At first, the Social Inclusion dimension was focused mainly on cities in the developing world. Later, we realized that the subject was relevant in almost any big city in the world today. The recent waves into Europe of exiled people, refugees, and asylum seekers (out of internal or international wars, tribal conflicts, and famine or natural disasters) have increased the pressure on existing cities to be able to cope with less privileged populations, minorities, and people with some kind of deficiency. The same is true of Cubans, Venezuelans, and South Sudanese into the United States.

Poverty

The mechanization (that is before automation!) of agriculture dislocated large contingents of unskilled labor and their families from the countryside to cities in many countries in the world during the last century. These people looked for better opportunities in the city, but they were totally unprepared for the new jobs available. Civil construction of houses and skyscrapers employed some of them at first but eventually even these jobs needed basic skills and training they did not have, since many were illiterate. The result was poverty and these dislocated families went to live in precarious regions in the city that became the infamous slums so common in large cities in Brazil, India, and so many other developing countries.

Slums have been overlooked by the cities for years almost as an unpleasant component of the city fabric. Over time though, youngsters in the slums became restless with the situation and started to react. Crime rates in the city increased, drug dealing became a way of living, and the proximity between the slums and the more developed parts of the city became a real problem. A classic photograph in the Tate Gallery in London depicts a sophisticated apartment building in São Paulo, in Brazil, with several suites and a private pool in the balcony of each apartment, just next door to one of the largest slums in town.

The pandemic of 2020/21 blew the situation in our faces even further as the number of "invisible" people in some cities, who used to live out of small jobs and street peddling, needed direct help from their governments in order not to starve after the lockdowns. It is still unclear what will be the cost to society of this huge demand of public funds, but the discussion about the need of a universal minimum wage for all, considered a utopia before (The New York Times, March 18, 2020), is now being seriously considered in the United States and in many other countries. And very rightly so.

In the city, we should look for Social Inclusion as a major dimension. But social inclusion should not look at the poor in a stereotyped fashion. For instance, training for youngsters in the slums should be geared toward what they really want to do as an occupation or profession and not toward occupations that our prejudices have boxed them in: Training should concentrate on, for instance, music, arts, and sports and not as cooking staff, hairdressers, janitors, and such.

There are many possible solutions for poverty in the city, but in the long term, most people agree, the one silver bullet is education. Those unlucky ones that were born in a poor background should have an opportunity to level their chances in life a bit by going through a good educational system. In the knowledge society we live today, education is even more important than before, and, as a society, we cannot afford to leave large numbers of citizens behind. It is costly of course but as the old Mark Twain's saying goes, "Every time you stop a school, you will have to build a jail. What you gain at one end you lose at the other. It's like feeding a dog on his own tail. It won't fatten the dog." Or, the more modern quote from Derek Bok, then president of Harvard University, "if you think education is expensive, try ignorance"!

Minorities and people with special needs

HSSC projects must contemplate minorities in general, including people with any kind of special needs. Chris Downey, who lost his eyesight suddenly in 2008, when interviewed by the American TV program "60 minutes" in 2019 summed it up very well: "In designing a city for the blind, I hope you realize that it actually would be a more inclusive, a more equitable, a more just city for all." Think of it for a moment. The same idea is true for children. What do children want in their minds (check, for instance, Suttie, 2019)? Parks to play, large sidewalks to go about, safe transport to go to school, secluded and safe bike lanes to enjoy... We do too!

Tales from our workshops

Another workshop we conducted in Florianópolis, in the South of Brazil, in 2019, was for the region of an old farm that belonged to the University and was just hidden at the back of the local airport. It just so happened that the airport had been privatized and the new administrators of the concession decided to build the new and very modern airport terminal at the other side of the runways, facing what was the former back of the airport before. With the change, the farm became very valuable land directly facing the new terminal, inaugurated in 2019, to be one of the best air terminals in the country.

The workshop focused on how to use this opportunity in the best possible way, keeping the original farm activities and experimental projects in place. Projects that came out of the workshop were very interesting but the one that called everyone's attention was the project proposed by the Social Inclusion working group that was called "straight ahead!".

Just adjacent to the farm, and separated from it by barbed and razor wire fences, there is a poor and problematic community (not a slum, but showing similar problems) and the working group tried to figure out what to propose for the borough. They interviewed several people locally and eventually came up with the project of a bike and pedestrian lane adorned with local plants and flowers, crossing right through the farm and connecting the borough with the new terminal. Planting and maintenance of the lane will be done by the people of the community and the plant bulbs will be provided by the farm. The bus commute between the community and the terminal takes 50 minutes today, including a bus change in a nearby bus terminal. With the new lane, they can walk there or ride by bike in 5 minutes! And not only that, the farm can sell bulbs of the beautiful flowers to visitors and tourists going through the airport or waiting for connections. They may also taste the local cooking style (originally from immigrants from the Açores, in Portugal) in the borough, generating a new source of income for local entrepreneurs.

Examples in the book

We selected examples of the SOC dimension in Chapter 5, Looking for Striking Humane and Sustainable Smart City Characteristics in Existing Cities, from cities as diverse as Melbourne, in Australia and Medellin, in Colombia. The Colombian case is particularly interesting, considering the former situation. Medellin was known internationally as the city dominated by the drug lords and their cartels, including infamous Pablo Escobar and his mafia. Through a series of urban projects that renovated the city, they managed to transform the city into a touristic place, an innovation hub, and a sought-after place for the installation of local headquarters of multinationals that want to operate in Latin America.

Your interventions

An interesting characteristic of the Social Inclusion dimension is the fact that the locals, in general, know or can indicate what they need and what should be done.

But they are wary and weary of outsiders and people who come with magical solutions to their problems. Wary because of lack of trust and, at the same time, weary of activities and projects that have already been tested in the past and did not work or were abandoned after the elections... It takes a great deal of conversation and a humble exercise of listening to them, but it is worth doing it!

The Mobility of People dimension

When one reads about mobility in the city, it is almost always related to mobility of cars, traffic jams, etc. We have seen this already, but once again, what is relevant is the mobility of people in the city, not the mobility of cars. A simple, but very often forgotten, concept!

Cities grew at a fast pace in the last century and this growth is still going on in several parts of the world, even more so in the developing world. This rapid growth has increased the demand for means of transport for commuters. Unfortunately, the private car was the preferred choice almost everywhere and this mistake resulted in unsustainable traffic in most cities. HSSCs study and implement alternatives to this model.

Public transport

Cities need a good and diverse public transport system in order to be able to improve the mobility of people. Public transport is a classic question of production engineering: How to move people efficiently from their residences to and from work and all their subsidiary trips. It would be easy to plan such a system on a clean sheet of paper. The trouble is that in most places a system is already working (in general, poorly) and changes must happen concomitantly with the existing system. Not easy. But considering the complexity of the solution, it is better to have a master plan and implement it in stages, starting with some novelty that shows clear advantages for the user.

For instance, a light-rail vehicle system: clean, efficient, and so silent, that when implemented in Rio, in Brazil, a motorbike had to precede the front vehicle on every trip in order to warn pedestrians (some using earplugs and totally unaware of the situation) of the oncoming danger.

The best systems that have been implemented, in places such as Geneva in Switzerland or Vancouver in Canada, are multimodal. Users commute from a transport modal such as suburban train to a light-rail or underground system seamlessly and have available all the necessary timetables and alternatives for connections.

Nonmotorized mobility

Special attention must be devoted to pedestrians (see below) and nonmotorized transport using bikes, skates, and roller skates. Bikes, in particular, are wonderful means of transport for commuting distances you find in a typical city—1—5 km, a short bike ride of 5 to 25 minutes, in places where the geography is favorable. Even when the city has small hills, such as in Barcelona, in Spain, people who live in the upper parts of the city commute down by shared bikes in the morning, leave them there, and return home by bus at night. The city must return some of the bikes to the hills at the end of each working day, but this is a small price to pay for not having more private cars downtown.

Intelligent mobility goes beyond the efficient management of the public transport system to the population. It also concerns a change in culture, habits, and strategies to move people about the city. Information management is key: Besides offering high availability, punctuality, and comfort, the public transport system must be easy to use with appropriate apps that show alternative routes, inform travel and expected arrival times, and be integrated, in a way that makes sense for the user.

Care and safety of pedestrians

Walking to work is a clean and healthy alternative wherever possible. But pedestrians should be taken care of. Large and well-kept sidewalks, streets that are closed to car traffic, and public safety for the pedestrians have all to be considered carefully and do encourage people to leave their private cars behind. But the city administration needs to look at pedestrians with due respect. They are doing their part to improve life in the city. Are you doing anything?

Changes in attitude and shared transport

Youngsters are changing their attitude toward cars, as we have seen. But not only that. They favor living close to where they work or close to the public transport system. The pandemic of 2020/21 may favor the "home-office" alternative at least for some days of the week in many companies. But even when workers "go to work," it may not be to the company's headquarter building downtown, but to a coworking facility close to the worker's residence where a company cell or project is developing their work.

Shared transport is another interesting phenomenon: As the new generations are not so keen on owning stuff but are happy just to experience the use of the stuff, shared transport alternatives are springing up all over the world in the forms of shared bikes and electric cars, car-pooling, and other systems.

Tales from our workshops

Another interesting structural project suggested in the aforementioned Primavera workshop in Florianópolis was the underpass in the main road facing the complex. The innovation hub is on one side of the main road, whilst the other side is almost irrelevant. The road works as a dividing wall between the two sides of the road. Building a viaduct over the four-lane major road in order to integrate the complex with the other side would be too expensive and so not a possibility at the time. Participants in the working group of the Mobility dimension came up with a simple but efficient idea (simpler ideas are sometimes the best ones). To lower the main road just for a few blocks in front of the innovation hub and cover it, at the ground level, with a prefabricated structure that could resist pedestrians and bikes, but not cars or any other kind of vehicle. Users of the complex could arrive there from either side of the road by bike, car, or public transport and go to their destination crossing the nice garden and plaza on top of the road. The difference in cost was calculated roughly as 10 times less expensive. And one can imagine the economic impact this project will have on the other side of the main road.

Examples in the book

There are novelties in Shanghai, in China, and a more traditional intervention in Rio. But the good thing about the Marvelous Port project in Rio is the aspect of integration. The modern light-rail system has been built and connects six other transport modals downtown: ferry boat, underground metro, local airport, suburban rail, intercity bus terminal, and regular bus. But although the project is a success, it has not developed its full potential because of politics (dear reader, does it sound familiar to you?): The project was associated with the former mayor by the population and the next mayor did not want to allow it to flourish...

Your interventions

There are obviously many possible MOB dimension projects to develop in your city. One word of caution here is not to think about improving the conditions of the car in the city. Nothing against the car (sorry, back at the subject again!), it is just a question of trying to do something different. There are many people in your city taking care of the car system, and there is probably a traffic department already in the city, they do not need you. Unless you are in the traffic department yourself. If that is the case, may I kindly suggest you go ask for a transfer to some other part of City Hall, where you can really make a difference to improve life in your city.

The Governance dimension (horizontal)

The management of an intelligent region is achieved by way of a set of partnerships and cooperative actions between government institutions, companies, nongovernment organizations, and the citizens themselves. There should be several channels of communication between these actors, and many actions are carried out through collaboration between government and society. A positive point for this relation on a city level is that the elected and nonelected municipal officials also live in the city. Their children go to the same schools as yours, they all suffer because of the same pollution and traffic jams as you do. That is strikingly different from the other two government levels (state or provincial and federal or national) whose officials are too far apart from local problems to develop an empathy with residents toward the solution of their problems.

An intelligent government values transparency, that is, all acts and information from public agencies and services are de facto public (except when, for specific and known reasons, they need to remain confidential). More than that, this new government facilitates access to data and public services—giving entrepreneurs the opportunity to develop solutions for the city based upon public data—making life easier for citizens and businesses. The population is engaged and uses political and nonpolitical spheres to draw attention to problems and claim solutions. But in many cases, there are solutions that emerge from society—and are implemented even without formal government support.

It is not easy to build the habit of shared governance in a city. On the side of the government, there is a sense of authority and "know-it-all" that must be curtailed. On the side of the citizens, there is a mixture of apathy (it is not going to work...) and mistrust of the government, feelings that also must be minimized. The pandemic of 2020/21 may again build a sense of community since we all had the opportunity to realize how vulnerable we are, and also to experiment a feeling that we are all in this together. "This" here meaning *the world*. But we can start with the city, since it is there where we can have an immediate impact.

Tales from our workshops

During the Lagoa da Conceição workshop, in the South of Brazil, in 2014, we invited all possible representatives from civil society to take part in the week-long discussion. One of them was the president of the resident's association called Associação dos Moradores da Lagoa (AMOLA), an old guy with a long white beard that looked like an old sage who would enlighten us all with his wisdom. His first intervention was disheartening: "Our association is called AMOLA for a reason (amola in Portuguese is a verb that means 'to nag' or 'to pester') — we are here to 'amola' you all and I want to start by saying that we have heard from people like you before — they come here with pre-conceived ideas and don't listen to us — and worse, nobody ever did anything to help us here, afterwards!".

What a start! But the key to a successful governance project is to do exactly what he suggested: "listen to us here" (good wisdom, after all). Governance has everything to do with listening to the locals, discussing projects and details, hearing past stories, and of course eventually proposing solutions. But it takes time. The main component of governance is trust. And you only build trust over time.

Examples in the book

We have examples from different cities in the world. But it is interesting to notice the level of participation of citizens in Reykjavik, in Iceland, on their Better Neighborhoods project. See also the European Union's My Neighborhood project (Oliveira and Campolargo, 2015). Another interesting example is the Doughnut Economy concept developed by Kate Raworth in Amsterdam. Think of the inclusive participation in the idea of a doughnut. There is no head table or centralized control, but a circle in a doughnut format, where everyone is looking at, talking to, and listening to everyone.

Your interventions

A good training exercise for a governance project is to experience a condo meeting in the building where you live (if that is the case). You will be surprised with how many different opinions there are in a place where you thought everyone was somewhat alike with the same wishes, interests, and needs. Well, no! People *are* different and their different opinions must be considered! Another interesting conclusion of the exercise will be to figure out how on earth is it easier to discuss difficult problems than to discuss trivia? For instance, a big-budget new sewage system needed by the building is approved in no time, while the discussion about what color should the entrance hall walls be painted can take a long time...

The implementation of governance projects takes time and demands a lot of discussions. Be prepared to listen to different opinions. Some you may deem absurd. But some will convince you they are better than the ones you held before.

References

Costa, E.M., 2020. Framework: smart cities can be more humane and sustainable too. In: Augusto, J. (Ed.), Handbook of Smart Cities. Springer, Cham.

Depiné, A., Eleutheriou, V., Vanzim, T., 2017. Creative class: why and how to attract it to the city. In: V International Congress on Creative Cities, Porto, Portugal. <http://via.ufsc.br/wp-content/uploads/2017/10/Actas-CC17-tomo2-OPT.pdf> (accessed June 2020).

DNAinfo, 2011. Cornell wins $100 million bid to build campus on Roosevelt Island. <https://www.dnainfo.com/new-york/20111219/midtown/cornell-wins-100-million-bid-build-campus-on-roosevelt-island> (accessed July 2020).

eia.gov, 2019. Biomass explained. <https://www.eia.gov/energyexplained/biomass/waste-to-energy.php> (accessed July 2020).

Giffinger, R., et al., 2007. Smart cities: ranking of European medium-sized cities. <http://www.smart-cities.eu>.

Gladwell, M., 2002. The Tipping Point. Back Bay Books, New York, p. 304.

Gladwell, M., 2006. Thoughts on freakonomics. Blog at Gladwell.com. <https://gladwell.typepad.com/gladwellcom/2006/03/thoughts-on-fre.html> (consulted in June 2020).

Glaeser, E., 2011. Triumph of the City. Penguin Books, New York.

Kohr, L., 1957. The Breakdown of Nations. Rinehart & Company, New York.

Levitt, S.D., Dubner, S.J., 2005. Freakonomics: A Rogue Economist Explores the Hidden Side of Everything. William Morrow, New York, p. 242.

Oliveira, A., Campolargo, M., 2015. From smart cities to human smart cities. In 2015 48th Hawaii International Conference on System Sciences (HICSS), HI, USA, pp. 2336–2344. https://doi.org/10.1109/HICSS.2015.281.

Sander, R., Taylor, S., Jr., 2012. Mismatch. Basic Books, New York.

Schumacher, E.F., 1975. Small is Beautiful: A Study of Economics as if People Mattered. Harper & Row, New York, p. 305.

Stanford News, May 2, 2019. Solar schools: Stanford research examines overlooked benefits of solar panels on U.S. campuses. <https://news.stanford.edu/2019/05/02/happens-schools-go-solar/> (accessed July 2020).

Suttie, J., 2019. What happens when kids help design our cities. Greater Good Magazine (March 11, 2019). <https://greatergood.berkeley.edu/article/item/what-happens-when-kids-help-design-our-cities> (accessed July 2020).

The Economist, July 4, 2020. After many false starts, hydrogen power might now bear fruit. <https://www.economist.com/science-and-technology/2020/07/04/after-many-false-starts-hydrogen-power-might-now-bear-fruit> (accessed July 2020).

Chapter 5

Looking for striking Humane and Sustainable Smart City characteristics in existing cities

"I see a beautiful city and a brilliant people rising from this abyss, and, in their struggles to be truly free, in their triumphs and defeats, through long years to come, I see the evil of this time and of the previous time of which this is the natural birth, gradually making expiation for itself and wearing out."

Charles Dickens

"None of us, including me, ever do great things. But we can all do small things, with great love, and together we can do something wonderful."

Mother Teresa

Introduction

It would be unwise today to try and declare a city, any large city in the world, as a "smart" city, a "creative" city or a "sustainable" city. Let us be humble about the results so far. Our large cities, *all of them*, are unintelligent not smart, repetitive not creative, and, even more sinful, unsustainable. Calling any of our large cities sustainable would be an anathema for which we could be cursed by some ecclesiastical authority. Our large cities are, in fact, putting our planet on a dangerous path that may lead to extinction. We will get back to this subject on Chapter 7, The Future: The Need for More HSSCs Postpandemic 2020/21, and Chapter 8, Conclusions and a Call to Action.

Having said that, efforts are underway to change the situation and we must shed light on them as well as learn from their interesting experiences. All the examples described here are projects that point in the right direction, in our view, and have not, so far, transformed a whole city. But it is a worthy beginning.

Examples were drawn from different parts of the world and each one focuses on one of the eight dimensions defined in the preceding chapter.

Humane and Sustainable Smart Cities. DOI: https://doi.org/10.1016/B978-0-12-819186-6.00009-9

A set of examples

City	Country	Dimension	Project
Addis Ababa	**Ethiopia**	**ENV**	**Green Legacy**

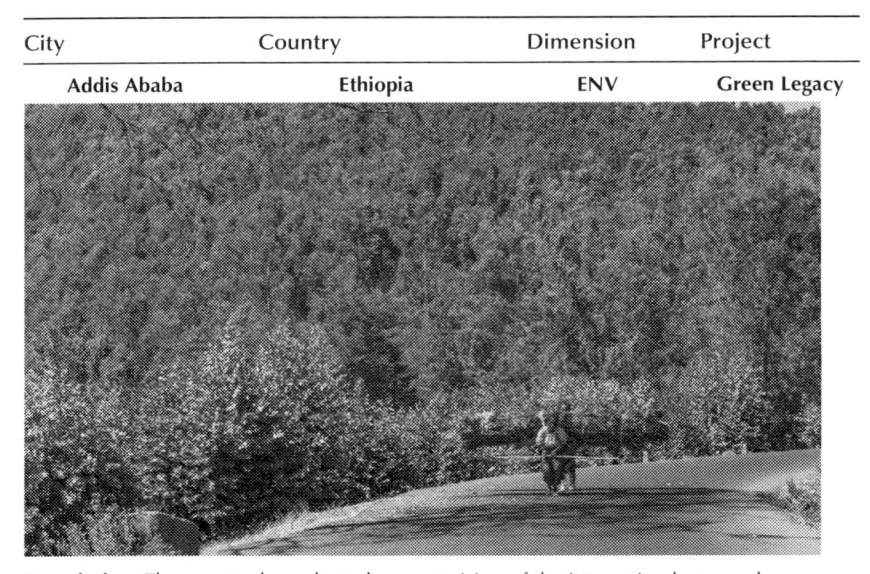

Description: The country has adopted a smart vision of the interaction between human health and biodiversity. They have been building a green and climate-resilient economy, which the Green Legacy Project is part of. This project has an ambitious plan to plant up to 5 billion seedlings, and the whole plan includes a goal to plant 20 billion trees, during a four-year period.

Dimension—Environment: The reason why the government decided for this project is not only to fight against climate change but also to improve people's health and well-being. According to the Prime Minister Abiy Ahmed, the one thing the pandemic made them realize is human vulnerability and the importance of health maintenance. Ethiopia is trying to reverse the heavy deforestation that led to only 4% of its area covered by forests.

Current situation: Even though the pandemic hit the country, planting is still going on. The country has already achieved a number of 4 billion seedlings planted in the year 2019, including the surprising goal to reach a rate of up to 350 million seedlings planting in a 12-hour period.

Results for the citizen and drawbacks: Millions of people have been mobilizing to take part in mass planting sessions in order to help transform the region into a green society. The aim also is to raise the public's awareness of Ethiopia's environmental degradation, educating the local society about the importance of adopting a "greener" behavior.

Future development: The Green Legacy Project has a goal to plant 20 billion trees, during a 4-year period, on the 11 regions of the country.

References:World Economic Forum at https://www.weforum.org/agenda/2020/06/ethiopia-is-going-to-plant-5-billion-seedlings-this-year/https://www.africanews.com/2020/05/13/green-legacy-initiative-ethiopia-targets-5-billion-trees-this-year/#:~:text = Ethiopia%20has%20announced%20efforts%20to,to%20plant%205%20billion%20trees. "IMG_5685 Addis Abeba, women carrying firewood." by Ninara is licensed under CC BY 2.0.

Data collected by: Fernanda E.D. Palandi   fernanda@labchis.com

City	Country	Dimension	Project
Almeida and Ciudad Rodrigo	**Portugal and Spain**	**HAC**	**Walled Cities**

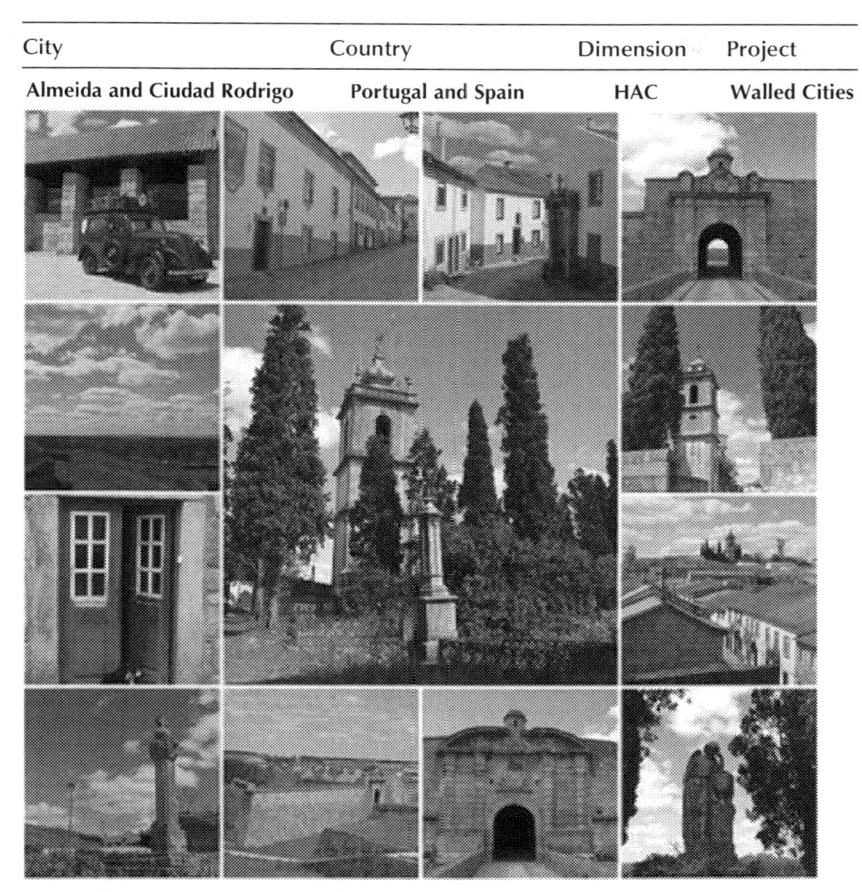

Description: The Transfronterizo Consortium of Walled Cities emerged as a result of the strong existing ties of union and territorial and architectural similarities between the City of Almeida (Portugal) and Ciudad Rodrigo (Spain). Both City Administrations are aware that the development of their municipalities involves joint actions that integrate and unite efforts to achieve common objectives and goals based on common planning and action.

Dimension—Historical, Artistic, and Cultural Heritage: The consortium of Walled Cities is the product of a border cooperation that Almeida (Portugal) and Ciudad Rodrigo (Spain) maintain, whose mission is to eliminate the border effect and transform the line that delimits both countries into an element of unity and development. This is based on its historical cultural heritage of defensive connotations faithfully represented by the walled enclosures, inserted as the Fortification of Raia Central.

Current situation: The first action was the creation of a Cultural and Tourist Dynamization Plan for the Spanish-Portuguese border area. It considers a series of interventions based on the definition and initial identification of the tourist product "Cidade Amuralhadas" with the intention of boosting the promotion, diffusion, and knowledge of local resources that grant a singularity to the border space that circumscribes its scope of intervention.

Results for the citizen and drawbacks: The rethinking of the urban management model based on maintenance and historical rescue × development has promoted the participation of the community in the discussions and a feeling of belonging in the process.

(*Continued*)

(Continued)

City	Country	Dimension	Project

Both cities promoted the growth of traditional local festivals such as the historical re-creation of the French siege and invasion in Almeida, and the Castela and Leão Theater Fair, Carnival of the Bull and Pilgrimage to Peña de Francia, in Ciudad Rodrigo (Spain). The main challenge for these cities is to offer attractiveness for the return of young people who leave to study elsewhere.

Future development: Provide tourism with business opportunities to attract new entrepreneurs, especially young people who have left the cities to study, and consecutively enter the portfolio of tourist routes of the main operators in both countries and an increase in tourists who seek itineraries with unique historical experiences. Also under discussion are joint government actions between Portugal and Spain to consolidate the Transfrontier Project.

References:http://www.ciudadesamuralladas.com/. Photo from https://amantesdeviagens. com/conhecer-portugal/distrito-guarda/aldeia-historica-almeida/http://www. ciudadesamuralladas.com/libro/AlmeidaCiudadRodrigo.pdf. Photo by "Almeida I" by Pedro Nuno Caetano is licensed under CC BY 2.0

Data collected by: Alexandre Augusto Biz alexandre.biz@ufsc.br

City	Country	Dimension	Project
Amsterdam	**Holland**	**GOV**	**The Amsterdam City Doughnut**

Description: Derived from the UN's sustainable development goals, the Doughnut Economy proposed by Kate Raworth consists of "a doughnut-shaped space in which it is possible to meet the needs of all people within the means of the living planet—an ecologically safe and socially just space in which humanity can thrive being: (1) healthy: with food, water, health, housing; (2) enabled: with education, energy, income, and employment; (3) connected: through mobility, community, digital connectivity, and

(Continued)

(Continued)

City	Country	Dimension	Project

culture; and (4) empowered: through social equity, political voice, equality in diversity, and peace and justice."

Governance dimension: It has been coordinated by the Amsterdam Donut Coalition, whose goal is to connect and stimulate collaboration, create the necessary conditions to "get the region into the donut," and publicly show the progress. The coalition is composed of a network of over 30 organizations—including community groups, commons-based organizations, small and medium-sized enterprises, businesses, academia, and local government. The coalition is also constituted by city dwellers who created a personal profile in the dedicated online platform—which means, having agreed with its goals and guiding principles.

Current situation: At the request of the municipality, Kate Raworth wrote the city doughnut for Amsterdam. Meanwhile, the municipality published its circular strategy, focusing on three promising categories of products, materials, and raw materials, the so-called value chains. With these categories, the municipality sees opportunities to influence and achieve results with: food and organic residual flows, consumer goods, and environment. Participants are invited to select an available condition, and check who is the condition's ambassador and which projects are running in order to engage.

Results for the citizen and drawbacks: Workshops were held in seven different neighborhoods, bringing municipality staff together with residents to hear their visions and priorities for a thriving Amsterdam. Another gain for the citizen is having Kate Raworth recently appointed as Professor of Practice at the Hogeschool van Amsterdam. For now, the posed challenge is to move the city within the doughnut's boundaries from both sides simultaneously, promoting the well-being of all people and the health of the whole planet. There is a concern that actions taken could increase the price and accessibility of public transport.

Future development: To put the City Portrait Tool into practice by the ongoing network of changemakers—which is an interative cocreation cycle, connecting analysis and action from the global to the household level, through innovation and learning, supported by the Doughnut's principles of practice. This tool will show the extent to which the city is currently exceeding planetary boundaries through its consumption patterns and use of Earth's resources. It is also at the core of the City of Amsterdam's broader ambitions to become a circular city, the Amsterdam Circular Strategy 2020—2025.

References:https://www.kateraworth.com/wp/wp-content/uploads/2020/04/20200416-AMS-portrait-EN-Spread-web-420x210mm.pdfhttps://amsterdamdonutcoalitie.nl/. Photo by "Amsterdam" by luca.sartoni is licensed under CC BY-SA 2.0

Data collected by:　　Tatiana Schreiner　　tatischreiner@gmail.com

City	Country	Dimension	Project
Ávila	Spain	HAC	SHCity

Description: Smart Heritage City (SHCity) implemented in Ávila, Spain, a technological platform that facilitates the management and conservation of the historical complex of the city, declared a World Heritage Site by UNESCO, in addition to contributing to its tourist dynamization. The project was a collaborative effort of a multidisciplinary team of professionals from Spain, France, and Portugal.

Dimension—Historic, Artistic, and Cultural Heritage: Strategically located alongside the City's platform for wealth managers, SHCity developed a tourist app that leverages the information captured by monitoring systems and provides a more informative approach to prospective visitors. The app also allows visitors to design their own routes through the city, assessing the time available, the points of interest closest to their current location, or those in which they will have to wait less time because of a smaller number of visits at that time. In addition, interactive panels were installed so that blind people could access certain data of interest.

Current situation: The SHCity project, which served to transform Ávila into a smart heritage city, is one of the finalists in the European ILUCIDARE awards, convened by the consortium of the same name, the European Commission and Europa Nostra.

Results for the citizen and drawbacks: The data collected by the sensors facilitate diagnosis and decision-making by city managers, including the important municipal archeologist. With objective and accurate information, improved diagnosis and decision-making are possible. In addition, the platform issues an alert in case of detecting any risk or uncontrolled parameter, so that authorities and operators can react immediately.

Future development: "By developing a network of sensors linked to an intelligent and open source management assessment tool, this project is a brilliant example of heritage-based technical innovation," the ILUCIDARE jury noted, adding that it was also "an intelligent and original solution that addresses different aspects of heritage management in a holistic way, including environmental and safety issues, leading to better decision-making." And points to an interesting future development for the project "to be applied in other contexts of urban heritage throughout Europe."

(*Continued*)

(Continued)

City	Country	Dimension	Project
References:http://shcity.eu/noticias.asp?language = enhttps://ilucidare.eu/news/discover-6-projects-shortlisted-ilucidare-special-prizes-2020. Photo by "Avila2" by Buho22 is licensed under CC BY-ND 2.0			
Data collected by:	Marciele Berger Bernardes	marcieleprojetos@gmail.com	

City	Country	Dimension	Project
Barcelona	**Spain**	**HAC**	**Sónar + D**

Description: Created in 1994, Sónar is a pioneering cultural event with a unique format and content. Its first-class reputation as a leading reference for international festivals is thanks to its attention in curation, combining a playful nature, the avant-garde, and experimentation with newest trends in dance and electronic music. Sónar + D is an interdisciplinary meeting that gathers in Barcelona leading artists, creative technologists, musicians, filmmakers, designers, thinkers, scientists, entrepreneurs, makers, and hackers to participate in a carefully commissioned program with the aim at inspiration and networking.

Dimension—Historic, Artistic, and Cultural Heritage: Sónar + D takes place along with Sónar, Barcelona's pioneering music festival created by Advanced Music, recognized since 1994 as one of the most important events for experimental culture in Europe. It extends Sónar's important role detecting emerging artists and languages into the space of creative and technological innovation. Sónar + D puts the Research and Development perspective into Sónar.

(*Continued*)

(Continued)

City	Country	Dimension	Project

Current situation: 4600 professionals, delegates from 61 countries, 2200 participating companies from the creative tech companies, 702 international journalists from 344 media from 28 countries, 250 creative communities educational and professional, 29 conferences attended by more than 3200 people, 425 participants in 22 workshops, and 20K interactions registered in the Sónar + D Networking App.

Results for the citizen and drawbacks: In 2019 they dedicated the event to artificial intelligence (AI) and how it is reshaping our world. From revolutionizing information technologies to its growing presence in their homes and daily lives. In this event, they gazed into the future to see how AI is opening new paths for the creative industries. They also had the chance to participate in a networking space that offered the possibility to establish new contacts and professional opportunities with companies and professionals in this field.

Future development: Sónar regrets to announce that due to the global crisis deriving from the Covid-19 pandemic, the 2020 editions of Sónar Barcelona and Sónar + D will not be able to take place and have been postponed until 2021. After carefully examining all of the alternatives and closely following the official guidelines, this decision has been reached as the only possible way to safeguard the health and well-being of all the festivalgoers, artists, and teams. This new edition, under the name Sónar + D CCCB, will have a format and content designed for the current cultural context, and with a focus on new and possible futures.

References:https://sonar.es/en/2021https://sonarplusd.com/em. Photo by "Barcelona, Spain" by dconvertini is licensed under CC BY-SA 2.0

Data collected by: Carlos Roberto Olsen   carlos.olsen@gmail.com

City	Country	Dimension	Project
Copenhagen	**Denmark**	**DEV**	**Copenhagen Capacity**

(*Continued*)

(Continued)

City	Country	Dimension	Project

Description: Copenhagen Capacity is the official organization for investment promotion and economic development in Greater Copenhagen. Copenhagen Capacity assists foreign businesses, investors, and new talent in identifying and capitalizing on business opportunities in Greater Copenhagen.

Dimension—Economic Development: The project supports new businesses entrants to identify business opportunities in Greater Copenhagen—from initial considerations to final establishment. They are the leading experts on developing business opportunities in Greater Copenhagen, and show a well-connected network of experts in the region to help the new entrants. Their services are free of charge for all foreign-owned companies who want to establish themselves or to invest in the city, and are provided in full confidentiality.

Current situation: The Danish government and a united Danish Parliament have passed several Relief Packages for all businesses in Denmark—including fully foreign-owned companies, in order to help them survive during the crisis. Information about the Relief package is updated continuously.

Results for the citizen and drawbacks: 2019 was a record-setting year for Copenhagen Capacity and Greater Copenhagen. The initiative helped attract and retain 50 foreign companies, and worked with 101 companies in Greater Copenhagen to fill 350 vacant positions with international talent. Altogether supported activities contributed with 4.6 billion DKK (circa US$675 million) to Denmark's GDP. The drawbacks is that some locals complain that the initiative is for foreign citizens only and only benefits the City indirectly, although local startups are also addressed by the project.

Future development: Denmark is one of the most digital economies in the world owing to excellent IT connectivity and one of the world's highest levels of IT literacy and e-readiness. It offers a comprehensive set of business data and provides international financial services companies with unique business opportunities. The highly developed digital infrastructure in Denmark is a product of the close cooperation between the public authorities and businesses, providing international financial services companies with unique access to developing new fintech solutions and services. According to Banco Mundial 2019, Denmark is Europe's best country for doing business.

References:https://www.copcap.com/. Photo by "Copenhagen Street Scene" by byzantiumbooks is licensed under CC BY 2.0

Data collected by: Clarissa Stefani Teixeira   clastefani@gmail.com

City	Country	Dimension	Project
Curitiba	**Brazil**	**DEV**	**Vale do Pinhão**

Description: The Curitiba's Innovation Ecosystem is a balanced approach of Humane and sustainable Smart Cities (HSSCs) and the organization of an environment for smart economic development. Curitiba is currently organizing itself to publicize worldwide as a city that houses startups. This is a brand strategy that takes advantage of the international projection that the city got during the term of Jaime Lerner mayor. Several actions are dedicated to foster the startups actually organized by Vale do Pinhão Agency. The success of the ecosystem is due to the presence of qualified professionals, good universities, and diversity of industries.

Economic dimension: Curitiba has a high profile in terms of performance, which takes into account the economic impact of the ecosystem on exit (settlement of the business), over a period of two and a half years. It is estimated that all companies based on city are currently valued at $2.2 billion. The most globally recognized enterprises are the unicorn Ebanx and the fintechs Contabilizei, Wuzu, and Juno. Curitiba was considered one of the most promising innovation ecosystems in the world for the first time in the Global Startup Ecosystem Report ranking 2020 that analyzes more than 140 cities in the world.

Current situation: The precise date of the beginning of the startup fostering movement in Curitiba is uncertain. However, the movement became ofcial with the advent of the Curitiba Technopark and intensïed with the implementation of the Vale do Pinhõ. The movement comprises a number of universities, incubators (UFPR Innovation Agency, Fiep System, Jupter, UTFPR Incubator, Hotmilk PUCPR, IBQP, Intec TECPAR), and accelerators (District, Fiep System, ACE, Hotmilk, Founder Institute, Orbital, Jupter, and Isae), mentors, mutual funds, and institutions that help to foster entrepreneurship.

Results for the citizen and drawbacks: A stronger knowledge-based economy, new business, and jobs. In 2018 and according to the 100 Open Startups Movement, 10 among the 100 most attractive startups in Brazil were from Curitiba. The startups and their ranking are: GoEpik (4th), Loox Studios (15th), Eruga (38th), Pipefy (41th), Beenoculus (43th), Vidya Technology (48th), Ubivis (51th), Send4 (68th), 33 Robotics (77th), and the Pollen (98th). Other internationally projected startups are Madeira, Contabilizei, and Olist.

(*Continued*)

(Continued)

City	Country	Dimension	Project

Future development: Establish a governance system to handle the economic development plan. This imposes several additional actions (workshops) to the planners to get the engagement of leaders from the city hall, industry, and academies. Second, federal economic policies in Brazil are not yet clear enough to support the investments. The city planners are working with public-private partnership models to replace the lack of investments.

References:Spinosa, L.M., Costa, E.M., 2020. Urban innovation ecosystem and Humane and Sustainable Smart City: a balanced approach in Curitiba. In: J. C. Augusto (Ed.), Handbook of Smart Cities. https://doi.org/10.1007/978-3-030-15145-4_15-1. The Global Startup Ecosystem Report 2020. https://startupgenome.com/reports/gser2020. Vale do Pinhão: www.valedopinhao.agenciacuritiba.com.br. Photo "Jardim Botânico de Curitiba" by Leandro's World Tour is licensed under CC BY 2.0

Data collected by: Luiz Marcio Spinosa   ms.knowin@gmail.com

City	Country	Dimension	Project
Florianópolis	**Brazil**	**MOB**	**Rota da Inovação**

Description: Route between the Airport and the largest tech park in town, Sapiens Parque, with five intermediate stops at the Federal University, the Madre Benvenuta region, the old tech park Parque Tech Alpha, and Primavera Tech park. Each one of the seven stops will be declared a Special Zone in the City Code, where the concept of a HSSC will be applied in full. Transport in the route will be served by modern buses powered by solar energy with high-speed Internet and space for bikes and other items. The region around every stop will favor mixed use of live, work, and play.

Dimension—Mobility of People: The route will be a testbed for everything new related to mobility in town. The basic electric bus will follow an innovative design that will

(Continued)

(Continued)

City	Country	Dimension	Project

distinguish them from anything seen in other places. The objective is to have people living in any of the seven regions be able to work and play in any of the other six regions without use of the car and doing every daily chores by bike or walking.

Current situation: Each one of the seven boroughs is developing some version of the live-work-play idea already. The project will integrate them all and give legal protection for investors who want to establish new facilities in the regions.

Results for the citizen and drawbacks: The project aims at improving the eight dimensions of an HSSC in Florianópolis and become a showcase for eventually transform the whole island into an innovation city.

Future development: detailing the concept of the special zoning for each one of the seven regions, based upon workshops and several other studies that have been conducted already.

References:https://medium.com/@bretwaters/florian%C3%B3polis-brazil-6f12714db992 https://www.researchgate.net/publication/329158742_Towards_Smart_Florianopolis_What_Does_It_Take_to_Transform_a_Tourist_Island_into_an_Innovation_Capital. Photo by Eduardo Trauer—permission granted

Data collected by: Eduardo Moreira da Costa   educostainovacao@gmail.com

City	Country	Dimension	Project
Guaporé	**Brazil**	**PEO**	**Cidade Escola Ayni**

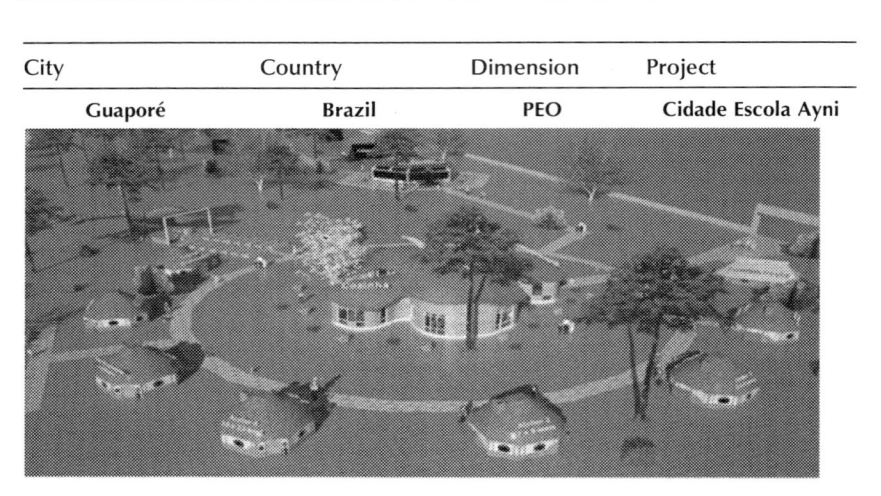

Description: Located in Guaporé, a Brazilian town located in Serra Gaúcha (Rio Grande do Sul), Cidade Escola Ayni's creation was based on the experiences and studies of its founder in communities and schools around the world, focusing on an education of the future. Ayni is a model school project that encompasses education, sustainability, and social transformation, emphasizing each student's potential. This new pedagogy (which is in itself a way of living) involves new concepts of social and economic organization, such as living education, bioconstruction and sustainability, nature and community, solidarity economy, collective financing, and gift economy.

Dimension—People: The project allows for social inclusion as parents, students, and members of the community become involved in its activities. All are included: people of various ethnicities, cultures, social classes, beliefs, and those who have some type of physical or cognitive disability, so that the importance of individuality and diversity in the integral development of the individual and his surroundings are embraced. The school

(Continued)

(Continued)

City	Country	Dimension	Project

carries out the maintenance of its infrastructure with the help of the students' parents and local and foreign volunteers that come to help and study the system.

Current situation: The free private school takes children from 3 to 7 years of age in the 18 spaces built in a 20,000 m^2 forest provided by the municipality, namely kindergarten atelier, children's expression workshops, library and astronomical observatory, land and water production systems, administration, hostel, guest house, visitation and tour area, rainwater collection systems, cultural space, arts house (music, theater, painting, and handicrafts), carpentry workshop, restaurant, huts, vegetable garden, ecological bathrooms, and systems for capturing solar energy and circuses. In addition, the school offers courses and retreats on the proposed pedagogy.

Results for the citizen and drawbacks: Ayni looks at a child as a wise being, full of potential. Its didactic methods work with the integration of the child, families, and community with the environment. This results in the students' great sense of autonomy. The environment is prepared to sharpen students' curiosities, exploring the practice of laboratories and workshops and the use of games as a way of learning. Local businesses are important as a means of automatic school funding encouraging the community to create a social support network.

Future development: The city school intends to serve students from 7 to 14 years old. In terms of structure and resources, plans are to provide a maker laboratory with a telescope, 3D printer, and robotics and physics artifacts for free learning practices. In terms of fundraising, the project plans to open a hotel and restaurant in an old house given by a family in the community, whose income is reverted to finance the school city project and whose collaborators will be the project volunteers and people with disabilities who will be trained and inserted into the labor market.

References:https://www.fundacaoayni.org/. Photo taken by the author

Data collected by: Suelen Lazaretti   suelen_lazaretti@hotmail.com

City	Country	Dimension	Project
London	**United Kingdom**	**GOV**	**London Councils**

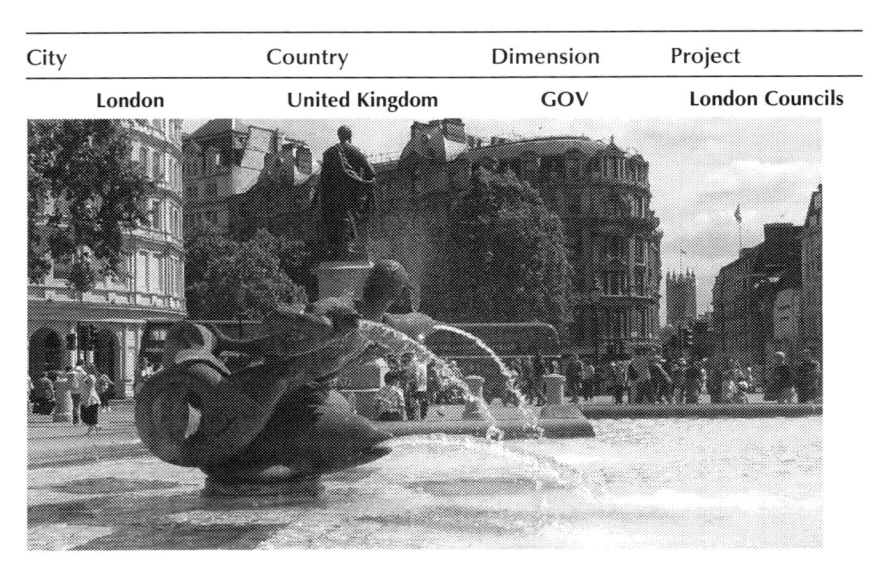

Description: London is the number one city in a new study from Eden Strategy Institute and OXD (ONG&ONG Experience Design) ranking the top 50 smart city governments globally on leadership and governance. Local government of London was carried out by the London Councils and the metropolitan borough councils, a structure that had existed since the end of the 19th century. London Councils represents London's 32 borough councils and the City of London. It is a cross-party organization that works on behalf of all of its member authorities regardless of political persuasion.

Dimension—Government: Since 1965, there have been 32 borough councils in London which provide the majority of day-to-day services for their local residents, including education, housing, social services, environmental services, local planning, and many arts and leisure services. London Councils is run by a committee made up of all the leaders of London's borough councils to discuss and agree on policy issues of importance to Londoners and their councils. The committee is supported by a cross-party executive of eleven senior members that acts as a forum for detailed policy development.

Current situation: London Councils is a think tank and lobbying organization, and also provides some services directly through legislation that allows multiple local authorities to pool responsibility and funding. The key themes are: asylum, migration, and refugees; children and young people; crime and public protection; culture, sports, and tourism; economic development; environment; health and social care; housing and planning; infrastructure; leadership, devolution, and democracy; local government finance; tracking welfare reforms; transport; London office of Technology and Innovation; London ventures.

Results for the citizen and drawbacks: London is a leading global city in the arts, commerce, education, entertainment, fashion, finance, healthcare, media, professional services, research and development, tourism, and transportation. It is crowned as the world's largest financial center and has the sixth-largest metropolitan area GDP in the world. It is the world's most-visited city as measured by international arrivals and has the world's largest city airport system measured by passenger traffic.

Future development: The challenges for London as well as for the world now is dealing with the outcomes from the Covid-19 pandemic. At this time of crisis, London has come together. As the threat of the coronavirus spread, communities have united to support one another to overcome this turbulent time together. The local government, along with private

(*Continued*)

(Continued)

City	Country	Dimension	Project

companies and residents, pooled their resources to deliver food parcels, medicines, and offer financial assistance for those in need.

References:https://www.londoncouncils.gov.ukhttps://en.wikipedia.org/wiki/London_Councilshttps://www.smartcitiesworld.net/news/news/report-ranks-top-50-smart-cities-on-leadership-and-governance-3100. Photo "London 2010" by Sean MacEntee is licensed under CC BY 2.0

Data collected by: Roberto Pacheco   r.pacheco@ufsc.br

City	Country	Dimension	Project
London	**United Kingdom**	**SOC**	**Camden Green Gym**

Description: Green Gym is a volunteer project created in 1999 by GP Dr. William Bird MBE and The Conservation Volunteers (TCV) in order to provide fun and free sessions where people are guided and take part in practical outdoor conservation activities. Unlike other conservation projects, the emphasis is very much on health and fitness. Green Gyms enhance mental and physical well-being through increased contact with nature and group activity. It makes people meet and work together to transform their local area, contributing something positive to their own community.

Dimension—Social Inclusion: Right now, a third of the UK's green places are in danger of being lost or degraded. Camden Green Gym is one of many TCV Green Gyms throughout the United Kingdom, and it works to ensure that outdoor spaces in the borough do not become neglected, overgrown, and unused, or even turn into magnets for vandalism, crime, and antisocial behavior. The project supports local people to develop the skills, knowledge, and confidence to take ownership of their public places. Green spaces are created, protected, and improved, for nature and for people.

(Continued)

(Continued)

City	Country	Dimension	Project

Current situation: In London, Camden Green Gym is one of 15 Green Gyms in the city. It runs for three and a half hours twice a week in the borough, working in small hidden nature areas generally unseen by the public, in urban woodlands, or in town greens. The Department of Health recognizes the invaluable impact that Green Gym sessions can have on those who take part and now prescribe it to patients with mental or physical disabilities to encourage them to improve their health and well-being. Camden Green Gym had 157 different volunteers in 2019, an average of 12 per session.

Results for the citizen and drawbacks: During its first 10 years Camden Green Gym ran 1034 sessions, had over 4000 people registered as volunteers (ranging from 16 to 84 years old), achieved 10,635 volunteering workdays, improved 65 Camden sites, and trained 52 volunteer officers. In the 2019 winter season TCV planted over 3000 trees in Camden alone and transformed 1500 green spaces nationwide. In 2017 a University of Westminster's study demonstrated that Green Gym participants reported higher levels of well-being and significantly lower levels of stress, anxiety, and depression.

Future development: Camden Green Gym is in regular consultation with Camden Council to develop green spaces, focusing currently on housing estate gardens in Somers Town and the Regent's Park Estates. Given the Covid pressure as this is written, there is additional uncertainty over the future. However, Camden recognizes the value of its parks and Green Gym in particular so there is hope of ingoing funding. Green Gym's aim is to scale up the project to have a Green Gym within 10 minutes of every UK home. Most Green Gyms are set up to become independently run by the volunteers themselves in due course.

References:https://www.tcv.org.uk/london/green-gym-london/camden-green-gym. for Camden Green Gym. https://www.tcv.org.uk/greengym/trust-me-im-a-doctor. for University of Westminster's findings. https://www.tcv.org.uk/greengym/health-benefits/green-gym-research. for National Evaluation of Green Gym 2016Photo by "Camden bridge" by mariosp is licensed under CC BY-SA 2.0

Data collected by: Anne Aune   anneaune@yahoo.com.br

City	Country	Dimension	Project
Lisbon	**Portugal**	**HAC**	**Parque das Nações**

(Continued)

City	Country	Dimension	Project

Description: The Parque da Nações (Park of Nations) is the striking modern side of historic Lisbon. The district was transformed from an industrial wasteland into the showground for Expo '98. Since the event, the area has undergone a second transformation, becoming a center for business and corporate Portugal. Today, the district is popular with both locals and tourists, filled with futuristic architecture, urban art, and unique gardens.

Dimension—Historical, Artistic, and Cultural Heritage: Expo Lisboa 1998 transformed the region today called Parque das Nações. Before the reforms, it was a vast decayed, degraded, and contaminated industrial and urban area. At the time, Expo '98 was considered the biggest urban conversion in Europe. Parque das Nações can be considered as a "city within the city," with: 31,000 residents, 30,000 workers, 10 hotels in operation, 25,000 parking spaces, 1000 students in public schools that include day care centers and kindergartens, and 979,405 m^2 of green spaces (in 2018).

Current situation: One-third of Parque das Nações is composed of trees and gardens and the site has urban creations of well-known architects. Among the works and spaces present are: Oriente Station, Lisbon International Fair, Marina Parque das Nações, Lisbon Oceanarium, Atlantic Pavilion | MEO Arena, Portugal Pavilion, Knowledge Pavilion, Vasco da Gama Bridge, Tagus River, Camões Theater, Cable Cars, and São Gabriel/São Rafael Towers.

Results for the citizen and drawbacks: Expo '98 was regarded as a great success for Portugal, promoting the new industrial might of the small country and even helped Portugal to join the Euro single currency. It is an open-air museum as urban art is found in the streets, squares, gardens, and sidewalks. Important details in relation to the Environment are: Pneumatic garbage collection from each building is carried out to the treatment center, as well as incentives for recycling and waste treatment, which results in greater hygiene and energy savings.

Future development: (1) Central accessibility to the intermodal transport network in order to encourage the use of public transport and make pedestrian use of the area viable, (2) lively and vibrant atmosphere throughout the year, (3) uniqueness and architectural quality of the buildings for the enhancement and consolidation of a new urban image, and (4) contribution of these buildings for a new relationship with the riverfront.

References:https://expresso.pt/multimedia/infografia/2018-05-21-Parque-das-Nacoes-a-cidade-de-todos-os-recordeshttp://www.portaldasnacoes.pt/category/arte-urbana/http://www.portaldasnacoes.pt/item/planeamento/. Photo by Edyardo Trauer—permission granted

Data collected by: Eduardo Trauer   eduardo@etrauer.com

City	Country	Dimension	Project
Madrid	**Spain**	**GOV**	**Decide Madrid**

Description: Decide Madrid is an ongoing project at Madrid City Council, aiming to engage the participation of its citizens in government policies. The platform utilizes the Consul open software, and was launched in 2015, allowing any citizen to make proposals, participate in online debates, and vote on other people's ideas. It is also possible to directly participate in the allocation of the municipal budget. It empowers the citizens to participate on its smart governance.

Dimension—Government: Proposals for improvements in public lighting, cleaning of parks, opening hours of common areas, or even hiring private security for certain neighborhoods are examples of proposals made on the platform.

Current situation: The project is still in progress. Today (June 13, 2020) there are more than 3700 discussions on the platform, and over 500 active proposals. The platform has already received awards and is now being made available in several cities around the world, including Montevideo, Lima, La Paz, and Rio.

Results for the citizen and drawbacks: Citizen demand for more direct citizen participation is attended, resulting in strong political support, Internet penetration, and integration in the policy-making processes. As drawbacks, it has been pointed out: decreasing citizen interest, lack of transparency, lack of feedback, lack of moderation or other mechanisms to organize debates and proposals, and concerns about the security of the platform.

Future development: Implementation of the platform in other countries.

References:https://decide.madrid.es/https://oidp.net/en/content.php?id = 1461#: ~ : text = The%20UN%20has%20awarded%20the,best%20public%20service%20of%202018. &text = The%20award%20was%20first%20held,of%20Economic%20and%20Social% 20Affairs. Photo "Palacio de Cristal" by Falling Outside The Normal Moral Constraints is licensed under CC BY 2.0

Data collected by:　　　Andreici Vedovatto　　　andreici@unochapeco.edu.br

City	Country	Dimension	Project
Málaga	Spain	HAC	Cidade Milenária

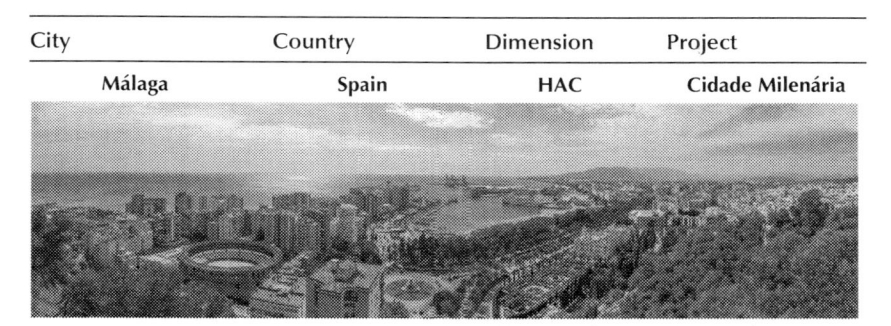

Description: The city of Málaga installed LED street lighting, offered over 20 bicycle rental stations, and more than 40 km of cycle paths. The parks and gardens have smart irrigation systems aimed at saving water and the city has a Sectorial Air Quality Plan that aims to reduce pollution, control pollen levels, and improve noise quality. Málaga also works in cleaning the streets and in waste separation processes in the city center. Malaga has 60 hectares of botanical gardens and 400 hectares of green spaces, bird watching, and nature walks.

Dimension—Historical, Artistic, and Cultural Heritage: Málaga is considered the "city of museums." In two decades, the city has grown from four museums and exhibition centers to 37 establishments. Old buildings and their surroundings have been transformed into vibrant historical and cultural spaces.

Current situation: The United Nations, through the UNITAR agency, established the CIFAL (International Training Center for Authorities and Leaders) in Malaga in 2018, dedicated especially to training in Sustainable Tourism.

Results for the citizen and drawbacks: Málaga incorporates the concepts of sustainability, innovation, and culture in its strategic plans and offers the right conditions for tourists and residents to enjoy the city.

Future development: Consolidate the city as an Intelligent Tourist Destination with the establishment of strategies for the reevaluation of the destination: This will increase competitiveness through a better use of its natural and cultural attractions, creation of innovative resources, improvement of the efficiency of the processing, and distribution processes so that they can boost sustainable development as well as facilitate the visitor's interaction with the destination.

References:http://www.malagaturismo.com/es/site/smarttourism/paginas/ciudad-milenaria/583http://www.malagaturismo.com/es/site/smarttourism/secciones/cultura-y-patrimonio/168http://www.malagaturismo.com/es/site/smarttourism/paginas/destino-turistico-inteligente/580Photo by "Malaga NZ7_1271_73" by Bengt Nyman is licensed under CC BY 2.0

Data collected by: Eduardo Trauer   eduardo@etrauer.com

City	Country	Dimension	Project
Lisboa	**Portugal**	**HAC**	**Parque das Nações**

Description: The Parque da Nações (Park of Nations) is the striking modern side to historic Lisbon. The district was transformed from an industrial wasteland into the showground for Expo '98. Since the event, the area has undergone a second transformation, becoming a center for business and corporate Portugal. Today, the district is popular with both locals and tourists, filled with futuristic architecture, urban art, and unique gardens.

Dimension—Intelligent use of Historical, Artistic, and Cultural Heritage: Expo Lisboa 1998 transformed the region today called Parque das Nações. Before the reforms, it was a vast decayed, degraded, and contaminated industrial and urban area. At the time, Expo '98 was considered the biggest urban conversion in Europe. Parque das Nações can be considered as a "city within the city," with: 31,000 residents, 30,000 workers, 10 hotels in operation, 25,000 parking spaces, 1000 students in public schools that include day care centers and kindergartens, and 979,405 m^2 of green spaces (in 2018).

Current situation: One-third of Parque das Nações is composed of trees and gardens and the site has urban creations of well-known architects. Among the works and spaces present are: Oriente Station, Lisbon International Fair, Marina Parque das Nações, Lisbon Oceanarium, Atlantic Pavilion | MEO Arena, Portugal Pavilion, Knowledge Pavilion, Vasco da Gama Bridge, Tagus River, Camões Theater, Cable Cars, and São Gabriel / São Rafael Towers.

Results for the citizen and drawbacks: Expo '98 was regarded as a great success for Portugal, promoting the new industrial might of the small country and even being considered as having helped Portugal to join the Euro single currency. It is an open-air museum as urban art is found in the streets, squares, gardens, and sidewalks. Important details in relation to the Environment are: Pneumatic garbage collection from each building is carried out to the treatment center, as well as incentives for recycling and waste treatment, which results in greater hygiene and energy savings.

Future development: (1) Central accessibility to the intermodal transport network in order to encourage the use of public transport and make pedestrian use of the area viable, (2) lively and vibrant atmosphere throughout the year, (3) uniqueness and architectural quality of the buildings for the enhancement and consolidation of a new urban image, and (4) contribution of these buildings for a new relationship with the riverfront.

(Continued)

(Continued)

City	Country	Dimension	Project
References:https://expresso.pt/multimedia/infografia/2018-05-21-Parque-das-Nacoes-a-cidade-de-todos-os-recordeshttp://www.portaldasnacoes.pt/category/arte-urbana/http://www.portaldasnacoes.pt/item/planeamento/.			
Data collected by:	name	email	
June 21, 2020	Eduardo Trauer	eduardo@etrauer.com	

City	country	dimension	project
Medellín	**Colombia**	**SOC**	**Cultura Metro**

Description: The Metro Culture in Medellin, Colombia, is the result of the social, educational, and cultural management model built by METRO to generate a culture of value and care among the stations' and the Metro lines' neighbors, developing an attitude of preservation of the transportation system. The Metro is seen as an important feature that separates Medellin from other areas, and contributes to the improvement of its citizens' lives.

Social dimension: The "Cultura Metro" includes educational programs, art projects, community engagements, and sustainability initiatives. Art projects include galleries within the stations featuring the works of local artists. The organization staffs trains youth leaders in the communities, helping them acquire skills to aid their personal and professional growth. As an example, one leadership development program educated over 2000 individuals, who subsequently coordinated community engagement days featuring art, music, and more.

Current situation: Currently Metro Culture has Educational Programs, User Training, Leaders Training School, METRO Friends Program, METRO Culture Apprentices, Driver

(*Continued*)

(Continued)

City	country	dimension	project

Training, Cultural Programs, Community Relations Programs, Metro Leaders School, Sustainable Mobility. The Meddellín Metro is one of the three (of almost 200 metros in the world) that is financially self-sustainable, without requiring state subsidies.

Results for the citizen and drawbacks: The beginning of the Metro operation, when first inaugurated in 1995, changed the identity of Medellín, as well as some of the cultural practices of its inhabitants. Each of the stations offers cultural spaces, recreational areas, water fountains, waiting benches, booths, and commercial premises.

Future development: One of the challenges of the Metro Culture in the present and future is to improve the forms of communication, to make them more appropriate to the needs and trends of today. This model can be adopted, totally or partially, by other cities and institutions whose purpose is to build a new citizen culture, which involves coexisting in harmony, solidarity, and respect for basic rules of use of public goods.

References:https://www.metrodemedellin.gov.co/cultura-metro. (accessed 18.06.20.) https://www.eltiempo.com/archivo/documento/MAM-677739https://repositImage. by Sylvia Currie is licensed under CC BY-SAPhoto by Image by Sylvia Currie is licensed under CC BY-SA 2.0

Data collected by: Mônica Ramos Carneiro   moni.carneiro@hotmail.com

City	Country	Dimension	Project
Mexico City	**Mexico**	**QOL**	**Chapultepec Park**

Description: Chapultepec Park, in downtown México City, was a retreat for Aztec rulers and later became the site of official residences for Mexican heads of state. It has always played an important historical and ecological role, as one the city's "lungs." Today it is one of the largest urban parks in the world (686 hectares) and a key element to social inclusion through several free activities that are open to the general public.

Dimension—Quality of Life: As well as a great example of SOC (Social Inclusion), its most prominent dimension is in the area of PHA (Intelligent use of Historic, Artistic, and Cultural Heritage).

(Continued)

(Continued)

City	Country	Dimension	Project

Current situation: After revitalization efforts at the beginning of 21st century, the oldest and largest urban park in Latin America offers entertainment for all. Its attractions include a walk through the Bosque of Chapultepec or the Botanical Garden, a visit to the zoo, to the castle, and to nine museums. It also contains several restaurants and food stands.

Results for the citizen and drawbacks: Its open green spaces and cultural attractions offer a sense of safety and enjoyment for its 18 million annual visitors. It is a successful example of an urban area that promotes social, cultural, civic, historical, and environmental value for Mexico city's residents and visitors.

Future development: The 19th-century gatehouse—which once served as entrance to a military school—is being transformed into a museum and operation center, providing information about the park's history, the rehabilitation program, and various cultural programs. It is a link between the origins of the Chapultepec Park and its use in the 21st century as an important urban park, known internationally.

References:https://www.smartcitiesdive.com/ex/sustainablecitiescollective/mexico-city-park-partnerships-role-urban-revitalization/228101/https://www.wmf.org/project/chapultepec-park. Photo by "Chapultepec Castle, downtown Mexico City" by Tatiana12 is licensed under CC BY 2.0

Data collected by: Patricia Pepper Costa   patriciagpepper@gmail.com

City	Country	Dimension	Project
Montreal	Canada	ENV	Green Alleyway

(Continued)

(Continued)

City	Country	Dimension	Project

Description: The Regroupment EcoQuartier (REQ) program was created in 1999 and aims to promote environmental citizenship and improve Montrealers' living environments through education and civic engagement. The main objective is to promote eco-citizenship and improve the living conditions through actions led by citizens, called to become real agents of change. REQ develops green lanes; distributes and sells eco-products; and promotes education and projects related to the environment, in collaboration with residents. Ruelles Vertes (photo) is part of REQ and develops innovatively alleyways that run through neighborhoods.

Dimension—Environment: The Green Alleyway is an environmental action anchored in local representatives and structured around the concepts of awareness, environmental education (ERE), information, training, and citizen participation. The borough and local organizations help to create the spaces, but then they become a responsibility of the residents committed to the project. City councilors give priority to areas known as urban heat islands, where temperatures are 5−10 degrees higher than in the surrounding area. By removing asphalt and planting trees temperatures are lowered, the air is purified, and soil quality is improved.

Current situation: More than 400 green alleyways across city neighborhoods have been transformed into lush gardens, safe play areas for children, and public meeting spaces, totaling around 15% of public spaces and more than 69 km throughout the city's 19 boroughs. It transforms soulless, trash-filled thoroughfares into green, ecological, vibrant and enliven spaces conducive to environmental actions, sharing, and playing. The success of the project relies on those involved in it and specialists says it helps to reduce heat islands, absorbing rainwater and bringing green spaces to underused corners of the city.

Results for the citizen and drawbacks: Through member services, network, and project coordination, the Green Alleyway Project revitalized what are often forgotten or abandoned spaces and also defends the right of citizens to have a healthy environment and an ecologically viable development of their community. It is mainly through ERE, underlying the resolution of environmental and social problems as well as a variety of learning strategies, that the REQ achieves its objectives. The city gives away plants to the inhabitants, who are to create gardens and green alleys.

Future development: Coordinated by the Montreal Urban Ecology Center the project wishes to support citizens to develop knowledge and skills to improve the quality of life in their environment and get citizens to actively participate in their community developing a constructive critical attitude. Urban planning experts say the success of Montreal's green alleyways project illustrates just what is possible when you give citizens a voice in the design of public assets. The democratization of urban planning has gained a lot of traction in university lecture halls and beyond, and is being tested in community-based projects.

References:https://www.eco-quartiers.org/http://greenalleymontreal.blogspot.com/https://www.landscapearchitecture.nz/landscape-architecture-aotearoa/2018/7/20/montreals-clean-green-alleyways. Photos of "Ruelle verte" by Villeray—Saint-Michel—Parc-Extension is licensed under CC BY-ND 2.0, and "Ruelle verte" by Villeray—Saint-Michel—Parc-Extension is licensed under CC BY-ND 2.0

Data collected by: Hans Michael van Bellen   hansmichael.vanbellen@gmail.com

City	Country	Dimension	Project
New York City	**United States**	**PEO**	**Roosevelt Island**

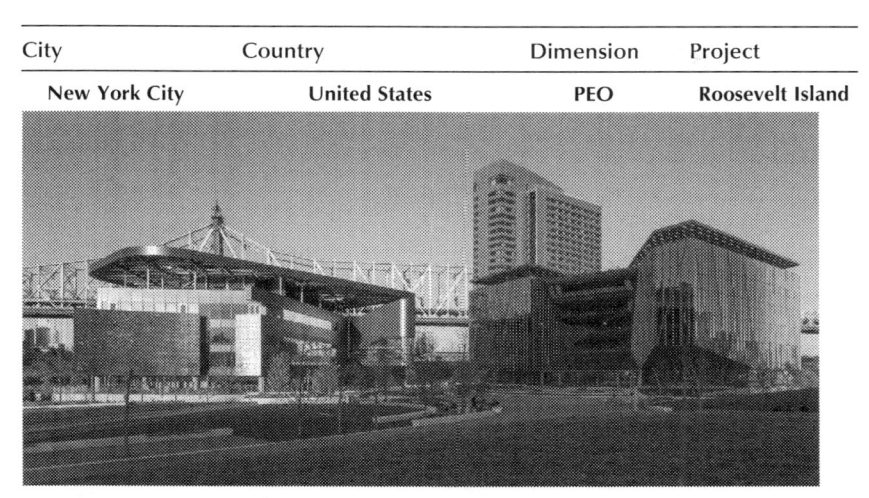

Description: Cornell is a project delineated by the City of New York, under then mayor Bloomberg, to transform New York into the new mecca for startups in the United States. The US$2 billion project was anchored by Cornell Tech, an ambitious project, now fully operational, to have a graduate course on Engineering and Applied Science geared toward the development of new companies by the students themselves. Students and professors live in the island to make the environment even more attuned to the sharing of knowledge.
Dimension—People: The project started by focusing on the attraction and retention of the best possible professors and graduate students, lured by generous salaries and grants for the development of new businesses. Besides the island itself, the small island is just next to the services and attractions of Manhattan, connected by a confortable cable car system and underground.
Current situation: Cornell Tech is fully operational and, besides the area dedicated directly to the project, the remainder of the island went through a wave of development with new residents and additional services. There are even some apartments dedicated to social housing in order to incentivize diversity in the island.
Results for the citizen and drawbacks: Roosevelt island is a feel good place both for the original residents and the new ones. Even considering the small area, there are sports complexes, gardens, and a limited cultural life. It is difficult, of course, to compete with neighbor Manhattan, but residents are in general very happy with their quality of life. Some residents complain of limited transport options to and from Manhattan at off-peak times.
Future development: There are still expansions underway in residential and commercial use. Roosevelt Island is fully operational and almost done.
References:http://rooseveltislander.blogspot.com/2020/. Photo by Rhododendrites—Own work, CC BY-SA 4.0. https://commons.wikimedia.org/w/index.php?curid = 64544182http://rooseveltislanddaily.prosepoint.net/.
Data collected by: Eduardo Moreira da Costa   educostainovacao@gmail.com

City	Country	Dimension	Project
New York City	**United States**	**QOL**	**Central Park**

Description: New York is the most populous and most densely populated major city in the United States. New York City has been described as the cultural, financial, and media capital of the world. Within New York, one of the most famous landmarks is Central Park. Central Park opened to the public in 1858 and is the most visited urban park in the United States, with an estimated 42 million visitors annually. It is the most filmed location in the world. The park is comprised of 843 acres, including 150 acres of water, 250 acres of lawn, and 80 acres of woodland.

Dimension—Quality of Life: Safety measures hold the number of crimes in the park to fewer than 100 per year as of 2019, down from approximately 1000 in the early 1980s. Once considered unsafe to enter after dark, now Central Park is safe and OK and is open from 6 a.m. to 1 a.m. As the world slowly recovers from the Covid pandemic, Central Park has become a safe haven for New Yorkers to enjoy the company of friends and family while still being socially distant.

Current situation: Central Park is, for New Yorkers and visitors alike, a green park, a sports complex, a beach, a forest, a complex of concert halls, and an amusement park. They simply love it.

Results for the citizen and drawbacks: Benefits to visitors include: protected bike lanes, designated running loops, 26 baseball fields, 12 tennis courts, 6 soccer fields, 4 basketball courts, 4 volleyball courts, 2 ice skating rinks, and a theater and concert hall.

Future development: A $150MM revamp will take place in the northern part of Central Park with building expected to begin in 2021 and conclude in 2024. Will include new pool and rink.

References:https://www.centralparknyc.org/park-history#: ~ :text = On%20July%2021%2C%201853%2C%20the,that%20the%20creation%20of%20a. Photo from http://assets.centralparknyc.org/pdfs/about/The_Central_Park_Effect.pdfhttps://ny.curbed.com/2019/9/18/20872349/central-park-nyc-north-harlem-meer-renovation.

Data collected by: Nando Pepper Costa   nando1costa@gmail.com

City	Country	Dimension	Project
Palhoça	**Brazil**	**QOL**	**Pedra Branca**

Description: A complete borough built from scratch on the former grounds of a cattle farm, not far from the tech-city of Florianópolis, in Brazil. The project encompasses 1.7 million m² of detailedly planned urban development with strict adherence to the live-work-play concept. It grew from two areas originally donated to build a large university campus and a modern hospital. Economic activities selected for the project contemplated those that needed the work contingent that was likely to live in the residential area of the complex. The borough has 50 services available at a very close distance, which avoids the use of private cars.

Dimension—Mobility of People: The complex is an all-encompassing exercise in the planning of HSSCs, involving all the eight dimensions and also a very interesting plan for local governance. But the most striking dimension is that of mobility of people and of economic development: The builders devised the actual prospective resident in detail. Since the region is influenced by the tech-city of Florianópolis. and residents tended to be young couples, commercial shops offer products, and services (by design) geared toward this group: So they present large coworking facilities, coffee shops, natural food places, bike shops, artisan beer, gyms, etc.

Current situation: The complex is 60% complete, with 2000 residents, 100 buildings of different sizes according to the original master plan, 30 companies, 50 service shops, a full operating university, primary and secondary schools, sports club, hospital and medical school, and even an operational small capacity airport. The range of services attracted also people from other regions. It was an instant hit and drew not only local people but also young professional from nearby Florianópolis and other neighboring towns.

Results for the citizen and drawbacks: Local residents are pleased to enjoy one of the main characteristics of HSSCs, which is living-working-playing in the same place. The number and quality of services offered are very well evaluated by them. Two drawbacks are that the number of companies installed in the area is still small and that the complex is a bit isolated from the capital city and innovation hub Florianópolis.

(*Continued*)

(Continued)

City	Country	Dimension	Project

Future development: The builders are on target to have the complex in full by 2023. The project's success propelled the company to start planning other complexes, both in Brazil and in other Latin American countries, and a major project is now under consideration for nearby city Florianópolis, which represents an excellent opportunity since the tech-city is expected to grow its population from the current 500,000 to close to 1 million inhabitants in the next few years.

References:https://www.passeiopedrabranca.com.br/http://www.ark7.com.br/us/projetos/. Photo by author

Data collected by: Eduardo Moreira da Costa   educostainovacao@gmail.com

City	Country	Dimension	Project
Paris	**France**	**DEV**	**Open Data**

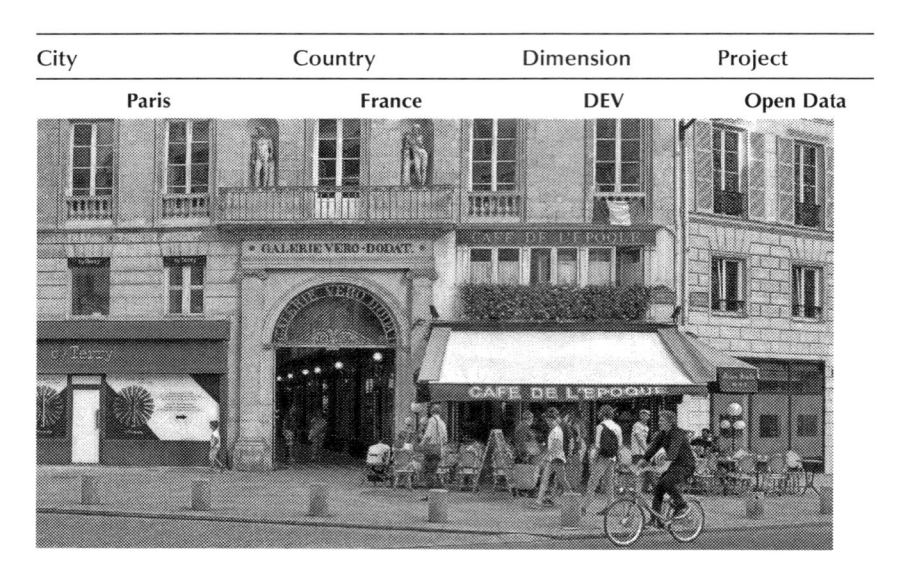

Description: Since 2010, the city of Paris has taken a pioneering position in open data policy with its open data platform. Its goal was to make all structured data accessible by open license to promote its reuse and generate new applications. In this sense, Paris supports big data analysis solutions, difficult to process with traditional tools, but which can be more personalized or participatory, and even transformed from reactive to proactive through predictive and preventive approaches, given new science methods data and innovative solutions. No aspect of urban life has escaped this digital transformation.

Dimension—Economic Development: Data is the new gold, as many people say. The availability and accessibility of open data for the development of new services is an important contribution for new companies and startups that can test and prototype their ideas and then offer them to the population in the city. It is difficult to measure how many and how startups have benefited from the open data project, since information about these companies is not readily available. But suffice it to point out that since the beginning of the project Paris has become one of the innovation hubs for ITC in Europe.

Current situation: Paris promotes open innovation with its partners through data exchanges that are kept secure and confidential according to the recommendations of the French Data Protection Authority (CNIL). Data is at the heart of numerous solutions currently being implemented or still under development, whether for energy and water management,

(Continued)

(Continued)

City	Country	Dimension	Project

mobility, use of waste as a resource, or new approaches, such as data-driven urbanism. They can also be central to new urban services for education, access to jobs, new sports, and cultural activities for all, and to ensure good health, well-being, and a better quality of life.

Results for the citizen and drawbacks: The main result of this project for the Parisian citizen will be accessibility and digital inclusion. This not only means maintaining a multichannel service offering with user-friendly interfaces, but also expanding access to digital uses. Public servants in the city of Paris will also be trained to ensure that they can help all the Parisian population and service providers in the use of the open data project. Besides reassuring by the government, some Parisians doubt that their data are secure in the new open data project.

Future development: Paris aims to be an inclusive city, a city that offers all its citizens the same (good) living conditions and a (positive) future outlook, regardless of their geographic, ethnic, religious, social, cultural, educational, or professional origin. Data is at the heart of this phenomenon and has become an essential resource because it is accessible to everyone. The spread of open data and coding for everyone also allows nonspecialists to imagine new applications. An infinite world of urban services will be within reach.

References:Paris Smart and Sustainable: Looking Ahead to 2020 and Beyond. Maire de Paris, 2020. https://www.data.gouv.fr/en/datasets/france-ile-de-france-paris/https://www.opendatasoft.com/data-on-board-2019. Photo by "Paris 2016 9 10 Saturday (12 v.1)" by Carl Campbell is licensed under CC BY-SA 2.0

Data collected by: Neri dos Santos   nerisantos@gmail.com

City	Country	Dimension	Project
Reykjavik	**Iceland**	**GOV**	**Better Neighborhoods**

Description: The Better Reykjavik/Better Neighborhoods platform is used to stimulate civic engagement in the decision-making process by giving citizens the opportunity to upload ideas and vote for them. The City Council has committed to reviewing the 15 most popular ideas each month, updating the citizens on the status of their implementation. Since 2010, about 16,000 registered users have submitted over 5000 ideas and posted over 11,000 comments; the City Council has processed 1045 ideas approved 220, rejected 289, and is still processing 336 proposals.

Dimension—Governance: Analyses of the platform have identified its integration with local government processes with the guaranteed review of proposals each month. That is a huge strength, compared to similar projects in other cities. The strong feedback loops also help build trust in the process amongst citizens. Finally, the platform interface encourages users to table arguments for or against a topic directed to a broader group, rather than to spawn debates on individual comments.

Current situation: It is unclear whether the platform is reaching a broad set of users, having reached university-educated citizens first. Some citizens believe that the platform is too small scale for them to contribute. Finally, citizens in general do not always have a clear understanding of government's capabilities.

Results for the citizen and drawbacks: The website gives residents of Reykjavik the opportunity to submit original ideas and solutions to municipal-level issues within the city. They are able to vocalize, debate, and amend a variety of ideas that they believe are crucial, and voters feel that they have a direct influence on the decision-making process. Four hundred and fifty ideas have been processed through the agenda setting part of Better Reykjavik.

Future development: The Better Reykjavík website is expected to be developed to become a venue for electronic surveys or consultation of various sorts, such as policy making or budgeting prioritization. An actual electronic voting system for individual issues is also a

(Continued)

(Continued)

City	Country	Dimension	Project
realistic goal, that is, with electronic identification. The Citizens Foundation (a nonprofit organization) operates this website for and in collaboration with the City of Reykjavík. **References**:https://reykjavik.is/en/better-reykjavik-0. Julie Simon, et al., February 2017. Digital Democracy: the tools transforming political engagement. Nesta. Available at: https://media.nesta.org.uk/documents/digital_democracy.pdf. Photo by "Reykjavik" by Chris Yunker is licensed under CC BY 2.0			
Data collected by: Marciele Berger Bernardes marcieleprojetos@gmail.com			

City	Country	Dimension	Project
Santiago	**Chile**	**SOC**	**Paseo Bandera**

Description: A public riding place that included a Tactical Urbanism Intervention (urbanism do-it-yourself and urban acupuncture) in 2017. An area, that due to the construction of the subway in the Historic Center of Santiago, blocks vehicle traffic through the street since 2013. The stretch of approximately 400 linear meter and 3300 square meters of street was painted and considered the largest "floor mural" in the world.

(Continued)

(Continued)

City	Country	Dimension	Project

Dimension—Social Inclusion: The street is affordable, playful, and rich in diversity and entertainment for all. The project began with quick changes, welcoming the population, encouraging the increase of social participation, and motivating the people to rethink their habits through different meetings and sharing experiences. It encourages people to work together, strengthen their relationships with neighbors, organizations, local commerce, and civic participation.

Current situation: Inaugurated in December 20, 2017, with an initial intervention period of 8 months, and a closure date of August 31, 2018. However, the transformation generated a great effect on the population that continues today and is part of the city's touristic route.

Results for the citizen and drawbacks: The opportunity to transform a public, urban, and historical space in decay into a "public and safe space for the people." The disadvantage is gentrification which, after the improvements made and the new visibility and tourism, increased the cost of living for residents in a way that it no longer fits the budget of poor residents. They are being taken from their original homes, and removed to less expensive areas.

Future development: Serving as inspiration for new spaces of conviviality and new uses of public space, promoting the reappropriation of urban space by its main user: the people, and finally, generating cities that are more vibrant and human. Also, public policies to avoid the problems of excessive gentrification.

References:La historia de calle Bandera. https://www.youtube.com/watch?v = XVbTtQ8bJ2Qhttp://www.santiagocapital.cl/fichas/home/calle-bandera/calles-y-su-historia/https://sala7design.com.br/2018/01/intervencao-urbana-enche-de-cores-e-transforma-rua-de-santiago-no-chile.html.

Data collected by: Estela Boiani   estelaboiani.arq@gmail.com

City	Country	Dimension	Project
Santiago	**Spain**	**HAC**	**Camino de Santiago**

Description: Camino de Santiago was a pilgrimage route since the 9th century. But during the plague in the 14th century it lost its importance until the 1980s when it started to pick up again as a route for people in search of solace, self-help, peace of mind, and mindfulness: a search for one's true self. The Camino is a network of ways nowadays, with starting points in France, Portugal, and Spain, but ending in the city of Santiago de Compostela, in Spain. There, an impressive old church waits the pilgrims for their prayers, and on Sundays, at 10 a.m. mass is preceded by a display of large censer that swings along the church main's nave.

Dimension—HAC Dimension: The Camino evolves from a Catholic pilgrimage to a route in search of self-knowledge. c.500,000 people use the routes annually and enjoy historic and cultural registers along the way. Pilgrims come from all parts of the world and interact with each other in whatever language they find possible. There is a brotherhood feeling along the way since everyone is doing more or less the same and there is no place for vanity; clothes are sort of torn apart by journey's end. A very unique experience indeed.

Current situation: The number of pilgrims went up from 1000 in the 1980s to the half a million of today. All the different routes have signposts along the way and the whole system is in place in order to help the pilgrim achieve his objective of arriving in Santiago de Compostela on a certain day, in order to return home or go to other places.

Results for the citizen and drawbacks: Every village and town along the various ways have benefited from the influx of tourists and the hospitality business thrives. Some of the "albergues" are official and charge very little for the night and for food, but pilgrims have to follow strict rules of what time to wake up and go, to make way for another pilgrim

(Continued)

(Continued)

City	Country	Dimension	Project

batch on the following day. There are also hotels and "pousadas" in the larger towns where pilgrims can enjoy a little more comfort along the way. But most of them choose to follow the official track. Some people complain that the religious origin has been forgotten over the years.

Future development: The Camino is being used for pilgrims on bikes as well. The number of bike routes has increased and are alternatives for those who want to shorten their journey on the Camino.

References:santiago-compostela.netOwn observation—done it twice by bike.Photo by "Finisterre - Galicia Navidad 2005" by blogefl is licensed under CC BY 2.0

Data collected by: Emídio Moreira da Costa   titocosta@outlook.com.br

City	Country	Dimension	Project
Seoul	**South Korea**	**QOL**	**Cheonggyecheon**

Description: The Cheonggyecheon is a River Park, 10.9 km—long, modern public recreation space in downtown Seoul, South Korea. The Park was an urban renewal project on the site of the Cheonggyecheon stream, which crosses downtown Seoul. The stream used to be covered by the transportation infrastructure and the area was very polluted and poor. The $900 million project initially attracted much public criticism but, since opening in 2005, has become very popular among residents and tourists. The Project has improved the quality of life in the City and promoted several leisure and economic activities in the area.

Dimension—Quality of Life: The renewal Project transformed the Cheonggyecheon Stream into an Urban Park integrated with the Culture and History of the Korean People, as it preserved the historical monuments along the new construction. At the same time, the project created a green corridor downtown Seoul and improved the public transportation system, prioritizing people instead of cars. It turned the area very competitive to attract new and qualified businesses, as residents, workers, and tourists can now enjoy walks, bike rides, and picnicking in an interesting surrounding atmosphere.

(Continued)

(Continued)

City	Country	Dimension	Project

Current situation: The project was initiated in 2003 and finished in 2005. The Cheonggyecheon River Park became an important international tourism location in Seoul, totally operational.

Results for the citizen and drawbacks: The Cheonggyecheon River Park transformed downtown Seoul. The Project revitalized the area and restored the river as a definitive local landmark. The implementation of organized multimodal transport systems reduced air pollution and even the city's annual average temperature. It also helps protect the area against eventual floods. On the down side, a few critics in Korean environmental organizations point out the high costs of the project and the apparent lack of ecological and historical authenticity.

Future development: The project has successfully enhanced opportunity for people to experience living ecosystems in downtown Seoul. It was not a restoration, but the construction of a large piece of green urban infrastructure that was successful in providing benefits for the citizens, inspiring others to think first about people and green infrastructure for them, rather than about cars and their costly infrastructure in new urban developments.

References:https://development.asia/case-study/revitalizing-city-reviving-streamhttps://en. wikipedia.org/wiki/Cheonggyecheonhttps://goodanthropocenes.net/restoration-of-cheonggyecheon-river/. Photo of "Cheonggyecheon" by bkusler is licensed under CC BY 2.0

Data collected by: Marcelo Ferreira Guimaraes   marceloguimaraes.tch@gmail.com

City	Country	Dimension	Project
Shanghai	**China**	**MOB**	**Urban Transport**

(Continued)

(Continued)

City	Country	Dimension	Project

Description: Located on the central coast of eastern China, at the mouth of the Yangtze River, the city, which once had great importance between the late 19th and beginning of the 20th century, resurfaced after the economic reforms introduced in 1990. It has become the largest commercial and financial center in China, also standing out as a tourist destination and cosmopolitan center. The rapid urbanization process overloaded the transport infrastructure, requiring that, even having the most extensive metro system in the world, the City started an ambitious new revolutionary urban transport system.

Dimension—Mobility of People: In order to organize the mobility of its 26 million inhabitants in a space of just over 6000 km^2, the new system followed the national guideline for sustainable urban transport: a significant reduction in the need for commuting, mobility on foot and by bicycle, investment in collective or shared electric modes, investment in the expansion and convergence of modes, and the introduction of technological services that guide the best way to get around in the city.

Current situation: The city was the 28th most congested in the world in 2016, producing a financial impact of a measurable loss of US$1120 annually per inhabitant, just in direct business loss, not considering the socio-environmental impacts on the quality of life and health of the city's population. Shanghai is now rapidly implementing the 2016 Design Guide that favors the mobility of people over cars, having won an international award in 2017 for a municipal model of bicycle sharing integrated with public transport. New private vehicles follow strict policies that limit licensing.

Results for the citizen and drawbacks: Reduced travel time wasted from 140 average annual hours per inhabitant to 133 average hours (2018/19). However, the reduction of congestion has not yet produced the positive impacts expected on air quality that is still poor.

Future development: It is predicted that the length of the metro should almost double in the next 5 years, reaching 1000 km in 2035. The increasing technological integration fosters the convergence and efficient use of modes, enabling joint action between the local government, technology and transportation companies, and the citizen. The introduction of automated systems in Big Data and AI will guide real-time rearrangements, in addition to supporting policies to improve transportation modals. It is expected that telecommuting will make a significant part of travel unnecessary. Cars should reduce from 40% to 10% of the transport matrix.

References:https://dialogochino.net/en/infrastructure/11025-chinas-sustainable-urban-transport-revolution/https://green-bri.org/how-china-should-push-green-transport-innovation-and-reduce-private-car-sales-by-75-to-5-millionhttps://www.coresponsibility.com/connecting-1-3-billion-changing-transportation-in-china/. Photo by "Model of Shanghai" by WordRidden is licensed under CC BY 2.0

Data collected by: Arthur Sanders   arthur@labchis.com

City	Country	Dimension	Project
Singapore	**Singapore**	**DEV**	**Marina Bay**

Description: A multibillion initiative to move downtown Singapore from its original limited area to a much broader, green and friendly location. The 360-hectare flat area was ready in 1990 with the conclusion of a major reclamation project that has started in the 1970s.

Dimension—Economic Development: Planning in Singapore is taken seriously and this project is no exception. The economic results are impressive since a former abandoned area has been transformed not only into a vibrant district, but is has been implemented with the all-important concept of live-work-play in the same area.

Current situation: The vision is to create a 24/7 live-work-play waterfront district but the initial focus has been on the construction of hotels, business offices, and areas of leisure. The first major development was the Marina Centre (Suntec City complex, Marina Square, and Millenia Tower) at the turn of the century. In 2010 the iconic Marina Bay Sands with an immense swimming pool on top of its three towers was open to public. The touristic and educational 100-hectare Gardens by the Bay with its massive Supertrees was inaugurated in 2012.

Results for the citizen and drawbacks: The area has become one of the prime areas for the Singaporeans to enjoy their leisure time, either at lunchtime on weekdays or as a family gathering on the weekends. They enjoy strolling on the 3.5 km waterfront promenade around the Bay easily accessible from many entrances.

Future development: Residential communities are planned as friendly neighborhoods. Shaded walkways and dedicated cycling paths will make walking and cycling the preferred choice for moving around. An intricate network of subway lines, cycling paths, and pedestrian walkways will serve the district.

References:https://www.ura.gov.sg/Corporate/Get-Involved/Shape-A-Distinctive-City/ Explore-Our-City/Marina-Bay/The-Marina-Bay-Storyhttps://www.gardensbythebay.com.sg/ en/the-gardens/our-story/introduction.html. Photo by "Singapore Marina Bay-02 = " by Sheba_Also 17,000,000 + views is licensed under CC BY-SA 2.0

Data collected by: Roberto and Monica Pinheiro   robertog.pinheiro@gmail.com

City	Country	Dimension	Project
Jyväskylä	Finland	PEO	Tiimiakatemia

Description: The quality of life and the future of the citizens of Jyväskylä (163,000 inhabitants), Finland, have been changed with an educational entrepreneurship project: "Tiimiakatemia" (1993). After an inspired teacher put a simple message on the university's messaging board: "Do you want to travel around the world and learn some marketing at the same time?" Twenty-four enthusiastic students applied. Their values were: learning by doing, practicality, continuous experimentation, continuous creation of the new, learning and traveling. The mission was eradication of unemployment.

Dimension—People: The Human Development Index depends upon four factors: good governance, secure property rights, sound economic policies, and, in this case, the education, which is the great transformation factor.

Current situation: The idea was to establish a Training Center in Tiimiakatemia to create an academy for excellent team coaches. After being a success in Finland for over 20 years, a company merged in to form Tiimiakatemia Global in 2011, reflecting the new status of the project that is now working in 12 other countries. The system continues to improve in leading the way for those who want to grow as professional team coaches and eradicate unemployment.

Results for the citizen and drawbacks: Creating a learning environment that supports multiculturalism—Education is no longer seen as just gaining knowledge but more as gaining knowledge that will enable individuals to deepen their understanding of the world and to recognize the roles they play in the world. Learning environments are undergoing transformations that will help them to be more flexible and acknowledge the needs of the society, students, and educational institutions.

Future development: Tiimiakatemia is a coaching method that is used to educate teampreneurs. It has been developed for almost 25 years and has over 10,000 different kinds of users in over 10 countries. In the future, it is hoped it can change the culture of citizens, producing more self-fulfilling people, self-sustainable enterprises, and a perennial nature, thereby changing cities and making them more human and intelligent. Finland

(Continued)

(Continued)

City	Country	Dimension	Project

changed a country through education and this can be an example for a small country to be the agent of change for the world.
References:Team Academy history. https://tiimiakatemia.com/en/tiimiakatemia/what-is-tiimiakatemia/. and Leinonen, Niina, Partanen, Timo and Palviainen, Petri, 2004. Team Academy: a true story of a community that learns by doing. PS-Kustannus Oy. Jyväskylä. https://tiimiakatemia.agileus.fi/en/tiimiakatemia/hist/https://jyx.jyu.fi/bitstream/handle/123456789/22341/1/9789513937133.pdf. Photo by "Jyväskylän yliopisto April 2007" by Pavel Kromer's Whole Lotta Trouble is licensed under CC BY-SA 2.0
Data collected by: José Alberto Sampaio Aranha   jasaranha@hotmail.com

City	Country	Dimension	Project
Vancouver	**Canada**	**GOV**	**GCAP 2020**

Description: Canada is a world leader in sustainable development. The City of Vancouver launched a few years back the "Greenest City 2020 Action plan (GCAP) for Vancouver," stating clearly that "to us, it's really important to know how Vancouver stacks up against other municipalities around the world." The plan was put in operation by a formal policy implementation and impact assessment with support of the Vancouver Council (local legislative). One of the main conclusions of the project is that smart cities need a smart legislative. Many good ideas in other cities have collapsed due to lack of support from legislators.
Dimension—Governance: The most striking dimension of "The Greenest City Action Plan for Vancouver" is the local governance dimension as it involves all the other seven
(Continued)

(Continued)

City	Country	Dimension	Project

dimensions of HSSCs. The strategy was set in motion by straight collaboration between the Council, residents, businesses, other organizations, and all levels of government, in order to implement the action plans. The vision is to create job opportunities today, while building and projecting a strong local economy for the future, along with vibrant and inclusive neighborhoods, in an internationally recognized city that is cool to work and live in.

Current situation: Since 2009, a group of local experts have researched best practices from leading green cities around the world and established goals and targets for the GCAP 2020 project. More than 35,000 people from around the world participated in the development of the resulting GCAP through social media, and in face-to-face workshops or events. The Action Plan was approved by City Council in 2011. Since then the high priority actions named in the plan have been completed, and new priorities have been set up.

Results for the citizen and drawbacks: Its citizens have a long tradition of participating in city government and Community affairs. It is one of the reasons why Vancouver has been ranked one of the best places in the world to live in. Public involvement is a vital part of any democratic process. Both City Council and other local Boards have social inclusion as a priority and accessibility by all citizens as a must. This practice results shows how that framework can be operationalized into formal planning, politics implementation, and impact assessment. "Who teaches learns when teaching. And who learns teaches by learning" (Paulo Freire)

Future development: The process to develop the Vancouver Plan that will guide the city to 2050 and beyond is being launched now in 2020. The people are invited to share their voices and sign up for updates. Vancouver Smart City is known for its Humane and Sustainable characteristics perspective. They look beyond 2020 with plans to green transportation through 2040 and to build a city that runs completely on renewable energy before 2050.

References:https://vancouver.ca/green-vancouver/greenest-city-action-plan.aspxhttps://vancouver.ca/files/cov/greenest-city-2020-action-plan-2015-2020.pdf. Photo from https://www.pexels.com/pt-br/foto/agua-alvorecer-amanhecer-ao-ar-livre-2782485/. Photo of "Downtown Vancouver" by PoYang is licensed under CC BY-ND 2.0

Data collected by: Marcelo Arno Nerling   mnerling@usp.br

City	Country	Dimension	Project
Vienna	**Austria**	**ENV**	**Smart Campus**

Description: The power network company Wiener Netze GmbH constructed a new headquarters next to the gas plant site, including areas for administration and operational functions. Since the summer of 2016, the Smart Campus offers a new workplace for around 1400 employees. The decision to build a completely new building and the centralization of the company was preceded by numerous investigations: The renovation of the previous buildings was not feasible, and the centralization of 10 company branches under one roof brought not only logistical advantages but also environmental benefits to the city.

Dimension—Environment: The building is designed to achieve ÖGNI Gold certification. ÖGNI certifies sustainable buildings and neighborhoods in accordance with European quality certificates. The certification systems can be adapted for different uses of buildings and specific to each country. It evaluates the following areas of study throughout the life cycle of the building: ecology, economics, sociocultural and functional quality, technology, processes, and location.

Current situation: From the planning stage, the multifunctional building complex, which combines offices and workshops, has ensured sustainability and energy efficiency. The Smart Campus, built according to passive house standards, is a result of 1200 photovoltaic modules, air-conditioning using ground water and heating using solar energy, along with 10,000 energy-efficient LED luminaires almost self-sufficient. The Smart Campus is one of the world's largest low-energy constructions worldwide. It also has solar-controlled shading, light-diverted louvers, and user-controlled regulation.

Results for the citizen and drawbacks: Apart from the reduction of the travel costs and emissions generated by traffic between the individual locations, the new office building

(*Continued*)

(Continued)

City	Country	Dimension	Project

also saves energy. The Smart Campus combines energy-saving automatisms and comfortable use with a smart user feedback. This intelligent house technology is intended to save operating costs, in particular energy costs, and to reduce energy and CO_2 emissions. In addition, the employees are left with sufficient space to make the individual workplace as comfortable as possible.

Future development: The group responsible for the Smart Campus has already developed other environmental projects in Vienna.The main focus of the company based in the city is the structural design of new buildings and conversion and renovation projects, combined with test engineering, on-site inspection, evidence preservation, expert reporting, and analysis of constructed structures.Concerned about environmental improvements for the planet, the environmentally intelligent solutions developed by the group can be customized and developed for other cities, countries, and continents, adapting to local specificities and problems.

References:https://smartcity.wien.gv.at/site/en/smart-campus/https://ic-group.org/en/technical-fields/buildings-structures/wu-vienna/smart-campus-viennahttps://www.ogni.at/leistungen/zertifizierung/. Photo by "The streets of Neubau, Vienna, Austria" by sarahsampsel is licensed under CC BY-ND 2.0

Data collected by: Thalita Bez Batti de Souza   thalitabbs@gmail.com

Chapter 6

Where and how to start in your city

Never doubt that a small group of thoughtful, committed citizens can change the world, indeed, it's the only thing that ever has.

Margaret Mead

Strategy

Several countries in the world are building new cities or boroughs from the ground up. Some of them, but not all, are planning these new projects according to the more Humane and Sustainable Smart City (HSSC) concepts (Songdo, in South Korea, and the Palm Tree complex, in Dubai, are interesting cases). These cases are rare and far apart, and will not solve the problem of our main cities today. The desired change in the world will not come from these projects, due to lack of resources in most countries. It will come from the implementation of HSSC projects in *existing* cities.

One way of starting this movement is to redo the city planning as a whole, change the city code, and execute the project in stages. A good opportunity to enact this change is when the city code is due for renewal. This happens every 10 or 20 years, in most cities. The trouble is, every change raises opposition from affected segments of the society that may hold legitimate or vested interests in the status quo. Because of this, decisions are delayed, the mayor changes, politicians change their minds, and the big plan may sit there for years. In many instances, forever.

We suggest another way of implementing change that may be much more effective. It is the guerrilla approach or city acupuncture that consists of choosing one region or borough of the city, studying, planning, and executing the change there, and then starting to gain hearts and minds in the city for interventions elsewhere. This procedure was executed by Cerdá in the Eixample in the 19th century that later on affected the whole city of Barcelona, and more recently by Janette Sadik-Khan in the Broadway project in New York City, whose side effects can be observed in several other parts of the Big Apple.

Humane and Sustainable Smart Cities. DOI: https://doi.org/10.1016/B978-0-12-819186-6.00002-6

In this chapter, we propose a practical methodology that has been applied successfully a few times in cities in Brazil and that may be useful to implement change in other cities around the world. The centerpiece of the methodology is a 1-week intensive workshop to propose showcase projects which, once implemented, will open transformation in that region and trigger change on a broader perspective in the city.

The following sections describe how to plan, execute, and evaluate the 1-week long workshop.

Choice of the target region in the city

This is a crucial decision for the success of the initiative. The place must be remarkable. In many senses. It may have an interesting history (not necessarily good) or past narrative or function. Place de la Concorde in Paris was the place where King Louis XVI and Queen Marie Antoinette were beheaded and became an enjoyable park and surroundings in the 19th century. The 22@barcelona project was a derelict former industrial region and port and became a featured initiative and showcase for new smart city projects all over the world. Old unused industrial regions are very good candidates. So are ports and harbors. Unused transport structures are also likely candidates. The former elevated railway, which transported meat from the "meat district" in New York City to the harbor, has been transformed into the "high line park" that hosts more than 5 million visitors yearly and has now been added to the touristic map of the city. The former highway that divided Seoul, in Korea, built on top of a river, is now a huge park and bike lane on the sides of the river (now open air) and is considered a landmark in the transformation of the city.

The region must also be dense and visible for impact. In order to have a new model borough, there must be enough people there to justify the investment. Think of the density of a Paris arrondissement or a Barcelona barrio of c.20,000 people per square kilometer.

And the area should not be too big, and lose its character, nor too small, which would make no impact. Think again of the medieval village measure of 1-mile radius, or c.8 km^2, so people can move around on foot and have enough services around, in the same area, that tend to their basic needs.

More likely candidates for target region

- Downtown
- Former harbor
- "Red-light" district
- Historical quarter
- Place of a recent intervention (airport, station, iconic building)
- University area

- Bar and restaurant cluster
- Tech park

Before you start

The leader

Find a leader! He/she might be yourself, of course, but there must be one, clearly identified. This person is key to the success of the initiative. The leader should navigate easily amongst all the parties involved in the transformation: City Hall, the Provincial Government, the university, the private sector, and all kinds of different stakeholders. The university is considered a more neutral entity and might be one of the pool sources for such a figure. It is probably not a good idea to source someone from the resident's association. They tend to be too biased and to believe that the region or borough *belongs* to them.

Partners

Then the leader has to partner with as many institutions related to the region as possible: resident's associations (in general, more than one); commercial associations; City Hall; Provincial Government; the police; large companies with interest in the region; and the National Heritage or administration of landmarks in the region such as churches, parks, museums, and monuments. Most of these people will need to be "sold" to the idea and that requires an individual face-to-face meeting. The process will take time. Think of 4 months before the event, at least. The good news is that people's reception to the idea of a workshop tends to be very friendly: You will not be proposing a plan; you will be asking for their valuable help in order to produce one. Simon Sinek, in one of his popular TED talks (Sinek, 2010), calls our attention for Dr. Luther King's famous speech in Washington facing 1 million civil rights activists: "I have a dream," he said. The great man did not say he had a plan.

Study the region

It is very important to study the target region in detail. Go there several times, at different times of the day and night and observe and feel how people live and move and what do they do. Frank Gehl (Gehl and Svarre, 2013) suggests you annotate everything you see. Count people, refer to similarities and differences, be aware of the circumstances, feel everything, and try to evaluate what is happening. Use your senses in full, not only your eyes. The good observer is at one time a statistician counting variables, a classifier identifying classes of people and of behavior, and an analyzer trying to make sense of it all. Jane Jacobs wrote her famous book observing the movement of people from the porch of her house at Greenwich Village in New York City (Jacobs, 1961). She commanded that cities should not be planned in the abstract form that the modernists so much liked at her time, but in the concrete form one gets from observing functioning, live, real people in real cities.

Planning the workshop

The workshop is a 5-day full-time intensive event that aims at identifying structural projects that may transform one region of a city and be the showcase to provoke change in the whole city. It involves organizers, partners, participants, facilitators, stakeholders, and the people who actually live or work in the region.

During the event, participants will be split into working groups (WGs) in order to tackle the eight different dimensions of more HSSCs described in Chapter 4, The eight dimensions of a more Humane and Sustainable Smart City.

Preparation for the workshop is key. One must talk to organizers and stakeholders, choose participants, set the infrastructure for the event, and work carefully with communication of the event's process to everyone involved. Ideally, the organizing group should have one person responsible for each one of the following dimensions.

Organizers

The workshop organizers are the main institutions that are or should be interested in its results. Following the quadruple helix idea (McAdam and Debackere, 2018), the group of organizers ideally should involve at least one institution each, from academia, the local government, an institutional representation of the private sector, and some institution representing the civil society or the citizen.

The leader must talk to each one of them individually. In the academic sector, it could be a graduate program on urban planning, innovation, knowledge management, or public administration, or maybe the institute of advanced studies or any other arrangement a local university has created in order to tackle interdisciplinary subjects. The involvement of a local university is also important to provide graduate students for the cohort of participants. But since the workshop is full time, students' participation must be negotiated with their original courses in order for them not to miss ordinary classes. In many of our cases in Brazil, the workshop was defined as a graduate course of a local university.

The private sector in different countries has different institutional representation but their involvement is, of course, very relevant. Think of the local industry federation, chambers of commerce and industry, or the local shopkeepers union (the closest the institution is to the target region the better), or maybe also a local company that is especially relevant to the region because of its size or location.

City Hall must be involved and sometimes with more than one sector. For instance, when the city has a planning unit, they must be there. But there are many other relevant stakeholders such as the local equivalent of the secretaries of Culture, Heritage, Ordinance Survey, Development, Innovation, Science and Technology, Police, Housing, etc.

The fourth blade of our quadruple helix is the representation of the civil society. This representation is in general a Nongovernment Organization such as the resident's association, the biker's association, the pedestrian association (in the unlikely case the region has one), the women's empowering group, and the social organization that works with inclusion of poor people. The leader must be prepared to get some angry or wary representatives that may be sick and tired of previous endeavors that unfortunately led to nothing concrete.

Participants

The workshop lasts 1 week and is full time. That means that participants should be really engaged with the idea and willing to dedicate that much amount of time to the project.

The first group of participants should be graduate students. They are in the process of academic research and are willing and used to conduct thorough research on related subjects and to search for relevant data for the workshop. Other participants include people directly affected by the study such as residents, local company owners, and all kinds of representatives of associations; local government officials; and people from other regions that want to learn from the experience. The number of full-time participants should be between 50 and 60 people. This is due to the fact that, during the workshop, participants will be split into the eight WGs (seven participants per group is a good count), one for each of the dimensions of more HSSC. Each dimension should be "localized" in the sense that dimension's topics relate to the most relevant themes for the target region. The suggested number of participants per group is a practical number from previous experiences: Smaller groups do not bring all the necessary different views on the subject; larger groups tend to drift from the topic under discussion and start parallel discussions amongst its members. And it is important to maximize individual participation.

Stakeholders

These are the people who are invited to speak to the participants. They can be invited to speak to the general audience of participants (general stakeholders) or to one or more WGs in particular (specific stakeholders). They should be invited well in advance in order to guarantee their agenda. It is interesting to invite them to attend the final presentation of results, at the end of day 5.

General stakeholders are the ones whose information and expertise interests every aspect of the workshop and every participant. An urban planner from City Hall or the provincial government, for instance. Or a historian that will describe the narrative of the region or borough. A graduate student who happens to have the facts and figures of the region in her research. Someone who has studied the region beforehand and that is willing to contribute with her knowledge to the workshop's success.

Specific stakeholders provide detailed knowledge about something that is only relevant for that particular WG. Their choice depends upon the main topics that were selected in each dimension of the WGs. A police officer, for instance, will talk to the public safety WG, if there is one. A building company owner, for instance, will talk to the economic development WG. A social worker will talk to the social inclusion WG. And so on and so forth. There should be at least three specific stakeholders per group before the workshop starts. The organization chooses and invites the original group of stakeholders to take part in the workshop. But more specific stakeholders will be added to each WG as the actual workshop week gets under way, as the group feels they need some more detail about a specific subject. Each WG may invite new specific stakeholders on their own, or ask for help from the organization to do it for them.

Facilitators

Facilitators (one per WG) are people who are part of the organization that is promoting the workshop and ideally have participated in other workshops. They are responsible for guiding the WGs through the week. Their role is to communicate the workshop process to the group, to inform them about the expected deliverables during the week, and to take back to the organizers a daily picture of what is happening in the group. Facilitators should not have hidden agendas that they try to impinge on the group. They are there to guide, to observe, and to keep quiet. Since they are in general more experienced than the other participants, they may be tempted to give ideas. The organizer should explain their role in detail before the event.

In the beginning, for the first workshop, organizers will have no experienced facilitators to rely on. In that case, they will have to be trained on the methodology beforehand. Training of facilitators should be carried out well before the workshop date. Two sessions of 4 hours each should be enough. Training is similar to the preevent class (see further down) for participants, only more in-depth knowledge of each of the subjects.

Relevant topics for the region

We have seen in Chapter 4, The eight dimensions of a more Humane and Sustainable Smart City, the (7 + 1) eight dimensions of more HSSCs:

- Sustainable Economic Development (DEV)
- People (PEO)
- Quality of Life (QOL)
- Historic, Artistic, and Cultural Heritage, and Tourism (HAC)
- Environment (ENV)
- Social Inclusion (SOC)
- Mobility of People (MOB)
- Governance (GOV)

For each workshop it is important to define with the other organizers and partners, which are the most relevant topics for each dimension in the target region. Besides that, there may be a special need to focus on one particular aspect of one dimension (maybe even have a specific WG for that topic) since it is important in that context. For instance, in the Hercílio Luz Bridge Workshop that will be reported below, the Identity topic of the Historic, Artistic, and Cultural Heritage dimension was brought to the forefront and treated in a different WG since the bridge is a national monument and is associated with the soul of the islanders.

Infrastructure

One strong recommendation from previous experiences is that the venue of the workshop should be inside the target region or at least as close as possible. Participants should walk and *feel* the place and observe the region several times in daytime and nighttime and talk to as many locals as possible.

The actual working venue needs a large comfortable conference room for, say, 80 people (up to 60 participants, plus stakeholders, organizers, and invited authorities) with access to the Internet and projection facilities. This room will be needed for the whole first day, and parts of days 3 and 5. Besides the big room, the workshop needs a small meeting room for each WG (between six and eight people) and a separate room for the organization. All rooms should have Internet access and not be very far from one another since that would make interaction between groups more difficult.

A single cafeteria is an interesting facility with no specific "coffee-break" times so that participants go there at random and interact as the workshop proceeds.

Communication

Communication about the realization of the workshop event is key to keep participants' interest and to help mobilize stakeholders. Depending on the actual status and regional or even national importance of the region being studied, the event may draw attention from local or national news, in both newspapers and radio/TV. The ideal situation is for the organizer to be interviewed by TV lunchtime news, when programs carry more of the local interest stuff. It is always important to remember that, since these programs carry large audiences, the interviewee must remember to cite all the organizers' names. One does not want to offend sensibilities before the event has even started!

Communication should involve:

- The announcement of the workshop, in order to attract suitable participants, to mobilize stakeholders, and to raise interest of potential partners. Depending on the region to be studied, besides all kinds of social media and a well-designed hot site, this phase might include radio and TV appearances.
- Planning interviews by radio and TV networks with the organizers and stakeholders during the workshop.
- Registering the making of the workshop in video, in a suitable format for distribution afterward in the social media.
- Planning the distribution channels of the workshop results in all sorts of media. This will potentialize its impact and the transformation of the potential projects, defined by the participants, into real projects in the shortest possible timeframe.

As in every project, the communication activity and its importance for the actual implementation of real projects should not be overlooked. It is crucial for success.

The 1-week intensive workshop

Preevent

It is a good idea to hold a preevent class to set all participants on the same page. The group of participants, as we have seen, is diverse, with different levels of knowledge about the concept of more HSSC and of the actual place to be studied, and with different levels of experience of participation in WGs. These dimensions of the work should be leveled up in order to transform the workshop into a fruitful exercise. We suggest at least four topics to be covered in this preevent:

- The concept of more HSSCs, with its main characteristics and plenty of examples;
- The description, history, and cartography of the region under study, explaining why the region was selected as a study subject in the first place;
- The design thinking methodology and the detailed workshop agenda, showing the expected deliverables at each day;
- Elinor's Ostrom concept of the Commons (Ostrom, 1990). Explain that the city is in fact a Commons—and its governance involves us all.

Ostrom's concept is directly connected to the vision of a city as a more Humane and Sustainable place (see Chapter 7: The future: the need for more Humane and Sustainable Smart Cities postpandemic 2020/21).

One of the main outcomes of this preevent is to really check participants' willingness to get involved full-time in the workshop. Give emphasis to the idea of a "workshop," meaning participants will really work toward the objective. The word *workshop* has been misused in many instances as just another designation for a traditional conference. Participants may get initially the wrong idea that they can go there, take a look, and come back later, as in any conference. In this workshop, that is certainly not the case. By the third day, participants in WGs are so involved in the project that they have no patience (and no time really) to explain to window-shoppers the previous activities and what is happening at that moment.

Participants that eventually drop from the full-time participation require-ment, for any reason, but are still interested in the workshop, may be invited to attend the first day of the workshop (the immersion day, in a traditional conference format, see below) and the end of the last day, for the presenta-tion, by participants, of the actual results of the workshop.

The preevent should last for something like 4 hours and be called a "warm-up" for the workshop. A typical agenda would be:

1. What is a more HSSC (by the Leader or an invited specialist, 60 m),
2. The region to be studied (by City Hall or an invited historian that will raise participants' interests even more, 30 m),
3. Ostrom (1990) studies of the Commons (by a local scholar, 30 m),
4. Description of the methodology and the detailed functioning of the 1-week workshop (by the organizer, 30 m),
5. The design thinking methodology (by an invited specialist, 30 m), and
6. Allocation of participants to WGs (by the organization, 30 m).

The last item should be preceded by the organizer's explanation, making clear that participants should indicate their preferences but avoid having more than one person from the same institution in the same WG in order to foster diverse opinions in every WG. Participants should also agree that some of them will be allocated to a different WG than the one originally chosen by them: It is important to distribute participants evenly in the WGs.

The number of participants in each WG should not be more than 7 or 8, and not less than 5 or 6. These are pragmatic numbers out of previous experiences: Too many people in the same group tend to start parallel con-versations that really disturb the work. Too few, participants tend to quickly adopt a single participant's point of view. As we have seen, if the number of participants is large, it is better to break a broad theme into two and create another WG. The ideal number of participants is thus seven times the number of WGs. Let us say between 50 and 60 people for the eight dimensions or WGs.

The workshop—charter of the week

This is how a typical workshop week agenda looks like:

	Immersion Day	Definition of the problem		Ideation and Prototyping	Project detail
	Day 1	**Day 2**	**Day 3**	**Day 4**	**Day 5**
9h	A. Opening	A. Preparation of the interview			A. Check project concept
9h30					
10h	B. The Leader	B1. Specific Stakeholder	A. Empathy maps	A. Brainstorming of new ideas and solutions	
10h30	C. The Place	B2. Specific Stakeholder			B. Project detail
11h	D. The city code	B3. Specific Stakeholder	B. Identification of main problems		C. Check project details
11h30	E. Surprise!	B4. Specific Stakeholder			
12h					
12h30	*Lunch Interval*	*Lunch Interval*	*Lunch Interval*	*Lunch Interval*	*Lunch Interval*
13h					
13h30	F. Examples everywhere		C. Prioritization of problems and threats	B. Consolidation of the ideas into projects	D. Preparation of presentation
14h		C. Indoor interviews / D. Outdoor interviews			
14h30	G. Legal constraints		D. Preparation of presentation		
15h	H. Economic view				
15h30	I. Resident's view	*Interval*	*Interval*	C. Choice of the project	*Interval*
16h	J. The public sector				
16h30		C. Indoor interviews / D. Outdoor interviews		*Interval*	
17h	K. WGs split		E. Presentation to the Plenary	D. Cross-fertilization with other WGs	E. Final presentation of results
17h30		E. Wrap-up interview day			
18h				E. Redefinition of the project	
18h30					
19h			F. Networking reception		F. Closing reception
19h30					
19h50					
20h10					
20h30					

Day 1—immersion day

The first day of any event is tense. Do not overlook details for the first day, in order to start on a high note. Keep time according to schedule. Although the first day looks more like an ordinary conference, remind participants, at all times, that they are there for a working exercise. The list of speakers and organizations will obviously vary from one workshop to the next, but consider these actors and stakeholders for the immersion day.

1. Opening session. The Leader and all organizers and partners sit and speak briefly welcoming the participants. Ask everyone to be brief and

not to name every single person on the table before they speak (a practice that everyone hates but that is repeated over and over).

2. The Leader. The Leader sets the tone for the event. Her mission is to inspire participants into being innovative, thinking out-of-the-box, and respecting everyone else's opinions and ideas.

3. The Place. Choose a local historian or an old and respected figure in the neighborhood to describe the region from the perspective of its narrative: what it is, where it came from, historical developments, etc.

4. The City Code. Once participants start to develop ideas, they have to bear in mind what is the City Code for the region and what are the urban planning projects that are or will be in place. Some places have a Planning company associated with City Hall; others have a Department. In any case, the speaker should be the highest-ranking officer possible.

5. Surprise! Before the meeting starts to look like an ordinary conference, it is a good idea to identify someone that will be able to surprise everyone and close the morning session on a good vibe. In a recent workshop in Florianópolis, we found out that Saint Exupéry (of *The Little Prince* fame) was a pilot with the French company Aeropostale and might have written parts of his worldly famous book in the Aerodrome of Campeche, within the region we were studying! The speaker was a university researcher who had unfolded the story as part of her Masters dissertation.

6. Examples elsewhere. Back from lunch, a specialist will describe examples of other regions in the same country or elsewhere that have gone through meaningful projects that might inspire participants for their own projects later.

7. Legal constraints. A legal specialist describes the laws and regulations that may affect projects in the region. For instance, is it possible to establish public-private-partnerships (PPPs)? How? What kind of money is available for initiatives in the region? Are there innovation laws that might apply? Under what conditions?

8. Economic view. Someone from a Trade Association brings the view of the private sector about the region. Are they interested? What would they like to see as a result of the Workshop?

9. Resident's view. A representative of a Resident's association brings their view about the future. Ideally, this person should talk with other associations first in order to present a consensus view. But they must be briefed in advance that the meeting is not an opportunity to bring in a roll of complaints against the administration. Otherwise, you may end up with the need for parking space, sewage systems, public lighting, and such. Encourage them to think about the future and bring their dreams for the region, not their daily acrimonies.

10. The Public sector. Depending upon the region being studied, there will be a need to hear some public officer about the region. The person can

be from any of the three levels of government, national, provincial, or local, or maybe someone from the judiciary.

The list of general stakeholders will change, and this is just a suggestion. But the organization should cover the most relevant actors in the region in a way that they all feel that you render them and their opinion important for the success of the event.

11. WGs split. At this point the group of participants is split into the eight WGs. Each group will gather around their facilitator, which will explain to them what to do and what is going to happen in the following days with the group. Then each group member describes what he/she does, their background, and their interest in the workshop. After this introduction, the Facilitator explains the roles to be assumed by the group members and, amongst them, they assign (without intervention by the Facilitator) which roles should be assumed by whom. The four Roles are: Coordinator, who controls the group, makes sure everyone is heard, curtails excesses, and controls time; Writer, who reports in writing all the group's findings; Presenter, who will present the WG's results in the plenary sessions; Designer, who will prepare the material for presentations; and Ambassador, who will establish dialogues with ambassadors from the other groups toward joint projects, call and fix meetings with specific stakeholders for the WG, and interface with the organizers.

By the end of the first day, participants will have a WG, a clear view of what is expected of them, and a schedule and location for their meeting on the second day.

Day 2—specific stakeholders

Days 2 and 3 of the workshop are dedicated to identifying the main problem of the region on the specific dimension of each WG. There we start to use the *designthinking* methodology of empathize, define-the-problem, ideate, prototype, and test. Day 2 gets information from specific stakeholders in order to draw the empathy map of each *persona* that characterizes stakeholders in the region. Some stakeholders will fit into the same persona. The objective is to have empathy maps of a few personas, not more than three.

1. Preparation of the interview. The interview aims at extracting from the stakeholder the information about what he sees, hears, thinks, and talks; and then concludes with what are his main worries and pains and what are his dreams. This is the information that will go into the empathy map and help identify the problem later on. The questions to be asked must be adapted to the situation so that they do not look personal or invasive. Since this is the first exercise in group work, the chosen (by the group) coordinator has to be careful to accept and pay attention to each member's ideas. At this time slot, the group reviews the stakeholder lineup for the morning session and suggests new stakeholders to be contacted by the Ambassador for the afternoon interviews.

2. (B1–B4) Specific Stakeholder Interviews. The first group of stakeholders to be interviewed by each WG will have been chosen and invited by the organizers. Other stakeholders will be chosen and invited directly by the members of the WG. Each interview should last half an hour and it is very important to keep the scheduled time: Several stakeholders are there to be interviewed by other WGs as well, and the rotation must be done at the pre-scribed time. At the end of the interview it is worthwhile to inquire the stakeholder what is, in his personal view, *the* problem of the region on that particular dimension or topic within the dimension. Try also to identify his personal dream. These last two questions will be very useful in identifying problems and solutions later on during the week. At the end of the morning interviews, each WG splits into two subgroups: One will follow on with the indoor interviews; the other will go for outside interviews in the region.

3. Indoor interviews. The subgroup that stays indoors will continue with the stakeholder interviews, in the same way that was done in the morning. Since these appointments were fixed on the same day, some stakeholders will not be available to go to the workshop office, but might be available for an interview over the phone. Use this tool when the stakeholder is key to the theme. On-site interviews are better and allow for a useful grasp of the interviewee's real opinions.

4. Outdoor interviews. The subgroup that goes to the field may conduct on-site interviews or get people at random. For instance, someone at the bus stop, someone at the school door, someone in the bar, etc. Photograph them for registration in the final report later. Whoever the interviewee, the ques-tions should follow the same pattern as before, so that opinions can be matched against each other in the consolidation phase back in the office.

5. Wrap-up the interview day. Members of the WG exchange impressions about whom they interviewed and what they learned from the experience.

One of the main problems with day 2 is to control participants' anxieties in trying to jump straight on to producing solutions instead of clearly identifying the problem. The Facilitator's role here is important to keep people on track: Although some members may think that they know what the problem is and can move on to the next phase, remind them that very seldom this is the case and the identification of the real and central problem is a worthwhile exercise.

Day 3—identification of *the* problem

There are many problems in any region on any of the topics of the dimension studied by the WGs in the workshop. But on day 3 participants should follow a predefined routine in order to single out what is the central problem of their dimension. At this point, they have all the information from the general stakeholders and the specific stakeholders on their hands. The work goes through four stages to pinpoint the problem. Then each problem is taken to the plenary session and takes suggestions from the other participants.

1. Empathy maps. Participants have fragments of the previous day's interviews to work on, and then draw the empathy maps of the personas they have identified. Some participants belong in the same persona. But they may characterize one persona that does not correspond to any of the interviewees. In that case, they can use their own collective imagination to describe that persona. They will eventually narrow down the group of different personas to a small number—no more than three.
2. Identification of main problems. From the empathy maps, it is now possible to identify the main problems of the region on that particular dimension. The definition of a problem should not be too broad (traffic jams or ugly streets, for instance) nor too narrow (no lighting in park X, for instance). A problem should be such that only a structural project will manage to face it. But again, there is a need for discipline here so that participants do not jump into solutions before clearly defining the problem.
3. Prioritization of problems and threats. An interesting way to prioritize problems here is to use the gravity-urgency-trend matrix in order to rank the list of problems. Gravity and urgency are self-explanatory. Trend refers to an evaluation of what happens to that problem if nothing is done. Will it get worse? Will it be fixed slowly or disappear in the future? Create a score for each dimension from, say, 1 to 5. The higher the number, the worse the situation. So, when you add the three numbers for each problem, the highest number will indicate *the* problem. The group now spends some time rephrasing the problem so that it is easily understandable by all participants and expresses exactly what the WG identified.
4. Preparation of presentation. The Designer of the WG now prepares the presentation to the plenary. It is important to refer to the list of stakeholders interviewed by the group and their findings in the walkabout in the region. When explaining the main problem identified, they must be careful and remember that the other participants in other WGs did not see or hear what they did: When one spends a long time discussing a subject in a group, they tend to present it to others as if they too were part of the group.
5. Presentation to the plenary. After each WG's presentation, there must be a time slot for suggestions or clarifications. It may also be a good time to start interacting with other WG's ideas. Some project results may encompass two of the main problems identified by the groups.
6. Networking reception. This is the time to exchange information amongst all participants. They should be advised to mingle with as many

participants as possible and not be restricted to their original group. High tables may help in making people move around and exchange ideas. This period may be important for the eventual merging of projects in the following days.

Day 4—ideation and prototyping

The day has arrived when participants can start pouring out their ideas and think about structural projects. The leader might want to come back on stage at this point and ask participants to be bold on their ideas. Instruct them not to limit themselves to budget constraints and disbelief in governments in general. One of the good things about cities is that money can be generated by the projects themselves. For instance, City Hall may allow for higher buildings in a certain area in exchange for project money for something that is worthwhile (sell the space above ordinary buildings) for the region.

1. Brainstorming of new ideas and solutions. Brainstorming should follow the common practice of not criticizing anyone, listening to everyone, building upon somebody else's opinion, etc. The WG's coordinator should take care of these points. Special care must be given to avoiding disheartening phrases such as "if that was possible, wouldn't anyone have done it before?", or "I have done this, it does not work," or "so and so would NEVER allow it to happen." Let ideas flow.
2. Consolidation of the ideas into projects. Some ideas sit in the same area and may be grouped together. Others may be dropped off. The coordinator should avoid the position by group members to "defend their ideas." She must make sure that, by this time, all the ideas belong in the group, not in a single member. Once ideas are clustered together, participants will devise projects. Maybe a project may contemplate two or more ideas. By the end of the session, the WG will have two or three projects to proceed.
3. Choice of *the* project. Now, what is the project to tackle? The best choice is the one that has the greater impact on the region. It not only solves the main problem identified by the group, but it has the possibility to spearhead other activities in the direction of the HSSC concept. It should be able to capture people's hearts and minds. In the words of one of the participants of one of the workshops, it must be able to enchant, surprise, and touch the people in the region.
4. Cross-fertilization with other WGs. The group is now divided into two: Half of the members stay in to answer questions by members of other groups, and the other half go around the other groups to ask questions and consider synergies or even mergers between projects. Participants must be warned to be open-minded about the exercise. The objective is

to have the best possible list of projects and they will belong to the entire group of participants.

5. Redefinition of project. With the information and discussions collected from the other groups, each WG redefines its project as the definitive contribution of the group. In case there is a merger between projects from different groups, the merged groups will conduct this last activity jointly.

Day 5—project detail and final presentation

1. Check project concept. The project idea is submitted back to the original stakeholders in order to get their feedback by phone. It is important to relate the main idea of the project to what he/she said or to what other stakeholders said, so that each stakeholder will feel that his/her participation was of some avail.

2. Project detail. Now the project is ready for detailing and inclusion of implementation facts and figures. In such a short period, there is no time to get definitive figures, but estimates are important. For instance, figures about chronogram and budget can be worked upon. Participants may phone specialists to help with these figures.

3. Check project details. Final check of the project details with some of the stakeholders that were interviewed by the group or that spoke to the larger audience on the first day.

4. Preparation of presentation. Participants of each WG receive instructions about format and content of the final presentation and prepare their work. It is important to call attention to the actual timing of the presentation. More time should be given to the project results than to the process of working toward that result. Presenters should also practice their presentation with colleagues in the group. Participants should also be warned that there will be people in the audience that were not involved in the workshop at all before, and so the context must be explained to a general audience.

5. Final presentation of results. Leader explains the workshop process to a possibly larger audience and calls presenters from each WG in turn. Presenters should identify and point to their colleagues in the presentation (ask them to raise, for instance) to acknowledge the collective work that was developed during the week. In the end, participants show some anxiety about what will happen next to their projects' ideas. So before closing the event, the Leader and the Organizers should point clearly to the planned activities for the day after the event.

6. Closing reception. A short closing cocktail or happy hour should be prepared by the Organizers. By the end of the week, participants are sorry to part with the group and a short celebration of the results of their endeavor is mandatory.

The final report

At the end of the week, the Organizers are left with a set of seven or eight presentations and lots of references. This material has now to be organized into a final report that makes sense to a general audience, which is the final report. Some of the participants in the WGs are members of the community and will go back to their daily affairs after the meeting. But a smaller group of 2 or 3 from each WG should be nominated to write the report of the group and to contribute to the final report. If the group of participants involves graduate students from a local university, they should be in charge of this task as part of the deliverables of the discipline associated with the workshop. We used this method in all of our nine workshop's experiences so far.

Each WG's report will contain participants in the group, stakeholders interviewed, sources that were consulted, information about the methodology used, photos of empathy maps and problems diagrams, photos of the group working, ideas raised in the brainstorming session, projects suggested, and detailed information about the proposed project. It is a long document and a full registration of the work developed during the week.

The final report, on the other hand, is a much more concise document with a short description of the methodology used and the list of participants, facilitators, and stakeholders, and a one-page description of the main projects that were suggested. The group in charge of the final report should have experience in preparing this kind of document. A journalist would help either a participant or someone consulted for the job. The final report should be clean, nice to look at and read, and have only the relevant information that will inspire the people who will have the resources to actually act and transform those project ideas into reality. They are not only government officials, by the way. The WGs should point to who is, in their case, the main actor that can execute the project. The Governance WG might also have indicated a way about how to proceed in the future.

The day after

With the final report in hand, the Leader and Organizers can now go and look for the respective actors for each project. Communication at this point is again key: The Leader should plan to show the workshop's results and distribute the final report in as many places as he can manage to. Distribution of the final report should start with the group of Organizers, Participants, Stakeholders, and everybody involved in the workshop during the intensive week.

The day after of our nine workshops so far varied widely amongst them. Some projects were implemented, some are in their final planning stages now, and some simply did not work at all. It is difficult to pinpoint the reasons for the greater or lesser impact of the workshops, but some of our lessons learned are described at the end of the chapter.

A sample case: the surroundings of Ponte Hercílio Luz in Florianópolis

Florianópolis is a state capital in the South of Brazil characterized by the fact that most of its territory is an island seven times the size of Manhattan (circa 400 km^2) and close to the continent. The island has been a tourist heaven for many decades with its 100 beaches and enchanting scenery of mountains, dunes, and lakes. At the turn of the century though, the city and the state suddenly awoke to the fact that the main source of tax income was not tourism anymore but information and communication technologies (ICTs) services! In a short time span of 40 years since the establishment of the Federal University there, the city became one of the most important innovation hubs in Brazil, with thousands of hopeful startups everywhere. Since the city code does not allow for any industrial activity on the island, graduate students, who did not want to leave in search of industrial jobs elsewhere, started to create new ICT companies of their own. Capitalizing this movement, a strong innovation support system was developed and the results are impressive. The movement is still strong and the number of new companies in ICT and other sectors continues to grow and the city now wants to be known as the "smart island" (Yigitcanlar et al, 2018).

The chosen region for the workshop

The 2017 edition of the Workshop chose the old bridge called Hercílio Luz and its surroundings as the object of study. The bridge was an engineering marvel when it was built in 1926 and was the first physical link between the island and the continent. It stretches for 800 m, the shortest path between the two areas. The bridge project designer built two bridges in the same format and the same technology. The other one is in the United States. But this sister bridge in the United States collapsed in the 1980s! The fact raised a lot of concern in Florianópolis although local studies did not show any immediate threat to the bridge's structure. In any case, the bridge was eventually closed completely in 1982 and remained closed for more than 20 years. But after a long discussion about the economics of tearing it down and building a new one, or reforming the existing structure, the state of Santa Catarina, who actually owns the bridge, decided to reform the bridge since it is a city symbol and a well-known postcard of Florianópolis and of the state of Santa Catarina.

The expensive reform was due to be ready by the end of 2018 and it looked like a good idea in 2017 to study how to transform the bridge and its surroundings into a more Humane and Sustainable borough. The bridge is listed as a historical, artistic, and architectonic monument in the National Heritage and there is a polygon around it where buildings cannot hide the bridge from straight view.

Organization of the workshop

As in some other editions of the workshop, this one was also set up as a discipline in the Graduate Program on Knowledge Management of the Federal University of Santa Catarina. This is a good start since students are interested in the subject and that provides an interesting group of participants that get credits for their work in something that they really like. Actually, the Bridge is meaningful to everyone that lives in the city.

Main partners were the City Hall and its Planning Institute, a trade association (Fecomercio—Commerce Federation) that is located in the surroundings, and an interesting representative from the civil society called "Friends of the Bridge Park," a group of residents in the area who took to themselves the job to protect the small park that faces the bridge on the island side. With the support of Fecomercio, the doors to the media were immediately open: The workshop became a constant piece of local news with weekly reports and interviews with the organizers.

The eight themes for the workshop were slightly modified from the eight dimensions list presented in Chapter 3, From smart cities to more Humane and Sustainable Smart Cities: the world in transformation, as we mentioned earlier. The "Smart People" dimension was dropped for not being that relevant in this case, and the "Local Identity" dimension was added, to take care of the importance of the bridge not only as a national monument but also as a cherished symbol for the population.

Fecomercio provided all the infrastructure for the event as well, which was handy: The place is four blocks away from the bridge, so participants could walk to the region and study the surroundings easily.

The workshop

The workshop was held from July 10 to 14, 2017, in Florianópolis, full-time, with 8 facilitators and 46 participants, of which 37 were graduate students from the Federal University of Santa Catarina and 11 were representatives from civil society.

Following the standard agenda described earlier, the first day was taken by lectures of general stakeholders and by the organization of participants into eight WGs with the dimensions listed in the table below.

Twenty-seven stakeholders participated in the interviews: 13 from the civil society, 9 from the state and municipal governments, 3 from different universities, and 2 from companies in the region. Some of these stakeholders were interviewed by more than one WG, so there were 35 interviews altogether. Besides that, participants also conducted random or guided interviews with passers-by on the streets of the region.

With the results from the interviews, they identified the main problems of the region that were then listed, prioritized, and grouped to become this final list of main problems:

1. No accessibility and poor connection between the bridge and the different transport systems in the city;
2. No monitoring system and very poor lighting in the region, leading to a feeling of insecurity (not demonstrated in crime statistics though);
3. Poor communication between institutions involved in the remodeling of the bridge (state, municipality, environmental organisms);
4. Public policy for the bridge does not consult or even consider, in many instances, the well-being of the population;
5. Although the bridge is the city's postcard, there are no specific actions to promote tourism in, or around, the bridge;
6. Lack of confidence or even total discredit of the population about the bridge ever returning to service;
7. Abandonment of public facilities in the area in terms of parks, public buildings, and museums;
8. Lack of significant or meaningful economic activity in the area around the bridge;
9. Lack of maintenance in the green areas and poor garbage collection in the whole region.

With the main problems identified, the WGs had the necessary tools to start looking for solutions based upon the empathy maps of personas identified during the process of stakeholders' interviews, the final list of problems, and the guiding question for each theme. The guiding questions are given in Table 6.1.

With this material, the group of participants worked quickly through a brainstorming session for ideas and solutions and then focused on a few ideas and evolved, through the design thinking methodology, toward the final list of suggested projects. These projects are described in the next section. Some photographs of participants and process phases are shown in Figs. 6.1−6.4.

Results—projects

During the discussions within the WGs and between WGs some projects were merged and the final list of suggested projects was reduced to 7.

1. (attending to problems 1, 4, 6 and 7) Regulate the use of the Bridge preferentially for pedestrians and nonmotorized forms of transport such as bikes and such. Then it may allow for public transport also but the

TABLE 6.1 List of dimensions and key questions.

Working group		Basic question
Number	Dimension	
1	DEV	How can the region and its main actors and institutions help foster the development of an inclusive and innovative economy, in line with the already existing characteristics of the city's economy?
2	Smart Identity	How to strengthen the sense of belonging that the population already have in relation to the bridge through the dissemination of the bridge's history and significance to the national heritage?
3	QOL	How to develop positive incentives toward reducing criminal action in the area, and also systems based on modern technology for monitoring and surveillance, in order to increase significantly the security and also the sense of security?
4	HAC	How to develop the local Historic, Artistic, and Cultural Heritage toward service offers for tourists, characterizing the region as a cool place?
5	ENV	How to develop the local economy taking into account and working toward the UN's 17 sustainable development goals for 2030?
6	SOC	How to develop work opportunities and facilitate access to the new economy for the less developed cohorts of society in the region?
7	MOB	How to move people around in a smarter, sustainable, and shared modern and connected transport system?
8	GOV	How to convince and engage politicians, public officials, and the population into a shared governance system at least in this one specific region of the city?

vehicle to be used should be unique and associated with the innovation spirit that the city wants to convey to the country and to the world: An electric vehicle, with large glass windows so that people can enjoy the beautiful views, with a design that surprises by being "exquisite."

2. (attending to problems 5, 7 and 8) Create a Living Lab and a LUZ Memorial: the first, as an opportunity to experiment and test new services that could then be deployed all over the city, and with a platform of city data that can be used by all the projects; the second, with all the modern technology to demonstrate the original and innovative design of the bridge at the time of construction, its evolution through time, the disaster

FIGURE 6.1 The bridge.

FIGURE 6.2 Workshop in progress.

with the sister bridge in the United States, and the design and structure used in this latest remodeling of the bridge. Both facilities would also become important tourist spots for the city.

FIGURE 6.3 Workshop results.

3. (attending to problems 3, 4, and 7) Establish an effective data collection and distribution system for all the different institutions involved in its operation and maintenance. Institutions would supply data knowing that what they get in return is worthwhile for their own work. At a later stage, the system could also be shared with companies toward the development of value-added services for visitors and users.

4. (attending to problems 1, 5, and 7) Transform the Bridge and its surrounding in the "exchange" place between transport modes. Make sure that the system is thought of as a means of resolving the transport endeavors of the main users of public transport, clearly identified in the system (a student that lives in the Continent and studies at a University in the island, for instance). The interconnection with the private car should be encouraged by the existence of public and cheap parking on both sides, in order to give incentives to car users to leave their cars there and cross the Bridge by other means.

5. (attending to problems 5, 6, 7, and 9) Promote the redevelopment of the public spaces in the area through new services. The place must become "cool," with several options for people to get together, like the old plazas used to be in the old towns. Think of all the functions of the old plazas transplanted to our days and to the available technologies. Instead of being only a bridge to connect two geographical areas, it becomes a

FIGURE 6.4 The author and a participant.

desired meeting point for both tourists and locals with all the services they need. As the use of the area increases, the area may spread to nearby streets with closed streets (only on weekends, or even definitively).

6. (attending to problems 2 and 7) Establish a source of clean energy in the area with a clear description of the benefits of this source and connecting everything that happens in the region to UN's 17 sustainable development goals (SDGs) for 2030. Maybe a token post for each one of the SDGs, explaining how the region and the city of Florianópolis are contributing toward those goals. In clear contrast with today's poor lighting in the region, the new lighting system should be a model of the possibilities of new lamps, posts, and artifacts. Play with the fact that the Bridge's name (Luz, in Portuguese, means Light) and turn the lighting system into something really remarkable. Consider the possibility of making the bridge self-sustainable and generator of energy for its use and distribution of its surplus.

7. (attending to problems 3, 4, and 7) Establish a managing council that is totally different from existing government structures. It will have representatives from all sectors of society, it will work and use social media to communicate and to deliberate. And it will be flexible to change whenever needed. Benchmark from experiences that have been tried elsewhere in the world in order to find the best alternative for the region. Since the structure will be different from ordinary government, it may also be used for novel approaches for PPPs, not only in terms of governance, but also in terms of creating value in economic activities that are difficult to organize and implement today.

Final report

Thanks to support by Fecomercio, the final report, prepared by the graduate students from The Federal University of Florianopolis, has been published and distributed to several relevant actors in the city. This was crucial for the subsequent results that impacted the city and the region.

Real impact on the day after

The Hercílio Luz Bridge Workshop was one of the most impactful so far. The main reason is that some officials from City Hall participated intensively during the week and took to them the initiative to put forward some of the ideas and projects designed during the workshop. As this book is being written, the following concrete results had been achieved and were being pursued by the administration:

- The totally remodeled Bridge was inaugurated in December of 2019 with segregated pedestrian and bike lanes, and authorized use for public transport only, as suggested by the workshop. Later on, as the rapid bus transit system is completed, it will be also used for public transport by bus. No private cars, as also prescribed by the workshop.
- The governance of the transport system by bus in the metropolitan area is being redesigned around the principles of the workshop, with a substantial reduction of parallel and redundant routes through the different towns of the metropolitan region. The facilitator of the Governance WG in the workshop is in charge of developing the new system for real.
- The green areas on both sides of the bridge are being kept and enhanced as suggested by the workshop. Even when the buses use the bridge, they will be circled around the parks in order not to diminish any green area already existing.
- The National Heritage has agreed to use parts of the protected areas for economic activities related to tourism, with preservation of the local characteristics and "shape and form" of the historical buildings.

Finally, and most importantly, the population started to believe that their ideas might become reality, and that they will be heard by the public administration. This is a considerable and very welcome novelty in the city's history.

Lessons learned

- Participants loved the workshops. The personal impact of living intensely with a diverse group for a week is almost always high and good, in any kind of subject. In this case though, they leave with a sense that their work and the project they developed *may be* important, and that *they* (and not the government or someone else) are contributing to the shape and form of their own future surroundings.
- The choice of stakeholders with good knowledge of the themes of the WGs is key to the success of the initiative. Look for knowledge everywhere, not only formal knowledge at universities. It is important to interview police officers, nonprofits, politicians, merchants, entrepreneurs, the clergy, and several different people at City Hall. Ask them the prescribed questions for the empathy map, but also about their pains (what really bothers them) and gains (their dreams and hopes).
- Cities are unique. Cities show a mosaic of different experiences and there are no definitive formulas ready to be applied everywhere. It is necessary to study the local history and the current situation of the city. Beware of context. And remember to listen to the locals more than show off your knowledge of the subject. Most good solutions are in the locals' minds already. Mine them carefully.
- Although the ideas are there already, locals are surprised to realize that the collective result of the workshop, merging their ideas into something more meaningful, is better than what they thought originally. Communication of the results of the workshop to all the people involved should be part of the day-after strategy.
- Participants learn to respect other people's opinions during the week of the workshop. Although they arrive with preconceived ideas and projects, the collective experience teaches them that the group work is capable of producing better results and projects than their own. It is an exercise of humbleness.
- Governance is a different dimension from the others. All the other seven dimensions propose executable projects. Governance is about how to transform them into real projects. One alternative that we are considering is to place the Governance dimension as a cross-dimension whose job is to ascertain that at least some of the projects bear actual fruits.
- The scientific literature about more HSSCs is getting bigger. So, the fundamental concept must be reviewed from time to time in order to guarantee that it does not become obsolete.

- The design thinking methodology is adequate for the workshop exercise. Its rule of listen-to-the-people and try to think as if you were a user of the project, applies correctly in this case.
- Some participants have asked for more time for one activity or another. This is a possibility of course, but we gather that the total time of 1 week is right. More time would perhaps make the group lose focus. The final presentation might last longer though, so that participants can criticize, comment, or give suggestions to other WG's projects.
- The historical background or some narrative associated with the target place must be detailed at the beginning of the workshop. It is much easier to implement projects later when they fit somehow with the previous history of the place.
- Involvement of City Hall officials is very important for the implementation of the projects. Not only as stakeholders and consultants but also as full participants of the workshop (Spinosa and Costa, 2020). Their involvement should be organized early in the preparation phase. A good thing about government officials at the municipal level is that they are as interested in the success of the initiative as everybody else there, since they also live in the same place, their children go to the same school, etc.

References

Gehl, J., Svarre, B., 2013. How to Study Public Life. Island Press, Washington.

Jacobs, J., 1961. The Death and Life of Great American Cities. Vintage Books, New York.

McAdam, M., Debackere, K., 2018. Beyond "triple helix" toward "quadruple helix" models in regional innovation systems: implications for theory and practice. R&D Manag. 48, 3−6. Available from: 10.1111/radm.12309.

Ostrom, E., 1990. Governing the Commons: The Evolution of Institutions for Collective Action. Cambridge University Press, Cambridge.

Sinek, S., 2010. How great leaders inspire action. TED talk available from: <https://www.youtube.com/watch?v = qp0HIF3SfI4>.

Chapter 7

The future: the need for more Humane and Sustainable Smart Cities postpandemic 2020/21

Historically, pandemics have forced humans to break with the past and imagine their world anew. This one is no different. It is a portal, a gateway between one world and the next.

Arundhati Roy.

Covid-19 is the nearest we have to a revelation for atheists.

Rabbi Jonathan Sacks.

If you want to make the Gods laugh, tell them about your future plans...

Origin unknown, found in a T-Shirt in Boston, 1999

The world was *not* well in January 2020

We were all talking about the pandemic 2020/21 during those terrible years and how it turned the world upside down. But when we look at the world with our lenses focused on January 2020, before the outbreak of Covid-19, what was the situation then? Were we in good shape, and then the new coronavirus came unexpectedly to spoil our party? Heads of state, presidents, kings, and queens addressed their constituents around that time with their annual speech known as something like "the state of the nation," "the state of the union," or simply "annual report." However optimistic they might have been (and they were), about the state of the world, if we had trusted someone with the responsibility to address us all with a summary of the situation of our entire world, it would not look as bright.

In fact, we were *not* well in January 2020, as we detail later in the chapter.

The point here is not to bring additional gloom to an already gloomy situation. The idea is to plan our future as a new society that really learned from

Humane and Sustainable Smart Cities. DOI: https://doi.org/10.1016/B978-0-12-819186-6.00006-3

the pandemic crisis and had the resolve to tackle the world's situation in a holistic sense: We need to reconstruct our world from the debris of the crisis, but correcting the mistakes that were entrenched in our society before that.

In doing so, we need a new city. A future city that develops itself on top of the existing one. A retrofit on the one we had before. In order to achieve this, we—citizens—need to change our attitudes toward many issues such as the attack on the environment, the indecent inequality we have been accustomed to live with, and our individualism—since we now realize we are in this world together. Seems easy. Change oneself. Change the city we live in. The new cities will propagate their new arrangements to other cities. The world will be better.

It is exactly that. Let us start by going back to January 2020.

Anthropocene

Scientists are still debating whether we should register the human impact on the planet as a new geological era, the Anthropocene. The word comes from a combination of two ancient Greek words meaning "man" and "new" or "recent." The fact is that this "recent man" is abusing the planet in such an accelerated way that we might be following a path that will lead the earth toward the sixth extinction—our own! (the fifth was the extinction of the dinosaurs—before that the planet did not have species we relate to today). The beginning of such an Anthropocene era is also part of the debate but most scientists agree to set it to some event connected to the atomic bomb— either its first testing or its first deployment.

The offenses we are practicing against the planet have had terrible consequences, of which global warming is only but one. The others are on the atmosphere (dissemination of aerosol and excess nitrogen and phosphor leading to the depletion of the ozone layer), on agricultural land (excessive consumption of water, undue use of the land, chemical contamination), and on other species such as wild animals that face extinction in frightening numbers (amongst them cheetahs, Asian elephants, red tuna, tigers, and rhinoceros).

Global warming is the most noticeable offense because we might have surpassed the "point-of-no-return" already! Scientists do not agree on the actual size of the disaster, but if you filter extremists on one side that deny global warming and those on the other that clamor that the end of the world is near, the average consensus is expressed in the United Nations Environmental Program call for a reduction of CO_2 emissions by c.8% a year through 2030. This increase would cap the planet's average temperature at an increase of 1.5°C over the average temperature experienced during the industrial era—the maximum the planet might withstand and would avoid or at least contain extreme weather disasters such as the rise in sea level that would flood highly populated coastal areas all over the globe (Carrillo, 2019).

Facing this kind of disaster and the threat of plain extinction or our species, what were our leaders concerned about in January 2020? The Queen's speech in the United Kingdom did mention an effort to curb CO_2 emissions by 2050, but US President Trump did not only refer to the subject in his annual speech but went on with his intention (announced in 2017) to formally leave the Paris Agreement. Brazilian President Bolsonaro downplayed the deforestation of the Amazon Forest and his Minister of the Environment continued his attack on environmentalists that insisted on global warming, referring to their data as gross exaggerations. The pack is enlarged by those world leaders that declare their intention to do something about global warming but do not convert their intention into practice (as in Mozambican poet Ruy Guerra's poem "if I carry my hands far from my chest, it is because there is a distance between intention and execution").

And why do we ignore such an overwhelming threat? The explanation belongs to the realm of Psychology. There is even a Psychology book dedicated to the subject "Why our brains are wired to ignore climate change" (Marshall, 2015). UCLA psychologist Per Espen Stoknes (2017) explains that we ignore climate change due to five factors: distance, doom, dissonance, denial, and identity. *Distance*, both geographical and in time, because the problem is too far away from most of us (white polar bears floating on a tiny plateau of ice) or too far in time (sea level will rise in 2100). *Doom*, because after hearing about the end-of-the-world for 30 years now, we feel sort of "Oh my, there they come again." *Dissonance*, because we justify our daily attitudes as "necessary" and tend to forget, or not even know of, their environmental costs (such as flying a jet plane for 6 hours to speak 15 minutes about the dangers of climate change in another country). *Denial*, because we know of the problem but prefer to ignore it and put the blame on someone else or some other country that is doing even worse on mitigation measures. And *identity*, because politics inserted the topic in the agenda and convinced conservative voters that this is nothing more than another attempt by the "left" to expand even further the interference of government in your life. In fact, given the importance of the subject, it should become not a dividing, but a unifying theme for every citizen…

So, how do we change this situation? The abovementioned psychologists point in the same direction: We need to present the case in a positive way, closer to our everyday life. "We need to cultivate positive emotions associated with climate actions rather than negative emotions coming from climate impacts" (Arcanjo, 2019). Talk about the health advantages of eating less and changing our diet to fresh and natural items and less meat. Develop an app that counts not how bad the fossil fuel consumption of your SUV is, but how impactful, in terms of less CO_2 emissions, is your commute by bike instead of by car. Publicize the beauty and the good of the atmosphere above us (Stoknes calls it the "fragile skin of planet earth") and what you can do to improve its quality for your own benefit and your kids'. Stop using scientific data and jargon predicting doomsday and create an engaging narrative.

And the city? Most of the actions suggested to improve the dreadful situation of our environment happen in the city. In the Humane and Sustainable Smart City (HSSC) proposal of a new city further down in this chapter, we will suggest a way forward.

Inequality

The final decade of the 19th century saw the end of slavery, the industrial revolution in full speed, and an expansion in international trade, which led to a redraw of the power balance between the dominant nations of the time (the United Kingdom, Germany, and Russia in the West, and China, India, and rising Japan in the East). The 20th century began with the hope that new socioeconomic models could improve the average quality of life (Bhattacharya et al., 2016) and do it with equity on the planet (which it did not eventually, as we saw earlier).

The 19th was a century that faced two major wars. It started with regional disputes and conflicts that led to the Great War of 1914−18 ("the war to end all wars," sadly to be renamed the First World War, 30 years hence, with the outbreak of the Second World War) followed by several smaller conflicts. It is mind-boggling that these tragic events that led to a bloodshed of 20 million people in World War I (WWI) and 75 million during World War II (WWII) involved the most educated societies in the world at the time!

During the century, we did enjoy novelties that improved our quality of life such as the air conditioning and other house appliances, the TV and the Internet. But, at the end of the century, not only did the goal of socioeconomic inclusion remain unreached, but the level of inequality started to increase (from 1980 onward). But the world's population definitely established itself in the city (more than 50% of the people). As a result, our natural resources were coming to a point of exhaustion.

At the outset of the new century, again, new hopes for equality were rekindled. With all the technical advances we had experienced, there certainly should be a global solution to the afflictions of hunger, poverty, and inequality.

The means of production in the agricultural and industrial eras were mostly tangible, related to land, capital, mineral resources, and labor. As industry lost its preeminence in the last few decades, we entered the *knowledge era*, where the most important means of production is knowledge (instead of tangible things, or even capital). We moved work from the "main d'ouevre" (workforce, which refers to manual work) to the "brain work." Smart, flexible, and innovative people are now key.

One of the hopes that many people held with the advent of the new era was that contrary to what was true with its predecessors as means of production, knowledge actually *grows* when shared! Hence, it was the best chance in decades for reducing the inequality between people. Knowledge would be spread to everyone interested, and that would be enough to level the playing field—and better still—the owners of the original knowledge would also have their own knowledge increased as it was spread to other people. A clear win-win scenario!

Did it actually happen?

Unfortunately, the answer is, no! Inequality only grew in the last four decades all over the world. Inequality is demonstrated in the accumulation of wealth of the top 10% of society in comparison with the rest, between the top wage earners and the rest, and between the ruling majority and the minorities (Piketty, 2017). This is true in the United States and Europe, in the East and the West, in socialist regimes, and in liberal and capitalist countries. The top 1% of society earn more than the bottom 50% together. The three richest people in the United States—Bezos, Gates, and Buffet, for instance—are worth more than the bottom 50% of their fellow countrymen (160,000,000 people) (Kirsch, 2018). What went wrong?

Thomas Piketty wrote his best-seller *Capital in the Twenty-First Century* in 2013 and tried to dissect the reasons for this absurd accumulation of wealth. In more than 700 pages of his book, he explains that there is a dominant coalition that is organized to explain the inequality tragedy as a situation that is necessary for society to progress. They promote the old theory that we have to make the cake grow first before thinking about distributing it. And with their clout on governments, rules, and taxes, they perpetuate the situation.

Although Piketty's ideas met with mixed reviews and some disdain from traditional economists, the book quickly became a best-seller. It explained to the layman that not only was the world's inequality bad, it was getting worse since the 1980s! For many people living in developing countries, the dreadful situation of the poor was no news. But the fact that the situation was worsening, even as economies were growing, came as a real shock!

The book is explanatory and nonprescriptive. But in his most recent book *Capital and Ideology* (Piketty, 2020), Piketty goes further: in more than 1000 pages, he details and explains, with detailed historical background, his original explanation for the world's inequality, and then concludes with a recipe for the solution.

Piketty's new book was released in March 2020, just as the pandemic crisis was unfolding all over the world. So, it was written *before* the crisis. It is interesting to realize that his suggestions for the solution of the world's inequality would sound as radical contributions if they were read before the crisis. After the crisis, they may seem almost reasonable. Solution to inequality has risen to the top of the world's priority for two reasons. First, during the crisis, poverty has been exposed to the rest of society in each country of the world, and made us experience, in general, an uncomfortable feeling of guilt. Governments, in many countries, had to distribute money directly to large contingents of society, in order to avoid social despair and unrest. These measures unearthed the intolerable situation and the actual numbers of the poor. The cost of these measures will be covered by society as a whole, of course, and the debate is about what to do to remedy the situation.

Second, during social distancing, we were left to reflect about what is and what is not relevant in life. Money, for instance, good as it is, could not buy many things during the pandemic. Your beautiful new car was left in the garage. Traveling was not a possibility. International travel, in particular, will probably not go back to previous numbers for many years. Can we do something else with *part* of our money? We will go back to this in the sequence.

As a conclusion, no, the world was not going well in January 2020. On top of it, between February and March 2020 the crisis hit us all right in the face. Plans, predictions, and economic forecasts became useless overnight. As Mike Tyson said once, "everyone has a plan, until they get punched in the mouth."

The pandemic of 2020/21

A surprising crisis hit the world in 2020, with unknown consequences so far. The new coronavirus is not so deadly as some of its previous mutations, but it spreads much more rapidly. The resulting disease, called Covid-19, has killed hundreds of thousands of people and will continue to do so until a proper vaccine is tested and all the world's population takes it, which is a daunting task.

The crisis is of large proportions, and may be compared to just a few other health pandemics in our times, such as the "Asian" flu of 1957 or the "swine" flu of 1968, but still not as bad as the "Spanish" flu of 1918−19, that killed c.50 million people worldwide after the First World War. The Covid-19 is estimated to kill more than 1 million people before it is controlled by a vaccine.

The novelty here is that the best way to combat the virus' rapid spread rate is for people to stay away from each other in order to avoid contagion. This was called "social distancing" and was highly debated along 2020, since many people argued that the economic impact of social distancing could send large groups of underprivileged people into extreme poverty and eventual death.

Social distancing, on the other hand, avoided peaks of simultaneous search for medical treatment and especially hospital intensive care units (ICUs), and avoided overcrowding the existing facilities in hospitals everywhere. We had to flatten the curve of infected people so that the medical system could be prepared to work with the more critical cases. One of the problems with this discussion is that it soon became a political issue and unfortunately was debated, not on technical terms, but on ideological lines in many countries, which only worsened the situation.

In any case, the pandemic 2020/21 will have a profound impact in our cities. Some of them might be positive, after the shocking awakening brought about by the crisis. We describe what happened and is happening in the world here as an introduction, since our focus is not on the disease, but on its effects on our cities.

What happened

At the end of 2019, beginning of 2020, first reports out of the Wuhan province, in China, indicated that a new coronavirus had been identified and was dangerous. International travelers started to spread the virus to many countries in the world. The World Health Organization called the virus Covid-19 and declared a pandemic in February. By mid-March, the virus had spread to almost all the countries in the world. The virus was different from its previous versions in that it spread easily from one person to another, but fortunately was not that lethal. The main concern with the new virus was that with its spread, the hospital system in many countries (eventually in almost every country) could not cope with the need for ICU for that many grave cases at the same time. There was a need to keep people apart in order to "flatten the curve" of infected patients per day, so that the health system had time to adapt to the sudden surge of demand.

The best measures against the disease, before a vaccine could be found, were identified as the use of individual masks and the practice of "social distancing." Social distancing kept people apart from one another, wherever possible, particularly those most vulnerable to the disease, which were elderly people and those suffering from obesity, diabetes, and respiratory conditions. Social distancing was put in practice everywhere with different levels of rigor and with different degrees of success in terms of putting a stop to the spread of the disease.

The implementation of social distancing implied that people could not move about in the city, go to work, go to school, etc. Workers in the service sector stayed at home and started practicing "home-office." School classes, at the various levels, moved to remote learning or distance learning whereby classes, exercises, and evaluation were done at home; students and teachers were in contact through the Internet. Public transport, where available, had to adopt new distancing rules and was severely reduced everywhere. Shops closed, and the economy came to a standstill.

The disease spread unevenly all over the world, and countries, one by one, had to face the first wave of the virus during the first semester of the year, with different rules for social distancing and lockdown. By the end of the first semester of 2020 the spread of the disease had been contained in

China, Europe, and a few other countries, but was raging in the United States, Brazil, Mexico, India, and others.

Scientists were looking frenetically for a cure to the disease and/or a vaccine against it. A cure could be found at any time and could be applied immediately when and if it were discovered. As for the vaccine, after being found, it had to be tested, produced in huge quantities, distributed worldwide, and given to the whole world's population, a daunting task. Immunization of the population as a whole could realistically be expected only for the end of 2021, but the predictions changed widely.

The effect of the pandemic on the world's economy was catastrophic. Prediction of growth rates for 2020 dived into negative territory and, in some countries, such as the United Kingdom and Spain, dropped to double-digit negative. Unemployment was the direct result of the crisis and hit record levels everywhere. With the economic crisis came a pressure from the private sector and employees to reopen the economy and reduce social distancing. Several cities eased the restrictions due to this pressure, only to watch the situation worsen again, and to be forced to reinstall the distancing measures, such as Barcelona did in July of 2020.

Knowledge about the disease was scarce at the beginning and during the year 2020. Scientists could not guarantee how the virus was transmitted from one person to another exactly, whether a person once cured of the disease would be immune afterward, why it hit some countries more than others, etc. The dissemination of information was confusing and sometimes produced conflicting pieces from different sources. To make things even worse, national leaders in places such as the United States, because of the election in that year, downplayed the gravity of the problem. In Brazil and in other countries, leaders also politicized the disease and intensified the problem.

In a word, a mess.

A few stats

Previous deadly pandemics of similar nature in the last 100 years were the terrible "Spanish Flu" of 1918−19 (between 40 and 50 million dead, exact numbers unknown due to information controls that were still in place after WWI), the "Asian Flu" of 1957 (1 million dead), the "Hong Kong Flu" of 1968 (1 million dead), and the tragic HIV/AIDS of 1981 (35 million dead) (LePan, 2020). These crises added up to the yearly deaths caused by ordinary flu "influenza," and respiratory complications from the flu, of c.600,000.

As for the new coronavirus, as it is still spreading as we write, we refer to estimates only. It will have infected more than 20 million people and have killed c.1 and 2 million people before the end of 2020. The crisis will increase the number of unemployed people worldwide by 200,000,000 by the end of 2020. A massacre.

Changes in our behavior

Because of the crisis, we had to change our behavior. Stay-at-home had several impacts on our daily lives, both in objective terms (purchases, classes, delivery of goods and services) and in subjective terms (tolerance, solidarity, questions about the meaning of life, etc.).

Let us look at "home-office" first. Since most of us started to work from home and could not go out, the actual location of your "home" could be anywhere. People who have a second home in the mountains or on the beach (and had a good Internet connection there) suddenly realized that they could live there permanently. Companies measured their employees' productivity as almost as good as before, or even better. Permanent home-office started to look like a viable alternative.

Let us question this scenario on both sides. On the employee's side, since they could not go anywhere during the more acute phase of the crisis, it really did not matter if people were at home or elsewhere. Permanent living out in the woods may also have looked attractive. But once the attractions and services of the city are fully operational again, people will want to get back to them: restaurants, bars, parks, entertainment, friends, etc.

On the employers' side, productivity of work at home has been measured by companies when there is nowhere to go to outside, and it looks good. But when they start to measure productivity when everything is open and working in the city, and the beach is just there, friends are around the corner, etc., results will be different. So, work at home is a distinct possibility but its results must be measured in a more "normal" time, even if it is a "new normal." We will get back to this in the last section of this chapter.

The outcome of the home-office experiment will probably be a combination of in-and-out of the office for most service companies. But there are side effects to the home-office experiment in that workers will need services around them. This opens a new opportunity for businesses to spread all over the city in decentralized boroughs where people live.

We discuss the digital transformation that is happening in the next section. But in terms of our behavior, one of the changes that happened during the crisis and will certainly remain in place is online sales. There are things people want to buy in-store, for instance, if they need to try on clothes and shoes. There are other things that people like to go to the store to handle, experience, or even taste. These items will probably resist in the traditional brick-and-mortar store. But there are other items that are bulky, heavy, and that "you know what you want to buy anyway," such as paper for the printer, milk (even if it is lactose-free, or low-fat), beer, juice, cleaning and bath items (soap, detergent, deodorant, tooth-paste, etc.), that you can buy online without any limitations of choice. These items will probably go online for good. Or, at least, there will be a trend in that direction. Which is good for online retailers like Amazon, and bad for the local supermarket.

The opportunity

With the shockwaves that hit us all with Covid-19, there is wide speculation now about whether this will be the wake-up call we needed to change society for the better. More Humane, more Sustainable. Using technology (being Smart). But will we? Some optimists agree that we are going there one way or another. Others point to the previous pandemics and demonstrate that no, the world will not correct its wrongdoings. We side on the court of the realists, somewhere in between. We may change and it depends upon you and all of us. Not the government, not the state. Us. Remember the often-quoted inaugural speech by the US President Kennedy: "Ask not what your country can do for you, ask what you can do for your country."

There are two main tools that will help us on this trajectory, and they are explained in detail next.

Accelerated digital transformation

We have seen in Chapter 3, From Smart Cities to More Humane and Sustainable Smart Cities: The World in Transformation, that digitalization is one of the 3 "D's" of conceptual trends that our society is facing. The other two are decentralization and decarbonization. Here we detail the same concept in more depth—the digital transformation process—as it now unfolds in companies and governments—and explain why the pandemic of 2020/21 accelerated the process of change.

Digital transformation—which is a structural change in society, economies, cities, and organizations, caused by the comprehensive application of digital technologies and disruptive digital business models to everything—has been a theme of academic and business interest worldwide for a number of years. Think of online sales and e-commerce. It has been around for a couple of decades already. IBM, for instance, at the turn of the century, used to call its global strategy as "e-business." Eventually, they dropped it, stating that there was no point in calling their business "e-business" since, from then on, every business would either be an e-business or risk becoming a *no* business. In 2008 the company's global strategy changed to "Smarter Planet" anticipating the smart city, smart country, and smart everything movement.

Acute futurists such as John Naisbitt (1982), one of the first to anticipate China's return as a protagonist in world affairs, pointed out that the following century would arrive transformed by phenomena such as dramatic demographic changes, economic globalization, and modification of production and commercial structures on global scales, all strongly influenced by information and communication technologies. The new century would put pressure on public and private managers on how to establish management models, plans, and processes that were appropriate to the challenges of an Information and Knowledge society, which was already being unfolded.

Change does not happen in the overall economy as fast as in the tech sector, though. At the beginning of 2020, most companies were still struggling to adapt their strategies to the digital world. And it is certainly not an easy task when you think of trying to reach a moving target: New technologies have been introduced almost every year. If we look back at the beginning of this century, household names such as Facebook, Skype, Instagram, or WhatsApp did not even exist! Observe the year that these companies were launched as services in the market: Skype (2003), Facebook (2004), Twitter (2006), WhatsApp (2009), Pinterest (2010), and Instagram (2010). TikTok, a Chinese short-video sharing service that is now in the center of an international dispute between the United States and China, was only launched in 2017!

So, digital transformation was already happening as we entered 2020, but at different paces of change. Then came the Pandemic of 2020/21 that brought instant acceleration to the process of change. Consultancy company McKinsey (Blackburn et al., 2020) confirmed, through a survey of their customers, that the digital transformation was already considered by them as a trend that was reaching all sectors of human activity in the prepandemic period—in the shape of a hurricane. But the pandemic brought in a significant acceleration—in the shape of a tsunami—forcing all organizations to implement their digitalization processes in a very short time. Companies had to transform their businesses in the new model of digital platforms, even small and medium-sized companies, as this move became the only way to survive in the postpandemic world.

In fact, the pandemic may become known in the future as the dividing line between the "Industrial Age" and the "Digital Age." If the pace of change in the precoronavirus world was already fast, the luxury of time for studying, planning, and deploying change seems to be completely gone now. Companies that had mapped their digital strategy in phases of one to several years needed to scale down their initiatives and implement them in a matter of weeks, or even days.

The acceleration is already evident in various sectors and in several geographical regions of the world. Asian banks that cared for the poor, for instance, have quickly switched their physical channels to digital (mostly cellular access). The Brazilian government managed to digitally include more than 30 million informal workers in 2 weeks, in order to provide them with direct assistance money during the crisis. In this case, online applications to receive assistance in the state bank registered 10 million people in just 6 hours!

All over the world, health-care providers moved quickly to tele-health (tele-consultation, telemedicine). Insurers had to accept self-service complaints and do their assessment online. Retailers, probably the most visible sector in the process of change, had to organize online sales and contactless deliveries in days.

The crisis apparently offered a sudden vision of the future world, in which "the digital" becomes central to all interactions, forcing organizations and individuals to move forward on the digital adoption curve almost overnight. A new world in which digital channels will become the main (and in some cases the only) customer engagement model. Automated processes will become the main factor of productivity—and the basis for flexible and transparent supply chains. A world in which agile forms of work are a prerequisite for meeting seemingly daily changes in each client's behavior.

This first shock of digital transformation in all sectors has only to do with physical absence of a person in the shop, in the counter, in the clinic, and in the local market. But this is just the beginning of the process of change. Executives from all sectors are using digital advances such as artificial intelligence—in particular, analytics—smart embedded devices, and other online and social media tools to change customer relationships, internal processes, and value propositions.

The digital transformation of a company, according to Shvertner (2017), can be grouped in three different levels:

- The transformation of customer experiences in the use of the organization's products and services, expressed in the in-depth study of market segments and their behavior in the marketing space, consumer behavior and loyalty, interactive communication with customers in the sales process, and many digital points of contact between the organization and their customers.
- The transformation of the organization's business processes includes the automation of the R&D, production, and distribution processes. Digital technologies also allow people to work at different levels in different functional areas. By automating, standardizing, and outsourcing processes globally, organizations can become more agile, more receptive to changes in demand and better able to increase and sustain profitability. By increasing the home-office work of its employees, decision-making based on real customer relationship data helps to speed up the decision on product availability in different production units.
- The transformation of the business model is based on digital platforms. In fact, digital platforms, which will further accelerate the pace of digital transformation, will incorporate millions (in some cases, billions) of users, applications, and sensors, allowing people to be omni-connected, amongst them, and also with sensors and machines equipped with artificial intelligence, through the Internet of Things (as we have seen in Chapter 3: From Smart Cities to More Humane and Sustainable Smart Cities: The World in Transformation).

What can companies do to face the challenge of digital transformation and use it as an opportunity and not a threat? Scott (Anthony et al. 2017) suggests a dual transformation strategy. The first is to adopt the new technologies to improve the quality, the efficiency, and the eventual margin of their products and services, but being in the same business they are, and attending to the same or slightly expanded customer base. Think of Netflix changing their business model from the physical delivery of DVDs over the mail service, to streaming the same content through the Internet. That happened in 2004 and was a bold move since the Internet speed at the time did not allow for the transfer of that much data in a reasonable amount of time. In fact, Netflix actually accelerated the rate of adoption of residential high-speed Internet by users who wanted access to its new service.

The second kind of transformation is the more radical, riskier, but that can bring more benefits to the company. It is to use the company's existing strengths (loyal customers, trademark, global reach, capillarity, financial clout, several delivery channels, etc.) to venture into new territory altogether. New customers, new markets, new offers. True innovation. This is more difficult and may face much more internal resistance. Think of Netflix again, going from delivery of content to the production of content, a totally different business. In 2019 alone Netflix launched almost 3000 hours of original movies, TV shows, and other productions.

It was a bold move by the company that was initially met with internal skepticism, and that was first authorized only as a short experiment. The Netflix internal proponents' argument was that they were the ones who knew what their customers wanted, and nobody was in a better position to produce content to their audience as they were themselves. The first experiment was the TV show "House of Cards," starring the then very popular actor Kevin Spacey. They tried the TV show in the United Kingdom first, and then offered it to the whole world. An amazing success. It was only after this blockbuster (a curious irony here, Blockbuster—the company—was sent to bankruptcy by Netflix's success) that Netflix decided to go in full force into production of content. The rest, as we know, is now history: The company became the world's most valuable company in the entertainment business.

In summary, dual transformation is about (1) adopting new technologies quickly in your existing line of products in and around the same market, and (2) capitalizing on your strengths to offer something different.

The changes we have seen in the market so far, related to digital transformation, and that were implemented in record times, all refer to the first kind of Scott's dual transformation. The benefits are still to be reaped by companies that go a step further to transformation number 2.

Likewise, in the public sector, elected and nonelected officials, particularly those who are more proactive, are also incorporating digital transformation into the public administration of their cities, both in order to increase their own productivity, and to improve the relationship and the provision of public services to the population. We will come back to the subject in the final section of the chapter.

The city as a "Commons"

In this century, cities became central to our collective well-being in most of the world. Contemporary urban development implies responsibilities that include, on the one hand, managing environmental impacts, such as their effects on biodiversity (Oliveira et al., 2011), monitoring climate change (Gouldson et al., 2016), and controlling the use of exhaustible natural resources (Yar, 2020). On the other hand, managing sustainability in the urban space also implies addressing social factors such as property value (Christensen, 2014), insecurity and social exclusion (Soyinka and Siu, 2018), health (Aizawa, 2019), employment (Mandisvika, 2015), mobility (Burinskiene et al., 2014), and innovation (Mieg, 2012). Cities are responsible for most of the world's problems today. But they also lodge the very people that will be able to solve them.

Amongst the existing proposals for a new vision of urban spaces, the notion of the Urban "Commons," discussed briefly in Chapter 3, From Smart Cities to More Humane and Sustainable Smart Cities: The World in Transformation, emerged in the last decades from the convergence of two fields of study: public management and urban development on the one hand, and the research about the Commons inspired by the discoveries of Elinor Ostrom (1990), on the other. The main contribution that was expected from this multidisciplinary vision of urban spaces was the application of the sustainability of the Commons, as demonstrated by Ostrom, on the challenges facing different areas of urban development.

In the following, we briefly revisit the views of Ostrom which, by contrast with Hardin before her, consolidated the Commons theory and the main foundations of the Urban Commons area, as a contemporary reference to the issue of the development of urban spaces.

The works of Hardin and Ostrom

In the late 1960s, Garret Hardin (1968) presented what he considered to be an inevitable tragedy of humanity in dealing with finite natural resources in free systems: in the face of freedom of exploration, individuals who want to explore the resource will seek to maximize their individual gains in detriment of losses to the collective group of individuals. With that, given that the resources are limited, they are inevitably depleted, even when the perpetrators face the prospect of everyone's ruin. The only remedy, according to Hardin, to prevent the depletion of these kinds of resources would be by some form of external control, either by the government or by privatization of the common resource, instead of leaving it to be governed by collectives of free individuals. Hardin's work called attention to a real problem of our society, which is the overpopulation of the planet, and suggested strict controls over people's rights to procreate. The trouble with his work is that he exaggerated in the "form" of the message, and potential followers were shied away from the importance of its content. For instance, he referred to having children as "breeding," which sounded offensive to many readers as the term is normally used for animals.

For Elinor Ostrom, Hardin's article arrived shortly after her doctoral defense and her seminal studies on collective action, environment, polycentric institutions, and common property resources (Capelary et al., 2017). Ostrom disagreed with Hardin's assumptions that, when using common resources, human collectives will *inevitably* be caught in the trap of individual use without possible collective preservation. She disagreed even more with the proposed solution of external intervention over the collective. And she went on to prove it.

Ostrom conducted her research locally. She traveled to different countries to observe the situation of interesting instances of collective governance which explored fisheries, forests, oil fields, irrigation, and grazing lands in different places in the United States, Asia, and Africa. In 2009 Ostrom received a Nobel Prize in Economics for demonstrating theoretically and practically that, based on a set of principles, human collectives *are capable* of solving Hardin's paradox, which then, as today, is known as "The Tragedy of the Commons." Ostrom's prize came as a surprise to economists the world over, for she was the first woman to get it, not very well known in economic circles, and, to add insult to injury, she was not an economist by training, but a political scientist!

Ostrom's contributions began with the very definition of a Commons ("shared resources subject to social conflicts") and included a conceptual framework, called the Institutional Analysis and Development (IAD) framework, which explained the collective use of the shared resources, and defined who had responsibility for decisions, actions, and restrictions. She also studied the actual returns of the Commons to the individuals. Application of this IAD framework and its instruments made it possible to identify the complex and aligned networks of relationships that can occur within the collectives themselves, and between collectives and government structures, which can combine local and regional levels.

In summary, Ostrom demonstrated, through case studies and the proposition of theoretical foundations, that the recipe for success was the institutionalization of collective action as the basis for Commons governance, allowing communities to self-organize themselves. Her work is often cited as the eponymous Ostrom's law:

> *"A resource arrangement that works in practice can work in theory."*

Ostrom's eight rules for Commons governance are:

1. Define clear boundaries.
2. Match rules governing use of common goods to local needs and conditions.

3. Ensure that those affected by the rules can participate in modifying the rules.
4. Make sure the rule-making rights of community members are respected by outside authorities.
5. Develop a system, carried out by community members, for monitoring members' behavior.
6. Use graduated sanctions for rule violators.
7. Provide accessible, low-cost means for dispute resolution.
8. Build responsibility for governing the common resource in nested tiers from the lowest level up to the entire interconnected system.

We will refer to these rules in our suggestions at the end of this chapter.

Since then, and especially after the expansion of the Commons concept to also include knowledge and information in the category of inexhaustible Commons (Hess and Ostrom, 2006), the Commons theory has composed theoretical and conceptual elements in several areas of studies related to coproduction. Hess and Ostrom (2006), for instance, identified what they called cultural Commons, neighborhood Commons, knowledge Commons, infrastructure Commons, market Commons, and global Commons.

Urban Commons

For Hess and Ostrom, Urban Commons are in fact neighborhood Commons, which include a variety of collectives associated with the urban space, such as homeless communities, residents, owners, community squares and gardens, neighborhood security, sidewalks, imposition of silence, a group of street trees and even the streets themselves.

Urban Commons may be physical places such as parks and sidewalks, but also virtual, based upon city data. The best-known examples are the physical ones when groups of people come together to claim their right-of-use over some area that they regard as public or even their own property due to a historical condition. In many places, citizens lost their faith in the government as an unbiased mediator of the needs of everyone concerned, and in the wisdom of the "market" in the provision of goods and services. And they decided to take action to protect their place and transform it into a "Commons" with collective governance.

An interesting Urban Commons instance is the Tempelhofer Feld, an abandoned city airport in Berlin, Germany. After the airport's closure, residents in the surrounding area started to use the place for leisure activities such as biking, kite surfing, and picnicking; and also for gardening. Then the local council decided to allow for private builders to erect upscale condos in the area. The residents got together and through collective action groups such as the "Squat Tempelhof" and the "100% Tempelhofer Feld" managed to press a city referendum: In 2014 the population voted to keep the area for public use (Dellenbaugh et al., 2015).

An example of the virtual Urban Commons is the 311 system, available in many cities in the United States. It is a nonemergency phone number that people can call to report problems, file complaints about road damage, unwanted graffiti, etc. In Boston it is a widely disseminated tool for communication between citizens and the local authorities. When hurricane Irene hit the city, in August 2011, a system log of the citizen's calls during the crisis (reporting falling poles or trees, street blocks, etc.) plotted on a city map showed the approximate shape, intensity, and form of the episode in the city (O'Brien, 2018). O'Brien refers to the system as "the pulse of the city" and claims that simple solutions such as this can significantly improve life in the city and should be implemented immediately—instead of planning for sophisticated systems that take a long time to show results for the citizen, such as, for instance, a camera-based surveillance system downtown.

This first phase of the Urban Commons studies, in the mid-1990s and early 2000s, was followed by studies in the context of urban capital accumulation (Maeyama, 2013). They include analyzes of gentrification projects (i.e., modification of urban spaces from the replacement of small stores and poor homes for the insertion of new building and commercial enterprises). For Harvey (2012), the main impact of the Urban Commons approach on cities is in the logic of re-urbanization, which should not be based on capital gains alone, but on the relationship of social groups with their environment, which they start to consider as a collective good. This has consequences for the local government because their decisions will no longer be based on the monetary return of the public space to the city, but on the actual return of the public space to the well-being of its residents and potential users.

But following Ostrom's inspiration, when the local government truly wishes to treat their assets as spaces for public uses and purposes—or Commons—they should also promote self-organization of the Commons. This new governance method will make each of the communities responsible for the space once they feel that it "belongs" to them.

The Urban Commons approach is not unanimous. It has been questioned, both in terms of the validity of the perception of urban space as a Commons, and also in the very way in which Ostrom's discoveries are incorporated into the city. In the first case, critics claim that cities are much more complex systems of networks of heterogeneous actors (Metzger, 2015) and do not carry the characteristics of a Commons, previously used for the collective sharing of natural resources. In relation to Ostrom's theories, the criticism is in the intrinsically virtuous perception with which the term is defined and positioned as a principle to be followed (almost religiously), instead of a phenomenon to be studied under the view and scientific methods of past and contemporary history (Jerram, 2015).

Praise and criticisms are typical consequences of new approaches to studies for existing scientific fields. This is particularly true when this new approach is characterized by the convergence of multiple disciplines and views, as is currently the case of the Urban Commons. We think the Urban Commons approach appears just natural when we think of the world as a Commons.

The world and the city as a Commons

Ostrom's first rule for the successful governance of a Commons is to "define clear boundaries." What if we defined our Commons as "the world"? Have we subtracted most available resources from this Common Pool of Resources? Would the planet be a striking evidence and sad confirmation of Hardin's "Tragedy of the Commons"? Maybe, if we follow the existing track. Maybe not, if we collectively change our behavior. This battle will be won or lost in the city, which, as we have seen, simultaneously concentrates the problem and the minds and the resources to solve it.

Our job of preserving the planet, so far, bore no really distinct fruit. But there are small examples everywhere (and we have seen a few in Chapter 5: Looking for Striking Humane and Sustainable Smart City Characteristics in Existing Cities) that point to the right direction. The city as a series of Urban Commons is one possible solution. And we have a collective right to act thus. We may use the United Nations' (UN) definition of collective right as "the right of "all citizens, present, and future, to occupy, use, and produce a fair, inclusive, and sustainable city, defined as a common good essential to the quality of life" (UN-Habitat, 2017, p. 60). The "future" citizen in this definition is a reinforcement and a reminder of the sustainability imperative.

Cities perceived as Urban Commons should promote their citizens' rights and opportunities (and duties) in the economic, social, cultural, environmental, and political dimensions (Garnett, 2011). In the city, each of these dimensions is also projected on different geographical (neighborhoods, districts) and socioeconomic (tourism, security, mobility, health, energy) subsystems, with different and sometimes overlapping composition of agents ("commoners") that include companies, citizens, civil servants, visitors, academics, etc. Thus when perceived as collective spaces for the exercise of rights and duties, cities become a macrosystem network of intertwined Commons systems and subsystems. Each dimension of rights and duties and, also, each regional delimitation in which these subsystems occur, make up different Commons, in the context of Ostrom's Theory. Curious to think that the historic period known as the "cold war" (from the end of WWII, in 1945, or more precisely after the Truman Doctrine of 1947, to the dissolution of the Soviet Union block, in 1991) between the United States and the Soviet Union (and respective allies on both sides) helped demonize Communism on the Western Block. This may have hindered the effective use of Ostrom's findings in practical instances in many countries, because the very mention of the prefix "common" as in Commons, Communes, or Commoners would raise eyebrows and demand a very detailed explanation.

For practical use, each Commons, for the purpose of city management and planning, should start precisely with the first rule of Ostrom for sustainable Commons: the delimitation of the space. After doing so, the Commons will spell out purpose, vision, protagonists, and other components of the urban system, which are essential elements for the institutionalization of the other principles discovered by Ostrom. This is exactly what we will propose in the next section.

Hope: the new Humane and Sustainable Smart City postpandemic 2020/21

We want to transform our cities into places that are more HSSCs. We now have the momentum (postpandemic 2020/21), the theory (the city as a series of Urban Commons), the framework (UN's 17 sustainable development goals), and the tools (brought to us by the accelerated digital transformation of society).

So, what do we do with it?

Going back to Piketty's prescription, we singled out four suggestions that are more relevant to our context and include some of our comments for each one.

1. Taxation

   Piketty suggests a progressive taxation on property, and even more on inheritance, which could finance social programs. He focuses on the national and international policies. But taxation on property, in many countries, is local. This would be a new source of income for social programs in the city. As we mentioned before, the impact of the pandemic can (maybe) transform this taxation (a heresy today) into something palatable.

2. Citizen participation

   Piketty defines his proposal as *participatory socialism* in which control of the companies would not be taken by the state, as in a traditional socialism dogma, but would be shared by workers who would occupy 50% of the seats of administrative boards of companies. In our case, the same principle could be applied to boards of local government.

3. The environment

   Piketty demands more formal and legal obligations of companies in relation to international treaties such as the Paris Agreement, and a progressive new green tax on the individual in proportion to his carbon emission. Taking the idea back to our HSSCs, as we suggested before, the full cost of the car to society (environmental and health costs) should be progressively taxed to the car owner, and not divided throughout society.

4. Education

Piketty prescribes a redefinition of educational expenses of the city in a way that it privileges the children who most need it. The end result would be that all children are offered more or less the same level of education from kindergarten throughout the formative years up to university. Since education is one of the top expenses in many cities, this suggestion would need additional funds, which could be supplied by the extra taxation suggested in Item 1. In fact, a direct link between the new taxation and education of children in the taxpayer's city itself might ease and maybe accelerate the approval of the new tax.

With these guidelines, we can propose the changes that we hope to see in our cities.

The new Humane and Sustainable Smart City "arrondissement," a Commons

The new borough we envisage for our HSSC "arrondissement" (French borough) is already being tried in several places. In Paris, it is called the "15′ City," proposed by Sorbonne's professor Carlos Moreno (Davidson, 2020) and adopted full-heartedly by mayor Anne Hidalgo. In Portland, in the United States, they call it the "20′ neighborhoods," and want them to cover 90% of the city area. In Melbourne, by the same name, they also want to transform the city into a series of localities within which general services will be available in a 20′ walk or a short bike ride.

Mayor Hidalgo implemented bold changes such as blocking cars on the road by the Seine river and creating segregated bike lanes on several streets. The plan has been expanded during the pandemic and the new bike lanes were nicknamed by the citizens of "Covid routes." But Parisians apparently liked what they saw and reelected Ms. Hidalgo as mayor for another term in July of 2020. Although mayors are in general afraid of bold moves in their constituencies, for fear of the political backlash, in this one instance it worked very well for Mayor Hidalgo.

The definition of a new centrality in the city, where one can walk or bike one's way to everything, varies from city to city. But it includes, besides the living-working-playing triad that we have mentioned before, also life-long learning, medical treatment, and basic shopping. Melbourne presents a comprehensive list in their city plan for the 20′ neighborhood (Melbourne, 2020): local shopping centers, local health facilities and services, local employment opportunities, local schools, life-long learning opportunities, safe cycling networks, walkability, housing diversity, services for senior people, affordable housing options, safe streets and spaces, sports and recreational facilities, community gardens, green streets and spaces, local playgrounds and parks, good connection to public transport, and jobs and services within the region.

People density of this locality should be enough to make the provision of all these services locally viable. It all sounds very good, but is it doable?

We claim that yes, it is. And the pandemic just opened a window of opportunity for its implementation in the short term. And the "Commons approach" may offer the conceptual framework to get locals involved in the discussions. As people will want or will be instructed to work on some weekdays at home, they will need services close to them. And they will be more willing to participate in activities that affect their surroundings, such as the development of a Commons in their borough. Cities, besides Paris, Melbourne, and Portland, can also do it. It is a question of a new vision that needs a new leadership. It will not happen without the involvement of the City Hall, of course. But pressure coming from citizens will be noticed by the elected officials and maybe acted upon.

The new services needed in the HSSC arrondissement are not in place yet in most places. Here there are opportunities for many of the people dislocated by the pandemic or who permanently lost their jobs by the sudden automation frenzy that hit the companies. Local institutions that are connected to job creation or the promotion of opportunities may identify these gaps in the list of services that are already available, and inform and train people (especially local residents) to be the providers of the new services required by the current situation.

An interesting place to start is a square, a park, a historical building, or any other landmark that captures the local's imagination. Next, we suggest the organization of a practical workshop, as we detailed in Chapter 6, Where and How to Start in Your City. Then the actual Commons area should be delimited. It takes time. But the discussions may be the start of a new sense of citizenship, which has been all but lost in many large cities in the world.

The new car: the Humane and Sustainable Smart City commuter

One of the "unintended consequences" (maybe one of the few trends that goes against the HSSC idea) of the crisis is a growth in the number of people in the city who want to buy a car. Since public transport is now "unsafe" because of the possibility of contagion, even youngsters that were not considering a private car in their lives might change their minds. This is very bad news for the city. We certainly do not need more people (besides us oldies) wanting to buy cars and, as a consequence, clogging our streets.

South African innovation guru and now billionaire Elon Musk designed a vehicle in his Tesla company that was revolutionary: electric, with all sorts of novelties and appliances, but still... a car! It came as a surprise to many of us in the innovation field that his car would show up without the one characteristic of the car that mostly needs real change: the concept!

The existing car, as we know it today, including Tesla's, was designed to be useful as the vehicle to go to work, to take the kids to school, and to go to the cabin log on the weekends. We need something radically different for the city: vehicle to move a single person (maybe two), in safety, in comfort, from home to work. It would become the HSSC commuter. It does not have to go from 0 to 100 km/hour in 7 seconds; it does not need 17 cup holders (one will do just fine), it does not need a top speed of 200 km/hour. It has to be electric, for sure, low speed (40 km/hour, for instance), quiet, low consumption of electricity, comfortable, and safe. It cannot go side by side a city tank such as a Hummer (a giant jeep), and it may need a different lane altogether. So be it. We planned our cities for cars in the past. We can now redesign them for the new era and divide the available public streets to contemplate segregated lanes for all kinds of vehicles—one for the HSSC commuters, one for bikes, and one for traditional cars.

The new Humane and Sustainable Smart City home

Change, in any area, is always difficult. Unless one is moving from a situation that is really bad, or going to a situation that is really amazing, one tends to procrastinate change. This is true of any kind of change. Our houses, for instance, in most countries, are certainly not prepared for the occupants they have. Think of these two examples: in the suburban dream house in the green belt of the US cities, the garage is not used for the car, but for something else, be it a spare room, a laundry, or a workbench for the owners favorite hobby. As another example, in other countries, the largest room in the house is the living room, used a few times a year to host a party or as a waiting room for a dinner party with friends. The most used space is, in general, the kitchen—and in many places it is a tiny corridor, a reminder of long time gone, when the owners had cooking maids. . .

With the pandemic, houses will have to change.

The "stay-at-home" office space is one immediate concern. It cannot be just the old table under the stairs, or the kitchen table, or the comfortable chair in front of the TV that you used during the quarantine. You will have to make room for a proper space (or maybe two independent different spaces for you and your spouse, if that is the case) where you will spend most of your waken hours at home. These places will need appropriate access to the Internet and several mains' plugs. Think also of the screen view, the image from your computer camera, the one that people who interact with you will see. The use of video communication is already and will be even more widespread in the next few months, thanks to Google's, Microsoft's, or Zoom's tools. Lighting is also a major attribute for the quality of your image and better to think of this from the outset. The last concern is noise. Your cutie little nephew bumping on your table and appearing on the screen of your board meeting may look nice today, as we are all adapting to the changes, but will be an unacceptable nuisance in "more normal" times. And your microphone has to capture only your own voice, not the noise from the blender in the kitchen.

In other words, the home will become again a place for production, not only for the family life, which is an interesting revival historically. We saw in Chapter 2, Historical Overview: Cities From Medieval to Modern Times—What Went Wrong, that the city should get inspiration for its urban plan from the old medieval villages where people lived-worked-played in and around an area of 1-mile radius. Now the organization of the home also needs inspiration from medieval villages where production (weaving, child-bearing, learning, trading) was also conducted inside the house.

Other changes will be concerned with keeping the family safe and providing our basic needs of breathing clean air, drinking clean water, eating proper food, and socializing. Quality of the incoming air and water will need special attention, more than we devote to it today. People will review their water and air supply and install appropriate filtering that avoids virus and bacteria contamination. One area that is expected to boom is the local production of groceries and fruit. For this reason and to enjoy fresh air, a backyard in the house or a larger balcony or veranda in the apartment may be needed.

Cleaner energy supplies will be in order. Photovoltaic solar panels will become more and more popular as they progressively reduce their purchase, installation, and maintenance costs. Also, a "greener" home will be in demand: recyclable rainwater, treatment of used water before being directed to the sewage system, separation of your daily garbage into distinct bins for recyclable materials, etc.

In the apartment building, besides all the changes mentioned for the house, which will also be needed in the apartments, the building itself will need a system for receiving deliveries. This is in place in several cities already, of course, but the number of people buying stuff online is growing fast. Most buildings will need to incorporate deliveries in their daily routines. Another concern will be the use of the shared spaces in the building (pool, playground, office space, gym, gardens). They will have to be planned according to a completely different set of rules and demands from the users, which are not at all clear now.

The new Humane and Sustainable Smart City

We propose that the planning and the implementation of the new HSSC be an exercise that starts with the definition of the localities that make sense in the particular context and start with one of them. Transform that one into an HSSC arrondissement with a Commons structure and local governance. This is not a recipe for success. It is a recipe for change. And a change does not guarantee success. It is, in our view, a good alternative scheme to try in our cities. A very different one to what we have today—plans are too big, too slow in arriving at consensus, and many never get implemented.

Another project for the city, which we would classify as a "low-hanging-fruit" is a modern, segregated, safe, and clean bike system. It should include a network of easily accessible bike lanes, mandatory (in the city code) bike parking in commercial buildings, availability of shared-bike systems, and a division at City Hall to take care of the system. Bikes may develop a new interest in the population after the pandemic due to their characteristics of good exercise, opportunity to enjoy fresh air, help the planet, and sheer fun. And, to cap it all, many bikes in some cities carry the proud logo "one less car in the street!".

Finally, a new HSSC city develops a social project to be proud of. A project that uses the best possible technologies to promote smart inclusion of people in some kind of distress. Social unrest used to be a problem of developing countries. But with the waves of refugees from poor countries to the most developed ones, and the widening gap of inequality all over the world, social inclusion became a problem for all. Every city in the world must do something to help solve this problem.

The new Humane and Sustainable Smart City "you"

Changes depend upon us. The transformation of our cities into more HSSCs is a job for you and me to do. Read on, as we conclude the argument in the final chapter of the book.

References

Aizawa, T., 2019. Urban developments and health: evidence from the distributional analysis of biomarkers in China. SSM Popul. Health 8, 100397.

Anthony, S., Gilbert, C., Johnson, M.W., 2017. Dual Transformation: How to Reposition Today's Business While Creating the Future. Harvard Business Review Press, Cambridge, p. 272.

Arcanjo, M., 2019. Why we ignore climate change. Blog available at <https://medium.com/@marcusarcanjo/why-we-ignore-climate-change-ed8f3c400e3a> (accessed July 2020).

Bhattacharya, S., et al., 2016. Localizing the gender equality goal through urban planning tools in South Asia. Center for Study of Science, Technology and Policy. <http://deliver2030.org/wp-content/uploads/2017/01/cstep_final.pdf>.

Blackburn, S., LaBerge, L., O'Toole, C., Schneider, J., April 2020. Digital strategy in a time of crisis: now is the time for bold learning at scale. McKinsey Digital.

Burinskiene, M., Gusaroviene, M., Bruleviciute-Skebiene, K., 2014. The impact of public transport lanes on the operating speed of buses. In: Proceedings of the International Conference on Environmental Engineering (ICEE). Vilnius Gediminas Technical University, Department of Construction Economics & Property.

Capelary, M.G., et al., 2017. Vincent and Elinor Ostrom: two confluent trajectories for the governance of common property resources. Ambient. Soc. 20 (1), 203–222.

Carrillo, F.J., 2019. Editorial: the Anthropocene turn in knowledge-based development. Int. J. Knowl. Dev. 10 (4), 293—296.

Christensen, F.K., 2014. Understanding value changes in the urban development process and the impact of municipal planning. Land Use Policy 36, 113—121.

Davidson, J., July 17, 2020. The 15-minute city: can New York be more like Paris? Intelligencer.

Dellenbaugh, M., et al., 2015. Urban Commons. Birkhauser, Berlin, Germany, p. 244.

Garnett, N., 2011. Managing the urban Commons. Univ. Pa. Law Rev. 160, 1995.

Gouldson, A., et al., 2016. Cities and climate change mitigation: economic opportunities and governance challenges in Asia. Cities 54, 11—19.

Hardin, G., 1968. The Tragedy of the Commons. Science 162 (3859), 1243—1248. Available from: 10.1126/science.162.3859.1243. 13 Dec 1968.

Harvey, D., 2012. The creation of the urban Commons. In: Rebel Cities: From the Right to the City to the Urban Revolution. Available at <https://mappingthecommons.wordpress.com/2012/11/13/the-creation-of-the-urban-commons-by-david-harvey/> (accessed June 2020).

Hess, C., Ostrom, E., 2006. A Framework for Analyzing the Knowledge Commons: A Chapter from Understanding Knowledge as a Commons: From Theory to Practice. MIT Press, Cambridge.

Jerram, L., 2015. The false promise of the Commons: historical fantasies, sexuality and the 'really-existing' urban common of modernity. Urban Commons. Routledge, pp. 57—77.

Kirsch, N., November 7, 2018. The 3 richest Americans hold more wealth than bottom 50% of the country, study finds. Forbes. Available at <https://www.forbes.com/sites/noahkirsch/2017/11/09/the-3-richest-americans-hold-more-wealth-than-bottom-50-of-country-study-finds/#70f5aa613cf8> (accessed July 2020).

LePan, N., March 14, 2020. Visualizing the history of pandemics. Visual Capitalist. Available at <https://www.visualcapitalist.com/history-of-pandemics-deadliest/> (accessed July 2020).

Maeyama, S., 2013. The role of community organizations for 'safety patrol'. In: 14th Global Conference of the International Association for the Study of Commons.

Mandisvika, G., 2015. The role and importance of local economic development in urban development: a case of Harare. J. Advocacy Res. Educ. 4 (3), 198—209.

Marshall, G., 2015. Don't Even Think About It: Why Our Brains Are Wired to Ignore Climate Change. Bloomsbury, New York, p. 272.

Melbourne, 2020. 20-Minute neighborhoods: create more inclusive, vibrant and healthy neighborhoods. Available at <https://www.planning.vic.gov.au/policy-and-strategy/planning-for-melbourne/plan-melbourne/20-minute-neighbourhoods> (accessed July 2020).

Metzger, J., 2015. The city is not a Menschenpark: rethinking the tragedy of the urban Commons beyond the human/non-human divide. Urban Commons. Routledge, pp. 32—56.

Mieg, H.A., 2012. Sustainability and innovation in urban development: concept and case. Sustain. Dev. 20 (4), 251—263.

Naisbitt, J., 1982. Megatrends. Warner Books, New York, p. 290.

O'Brien, D.T., 2018. The Urban Commons: How Data and Technology Can Rebuild Our Communities. Harvard University Press, Cambridge, p. 336.

Oliveira, J.A., et al., 2011. Cities and biodiversity: perspectives and governance challenges for implementing the convention on biological diversity (CBD) at the city level. Biol. Conserv. 144 (5), 1302—1313.

Ostrom, E., 1990. Governing the Commons: The Evolution of Institutions for Collective Action. Cambridge University Press, p. 290.

Piketty, T., 2017. Capital in the Twenty-First Century. Harvard University Press, Cambridge, p. 793.

Piketty, T., 2020. Capital and Ideology. Harvard University Press, Cambridge, p. 1104.

Shvertner, K., 2017. Digital transformation of business. Trakia J. Sci. 15, 388–393. Available from: 10.15547/tjs.2017.s.01.065.

Soyinka, O., Siu, K.W.M., 2018. Urban informality, housing insecurity, and social exclusion; concept and case study assessment for sustainable urban development. City Cult. Soc. 15, 23–36.

Stoknes, P.E., 2017. How to transform apocalypse fatigue into action on global warming. Ted Talks. Available at <https://www.ted.com/talks/per_espen_stoknes_how_to_transform_apocalypse_fatigue_into_action_on_global_warming?language = en> (accessed July 2020).

UN-Habitat, 2017. United Nations Conference on Housing and Sustainable Urban Development, Habitat III Policy Papers: Policy Paper 1: The Right to the City and Cities for All. United Nations, New York. <www.habitat3.org>.

Yar, P., 2020. Urban development and its impact on the depletion of groundwater aquifers in Mardan City, Pakistan. Groundw. Sustain. Dev. 11, 100426.

Chapter 8

Conclusions and a call to action

"We but mirror the world. All the tendencies present in the outer world are to be found in the world of our body. If we could change ourselves, the tendencies in the world would also change. As a man changes his own nature, so does the attitude of the world change towards him. This is the divine mystery supreme. A wonderful thing it is and the source of our happiness. We need not wait to see what others do."

Mahatma Gandhi

Introduction

I wrote my first book at Harvard University in 2001, with the title "Global E-commerce Strategies for small businesses," published by the MIT Press, and later translated to Japanese and to Chinese. This is the opening paragraph of the final chapter of that book:

"This is an opinionated chapter. To this point in the book, I have tried to be factual, true to the sources, scholarly. Not here. The whole purpose of this book is to raise awareness about the opportunities for ~~small companies in the international market~~. That is what you read about in the preceding chapters. In this one, I convey my ideas and try to instill in you, the reader, the same hope and enthusiasm that I am feeling about the new economy. Here is where I make clear the main motivation for the book: I do indeed think that we have a good chance of transforming this place in which we live into a better world."

If we swap the scored words in this paragraph for "our cities in the post-pandemic world," it is valid here verbatim.

Because of the nature of this final chapter, I will change the narrative to the *first person*. It is a collection of opinions, hopes, and credos, and it would make no sense to use the impersonal *we*. Thus when I write *we* here, I mean you and I, or all of us in this world. The chapter will have no references, for the same reason. What you read here is what I think, believe, and practice.

Humane and Sustainable Smart Cities. DOI: https://doi.org/10.1016/B978-0-12-819186-6.00012-9

Hope

The new world after the pandemic will be about things that matter. There is no certainty of this statement, for sure. It is a hope. But it is a reasoned hope. We have seen that the tools to be used in order to promote change are in place and simultaneously aligned by the pandemic 2020/21: a new feeling of solidarity, of "we are in this world together," for better or worse; an already existing theoretical support system in the Commons; a previous international endeavor and agreement, materialized in the UN's sustainable development goals (SDGs) for 2030 to tackle the missteps of the Anthropocene era; and a tech-based accelerated digital transformation that enables several key activities at a distance, such as learning and medical treatment.

What is missing is the resolve. My claim is that the city should be the locus of the change, and that you and I should take the helm. Not blame the governments at all levels for our misfortunes. The change needed is about us, and it is our job to execute it.

What you read in the book so far

You have come a long way up to here. Even if you are a hasty reader who jumped to this section following my suggestion in Chapter 1, The Concept of More Humane and Sustainable Smart Cities, to read the book's summary that is presented here, the fact is that you became interested in the subject. Welcome aboard!

Chapter 1

I described the various names by which the work on the transformation of our cities has been classified. Then I introduce the concept of a more Humane and Sustainable Smart City (HSSC). The point is not just to find another denomination. There is a change in focus. In our case, it is the citizen. This may seem obvious, since each and every mayor say they are working for the citizen, but no, we indicated that they might just be inebriated by the juggernaut of Technology. So, the important concept in HSSC is the "Humane" declaration in the denomination. Projects should aim the well-being of the citizen and their results' metrics should be measured against goals related directly to the citizen. The number of kilometers of fiber optics in the city or the number of surveillance cameras downtown is irrelevant; what is important is how many citizens have access to broadband Internet and how safe it is for the citizen to walk alone downtown at night.

Another important message in the chapter is the need for a *more* HSSC. This means that the changes in the city toward an HSSC are a process, not a project with an end in sight. A corollary of this statement is that we cannot say a city *is or is not* an HSSC—either it is in the process of pursuing it or it is not.

Then I briefly introduced three attributes of an HSSC city in the process of change toward a more HSSC: the concept of live-work-play in the same small area (1 mile of radius, the size of medieval villages); the observation of the "citizens" wishes, interests, and needs" imperative; and the "mental de-industrialization" of our thinking.

Chapter 2

I presented a historical perspective of the development of our cities setting the observation points in three historical periods that I nominate as the "good," the "bad," and the "ugly." The "good" period is from the medieval times up to the transformation of Paris in 1860, when the basic functions of the city life were performed in a small area of around 1 mile of radius. In the medieval village, this was the average area of the whole village. In a big city such as Paris, every arrondissement was designed as if it were a medieval village. Unfortunately, no other major city followed this path after that, for reasons we explained in the sequence. Paris was the last city to be designed according to this concept.

The "bad" period goes from the end of the 19th century to the end of the 20th century. The industrial revolution brought with it the need to segregate the daily functions of living, working, and playing into separate areas in town. The reason for that was the fact that the new industries were polluting the city with waste and toxic material, and they had to be set apart from the living area. But the enabler for this segregation was the car, the poster child of the industrial revolution. With the availability of the private car, the cities could be spread over a larger area and the car could take citizens from one area to the other. It worked for a time, when not many people had cars (worked for those who had cars, of course). With the increase in the number of cars in the city, traffic jams became a nightmare and polluted the city even more than the industries in the outskirts. Urban planning concentrated all of its efforts in how to improve the city for the car—and the City Hall started to plan the city for the car instead of for the people. A costly mistake.

It did not work, of course, and we went from "bad" to "ugly." This is the situation where we are in today. The need for a new approach is urgent.

Then I detailed the three important attributes of HSSCs that were introduced in the previous chapter.

I do not own a car and have stayed carless for more than 15 years. But throughout the text, I tried not to be regarded as an anticar greenhead. Although I indicated that, in my opinion, the car became much more powerful and worthy of consideration that it really deserves.

Car lovers may have found this annoying and I apologize for the eventual insistence on the subject. But I hope to have conveyed the idea that I believe we have all been brainwashed by the car industry (and its powerful interrelated sectors) and that now is the time to get hold of the reigns of our cities back to us, away from what I referred to as *motordom* (the kingdom of the motorcar).

Chapter 3

I went deeper into the "smart city" concept in order to explain how important the new technologies can be for the solution of real problems in the city. Artificial intelligence, in particular, may become a game changer with the use, by the administration, of the vast amount of data produced by the city. Both for the administration's internal needs and planning, and also for the private sector to develop new applications for citizens, once the administration adheres to the "open data" concept.

Then I joined the bandwagon of those who are questioning the smart city concept and asked: smart for whom? The whole idea is that the companies that control our data may be exacerbating their power and financial clout to get rid of the competition and to control our lives in a way that may have escaped out of our control.

After that, I describe the changes that are happening in our society both in terms of the new generations and new social movements. And I go back to the car industry, but this time to describe the "perfect storm" the industry is facing. Uninterested youngsters, radical tech changes, and a much more difficult relation with their customers. A daunting scenario if you ask me.

Then I proceeded to differentiate the HSSC and the original smart city concepts. And to touch ground from theory to practice, I went on to describe practical examples of projects to be implemented in the city that will set the changing process in motion, with a clear reference to what an interested person can do, instead of just complaining to the local authorities.

Chapter 4

In this chapter, I define the eight most important dimensions of more HSSCs. They are Sustainable Economic Development (DEV); People (PEO); Quality of Life (QOL); Historic, Artistic, and Cultural Heritage, and Tourism (HAC); Environment (ENV); Social Inclusion (SOC); Mobility of People (MOB); and Governance (GOV). The first seven dimensions are real characteristics; the eighth is a horizontal dimension that is an enabler for the others.

This list of dimensions was not invented in the lab; it came out of sheer experience with the application of a workshop methodology in nine different instances in Brazil from 2013 through 2019. These are the dimensions that have repeatedly been appointed by local stakeholders as their main concerns.

Chapter 5

Here I asked a group of people in the family, friends, and colleagues to send me an example of a project anywhere in the world that came to their attention in terms of the HSSC concept. The results are there. In these 30 examples, I showed a sample of city changes that may inspire other people who want to make a difference in their own city. Such as you.

Chapter 6

This is a summary of the methodology we used in the implementation of our workshops in Brazil. Each workshop is a collective search for a list of structural projects that will make a change in the city. I organize a group of graduate students who participate in it as a graduate course for their graduate requirements (1/2 the group) and people who are really interested in making a change in their "arrondissement." The 5-day intensive workshop uses the design thinking methodology and normally produces such good results, that the participants and other stakeholders in the region end the experience surprised and really happy to have taken part in the event.

Then I showcased one of the workshops, which treated the surroundings of the Hercílio Luz Bridge in Florianópolis, South of Brazil, as a case study to illustrate the methodology.

Chapter 7

In this chapter I tried to point out that we have a rare opportunity to change our city based upon the combination of the theory of the commons, the accelerated rate of adoption of digital transformation in our society brought by the pandemic, the ambience created by the Paris Agreement with the UN's 17 SDGs, and the change in attitude that we all faced during the social distancing period of the pandemic in 2020.

Then I pointed out what we can do immediately in our cities with this opportunity. In the city, in the borough, and in the house. I suggest that it is a change that you and I must experience as well. But I left this final consideration to tackle here in the concluding chapter.

Suggestions for the new HSSC "you"

It might seem presumptuous to give suggestions for you or anyone else. But it just so happens that, when I talk about the subject publicly, which I do often, someone asks me at the end: "It is all very well, but what do I do with it?" So, here goes my suggestions for you.

Engagement

1. Become engaged with an association that represents the civil society around you. It might be the resident's association, the "friends of the park" association, the historical society of landmark X, the women empowerment group, the shop owners' association of street X, the church group, etc. If you cannot think of any such organization that attracts you, why not start a new one?
2. Choose one area in the city you care for and would like to see changed or improved. As we have seen in the book, it must be an interesting region that will sport a demonstration effect for the whole city. It must also be dense to make sense. As a rule-of-thumb, it should be an area that covers c.1 mile of radius and that gathers 20,000 people daily, either permanently (residents) or daily (commuters, visitors).
3. Make a connection with someone mid-level in the hierarchy of the City Hall who might be interested in becoming involved with an HSSC project. Bring her in for a brainstorming session with the organization.
4. Consider the possibility of conducting a workshop as I proposed in Chapter 6, Where and How to Start in Your City. Remember that the methodology applies to a real need for change in an area of the city in which you do not know beforehand what are the possible alternatives of solution. And the workshop's results will indicate the structural projects that will contribute to the improvement of the existing situation. It is *not* a methodology to convince recalcitrant stakeholders of something that you or someone else is willing to do in that region in the city.

Social inclusion

Alternatively, you might want to get involved with some kind of social inclusion project. During the pandemic, we were impacted by the amount of people who needed help, even in the more developed societies. It is all very well that many people distributed food and food baskets to poor people in the city. But that is an episodic remedy; it does not solve the problem (remember the famous proverb, "to help a starving person, give him fish. To solve his problem, teach him how to fish").

Other areas of social inclusion are related to minorities or people with disabilities, where almost everything is yet to be developed. Think of something you can do in your area of expertise, whatever that might be. You surely know something that is useful to someone else, particularly to the group above.

Do not be discouraged if your project does not seem big enough to be worthy. The point is to start doing *something*. I once learned the "starfish story," during a seminar, which goes something like this: An old man watches a boy playing on a long beach. As the waves wash ashore, some starfish are left in the sand. As the tide recedes, these starfish will die on the sand under the blazing sun. The boy waits for the starfishes to settle on the sand, picks one up carefully, and puts it back in the water. The old man calls him and says: "young man, this beach has almost one kilometer of extension. There are thousands of starfish left in the sand. Your action will not make any difference." The boy looks back at him, puts another starfish back in the water, and says: "It made a difference to that one!"

Environment

We all need to be more environmentally conscious. You can also help. On a personal basis. We are against the deforestation of the Amazon, or the industrial pollution in city X, or the oil spill in the ocean. But what are we doing on a personal level? Be sure that there are many things you can do. Change the old lamps from incandescent to LED in your house or building. Share your kids' ride to school. Change your gasoline drunkard SUV for an electric car. Plant trees. Top model Gisele Bündchen paid for the plantation of 40,000 trees on her 40th birthday. A good gesture. If your pocket is not the same size, plant one tree (remember the starfish). Carefully watch what you eat, and the packing used to bring it to your house. I am amazed by the amount of packing material we waste for everything we buy. Maybe you can do something there. And so on, and so forth.

Besides doing your bit at a personal level, also consider some kind of project related to the environment or any other aspect of the UN's 17 development goals. This project would fit perfectly in the engagement strategy described earlier.

Education

We all know that in the city, province, or country, given a problem, the answer, or maybe part of the answer, is education. So, in the process of change is there anything you can do in terms of education? Take something that you know, or practice, or do well, and share that knowledge with others.

This idea is different from voluntary work. Voluntary work deserves all the credits, for sure, and I praise everyone who is involved in it. But what I am suggesting here is slightly different (although it may also be voluntary). It is to share what you know with somebody else. Think of it.

The new HSSC "I"

A friend of mine in Campinas, Brazil, was building his house with a mortgage financed by the Federal Bank. Money for the construction was disbursed by the bank according to the construction phases. The building had just been completed and he desperately needed the final installment to pay for his expenses. But the bank's condition was that the municipal inspector go there in person and approve the construction. The officer went there and noticed an irregularity in the building that had to be fixed before his final approval. My friend was furious. He contracted a middleman who could "ease" the approval process giving money to clerks at City Hall. This middleman went there and came back saying that, with the new administration, they were not accepting bribes anymore. My friend told me this story and said, "Isn't it an absurd?". I tried to reason, "But friend, isn't this what we always wanted?!?" He replied, "Yes, but not on my turn!" We want to correct the world but not to correct ourselves...

So, in this context, we must change and do it ourselves. The often-quoted Ghandi's words, "be the change you want to see in the world," is actually a short version of the great man's words that are referred to, in full, at the outset of this chapter. But the meaning is the same. I, not everyone else, must do it.

When I do become really engaged with the implementation of the ideas I believe in (and I do)—besides teaching, giving talks and interviews, and writing, which I already do—there are several personal gains. First, I will stop judging others. I know we are going through a particularly bad spell of world leaders but let us leave that aside for the moment and do something ourselves. Second, it leaves time to reflect about myself instead of just complaining about every person who was supposed to do something and did not. Third, and much more importantly, I can act upon a circumstance that is under my control, which is to set myself in motion.

Engagement

I do provoke engagement in the workshops I organize annually. But I want to do something myself, in my environment. And I want to start small.

I live in a building in Rio that is very old, 100 years (people living in really old towns will not consider that "old"). Old buildings require maintenance much more often, and there is always some re-decoration, or maintenance, or retrofit work going on, with problems of noise, dust, debris, etc. The building is small, with just 12 apartments. When we meet with the other owners, it is usually about some kind of complaint or discussion about the monthly maintenance budget. Very few of my neighbors attend these meetings, maybe half of them on average. They just do not want to be bothered, even though the decisions of the group bind every owner. We only see each other on the way in or out, in the elevator, and even that is very seldom. The building has a live-in doorman, whom I like, but I do not know his wife's name... We also have a common terrace, at the top of the building, with a beautiful view of the Sugar Loaf and The Redeemer (two of Rio's most magnificent landmarks), which is not used at all.

I will make a move to become engaged with my fellow neighbors, for such things as a biweekly happy hour on Friday at 5 p.m., or a bike tour in the park. Pleasant meetings, not the ones to solve problems. Apart from the social side of it, there are interesting and positive things that we can think of in terms of the small square we have in front of our building (which is not used for anything either), in terms of the social use of the terrace, and in terms of, for instance, the neighborhood watch (and care) initiative, which is nonexistent.

Projects do not have to be big. Even such a small move can produce most interesting results.

Social inclusion

Kids coming out of the public education system in Brazil are at a much bigger disadvantage compared with their peers that go to private schools, where the infrastructure and academic dedication of teachers are much better. This is a huge social injustice in the country and partially explains the level of inequality we face today.

Most public schools (to the readers from England, "public school" here means literally a school supported by the government), and some private schools also, are attended by the kids during one period only, either morning or afternoon.

For some time, I have entertained the idea that a distinct knowledge of English and information and communication technologies (ICTs) could make a major difference in these kids' perspectives in life. The trouble with the English language is that some people resent the fact that English became the de facto international communication language. School teachers and their unions would probably cringe at the idea of expanding significantly the English language space in the school's curriculum. But we have to try it.

ICTs are a no-brainer as a leverage in today's world. But what is needed is not a computer lab where kids can taste technology. It is a radical change in the learning methodology in which students use the computer as a learning tool and develop a completely new degree of intimacy with technology.

The new classes of English and ICTs could be offered during the other period of the school (afternoon or morning), which would imply lunch for the students. This would be expensive for the school and would need external finance. Again, funding may come from the private sector.

I will try to set up such a scheme in Florianópolis for one school close to one of the city's tech hubs and to the university where I teach. The private companies in the hub could finance the school and professionals from the tech hub, and language students from the university, could be the voluntary teachers. It is certainly worth a try.

Environment

Rio is a beautiful city, as you probably know already, blessed with the most extraordinary geography. It has the largest urban forest in the world (Tijuca Forest). And several parks and gardens. In the place where I live, besides the small square in front of my building that I mentioned earlier, there is a sequence of parks that stretch out to the city center. They are all separated by roads and avenues and most parks are underutilized.

The birds' eye view of the area indicates that, with a few interventions, the green area could become continuous and compose a beautiful promenade of c.1 km. It would need a few underpasses built and very little else. It is a question of looking at the city as a place for the citizens and not only for their cars. The municipal elections will happen at the end of the year and, with the support of a few friends, I will propose this project to the main candidates.

Education

This is my largest project. I live in Rio and rent a small supporting apartment in Florianópolis, where I teach at the Federal University. Florianópolis is an innovation hub in Brazil and some sort of a dreamland for youngsters from all over the country, and also from neighboring countries, because of the island's beauty, several beaches, and other natural resources, plus the job opportunities in the tech sector. Many workers also launched entrepreneurial activities that led to startups that thrived, with a few "unicorns" (new companies worth more than US$1 billion) already in sight. This perspective makes the city even more alluring to the youngsters.

I hope to transform these youngsters' dreams into reality by designing a completely new, innovative, and daring undergraduate course for students coming from poorer backgrounds in Brazil and other neighboring countries. Students will do part-time work in the local companies that will pay for their tuition fees. For those who need it, there will be living expenses scholarships provided by grants donated by wealthy people in the country. The course's syllabus will contemplate the best part of engineering and computer science programs (and not the more irrelevant parts of it for today's world, which are required by the minimum curricula set by the federal bureaucracy long time ago), the best part of design and marketing programs, and all the new disciplines on "soft skills" (creativity, adaptability, group work, etc.) that will be required of the new professionals. The UN's 17 SDGs will be pursued to the possible limit. And the student selection process will privilege diversity of gender, ethnic origin, country origin, and disabilities. Students will be able to fluently express themselves in Portuguese, Spanish, and English.

During the setup of the project, which just started its planning phase, I am talking to all possible stakeholders to make sure the idea is viable. And the return from them, so far, has been very positive.

The new HSSC "us"

I used to work for the Federal Government in Brazil, in the National Council for Scientific and Technological Development. One of the things under my supervision was anything related to ICTs. Once in a meeting with other top officials in the government, also involved with ICTs, we were discussing an issue, and one of the participants angrily shouted: "This cannot go on! The government must do something!" I looked around and thought, everyone in the government who has anything to do with the subject is here! What the hell does he mean by "government"?

We tend to look at the government as a father figure that can do anything to solve our problems. I have worked for the Government on two occasions in Brazil. One of the things I learned during these two experiences, is that governments, in general, do not have the capacity (in the Physics sense of the word) to do what we expect of them. Either for lack of money (many people still believe the government is a bottomless bag of money), or talent, or time, or will, or all of the above. So, if we want the local government to do something (and we do), it is better to work our collective power to develop a project in detail, stating what we want, and then present it, ready for execution, to the government. To a point that the government will just need the will to implement it. If a new zoning law, for instance, is needed for the project, the actual text of the law must be part of the package that is delivered to the administration. And, contrary to popular belief, the will to get involved with worthy projects is something, for all I have learned, many people in government do have, especially the mid-level professional managers. The ball is in our court and we can indeed change our cities. We have seen that the municipal level is ideal for change because it is the government level that is directly interested in the results of local projects. City officials live and experience some of the problems we all face in our city. Traffic jams, pollution, lack of green spaces. Their children go to the same schools as ours. They are just as interested in having a more HSSC as we are.

I really would like to share all the experiences we develop individually and collectively with other cities in the world. To that end, you are invited to read the QR code just below and become a member of the HSSC "bandwagon" by registering your name and affiliation in order for us to be able to contact you.

Invitation

Click here to learn more about HSSC cities: www.labchis.com/HSSCbook

Conclusion

It has been a long journey up to here but worth each and every hour of it. It is funny to realize that many self-help consultants state that once you work on what you really like, it is not work anymore, but it is pleasure. Indeed, it has been my pleasure to organize the findings we developed on the subject and describe them here to you.

My goal was not only to write an interesting book, but to entice you to join this movement of people who want to change their cities through "a personal roadmap to transform your city after the pandemic" (the book's subtitle). I hope to have achieved this goal. Please sign up to be part of the band, by clicking on the QR code just above and registering. There is a lot we can learn from one another and be sure that this group will be used for this purpose only, not for merchandise or anything else.

You all read that I also committed to my personal change in the list above. I will be busy doing just that in the next few years. But feel free to get in touch and send me your thoughts on the subject. I work in a department that is called Knowledge Management. In the department we understand, as mentioned before, that knowledge actually grows when it is shared. Let us do this together. And while we do it, let us help transform our cities into better places for us people, our children, and everybody else that give us the pleasure of a visit. Not only our cities need it. The planet needs it.

Right Now.

Index

Note: Page numbers followed by "*f*" and "*t*" refer to figures and tables, respectively.

Printed in the United States
By Bookmasters